PRAISE FOR *STEM FOR ALL*

Bakshi has created a roadmap for educators who are beginning to braid together NGSS-aligned standards, principles of belonging, and culturally responsive pedagogy. She offers a call to action to find our professional learning squad so we can collectively uplevel STEM instruction to meet the needs of all students, with a steady eye on those who have been historically marginalized.

—Zaretta Hammond,
teacher-educator and author of *Culturally Responsive Teaching and the Brain*

Dr. Leena Bakshi McLean's *STEM for All* underscores the belief that every student is capable of greatness in STEM when educators truly know their learners, families, and communities and provide rigorous, engaging, student-centered learning. Her insights on rejecting one-size-fits-all curricula and embracing youth action for social justice are both practical and innovative. This book is essential for educators committed to equity and inclusion, offering clear next steps to eliminate barriers in STEM education. It is a must-read for fostering choice, voice, and societal impact.

—Katie Novak, Ed.D.,
educational consultant

STEM teachers and administrators need this book, especially in today's climate of resisting conversations about racism and historical harm. Not only does this book lead the necessary conversations about barriers to effective STEM instruction, but it builds bridges with the actions necessary for personal and systemic access. This book fearlessly faces resistance head on with truths that dismantle racism and it equips readers with actionable steps that open up the doors to STEM learning for all.

—Andratesha Fitzgerald,
author of *Antiracism and Universal Design for Learning: Building Expressways to Success*, CEO of Building Blocks of Brilliance Educational Consulting Firm

STEM for All poignantly addresses the significant gaps in access and opportunities for historically marginalized communities in the STEM field. With profound insights from Leena Bakshi McLean on the transformative value of STEM education and her guidance on changing systemic inequities in the field, we can truly pave the way forward in building a better future in STEM.

—Sara Stone,
assistant superintendent of teaching and learning,
Ravenswood City School District and LEAD Educational Doctoral Student at UC Berkeley

Dr. Leena Bakshi McLean's groundbreaking work is a must-read for anyone in education who is passionate about fostering equity and justice in STEM. Her innovative approach combines rigorous STEM content with principles of culturally responsive teaching, creating pathways for all students to succeed regardless of their background. Dr. McLean's dedication to inclusivity and her vision for a more equitable education system are both inspiring and essential for the future of our schools. This book is not just a guide; it's a movement that invites educators to reflect, connect, and take action for justice in STEM education.

—Charles Cole, III,
author of *Beyond Grit & Resilience: How Black Men Impacted by the Crack Epidemic Succeeded Against the Odds and Obtained Doctoral Degrees*

STEM for All as a concept is simultaneously morally right and socially just. It is also, somewhat paradoxically, aspirational and exigent. Right now, justice-centered STEM education is not equitably distributed. Dr. Bakshi wants to change that by equipping readers to begin identifying, interrogating, and interrupting stultifying, dehumanizing STEM Pedagogies. Sometimes "text" books in this vein leave you with more questions than answers. That is not the case with *STEM for All* as it seamlessly interweaves both the theory and the practice (praxis) in justice-centered STEM education, generally, and justice-advancing pedagogy more specifically. Therefore, the most pressing question is this: Are you in? Are you ready to reimagine your pedagogy so that it reaches all of the students you serve? Read this book and you will be imminently more prepared to do just that!

—Jeremiah J. Sims, PhD,
author of *Revolutionary STEM Education: Critical-reality Pedagogy and Social Justice in STEM for Black Males*

In a time where terms like *equity* and *anti-racism* are misrepresented and even banned, this book stands as a beacon of clarity and commitment to fostering inclusive pathways in STEM education. This book is a must-read for anyone willing to make STEM a reality for ALL!

—Sheldon L. Eakins, PhD,
author and founder of the Leading Equity Center

In this book, Leena shares the gift of helping educators find ways to elevate their pedagogy through the pursuits of connecting, creating, cultivating, and committing to a justice-centered STEM education. While expanding notions of what STEM is and its possibilities, Leena contextualizes problems of practice and offers necessary (and practical) solutions for transformative learning experiences—that center on anti-racism, disruption, and repair from historical harms. Leena reminds us that our students deserve nothing but excellence in STEM, and this book provides a pathway forward.

—Dr. Gholdy Muhammad,
professor of literacy, language, and culture at the University of Illinois at Chicago

STEM for All

STEM for All

How to Connect, Create, and Cultivate STEM Education for All Learners

LEENA BAKSHI MCLEAN

Foreword by
TYRONE B. HAYES, Ph.D

Afterword by
RAVEN BAXTER, Ph.D

JB JOSSEY-BASS™
A Wiley Brand

Published by John Wiley & Sons, Inc., Hoboken, New Jersey.
Published simultaneously in Canada.

ISBN: 9781394221448 (Paperback), 9781394221462 (ePDF), 9781394221455 (ePub)

For general information on our other products and services or for technical support, please contact our Customer Care Department within the United States at (800) 762-2974, outside the United States at (317) 572-3993 or fax (317) 572-4002.

If you believe you've found a mistake in this book, please bring it to our attention by emailing our reader support team at **wileysupport@wiley.com** with the subject line "Possible Book Errata Submission."

Wiley also publishes its books in a variety of electronic formats. Some content that appears in print may not be available in electronic formats. For more information about Wiley products, visit our web site at **www.wiley.com**.

Library of Congress Control Number : LCCN 2024021649 (print) | LCCN 2024021650 (ebook)

Cover Design: Wiley
Cover Image : © Umer Khan/Getty Images

SKY10084105_091024

This book is dedicated to every single one of my students from elementary, middle school, and high school, and to university pre-service teachers. This book is also dedicated to all the students of our STEM educators. Whether in your career or in your life as a global citizen, may you find your pathway to STEM, #4Real!

Contents

About the Author

Leena Bakshi McLean, Ed.D., is the founder of STEM4Real, a nonprofit professional learning organization committed to combining STEM and NGSS content learning with principles of justice-centered teaching methods and leadership. She has worked as an adjunct professor of teaching methods and Universal Design for Learning at UC Berkeley and Claremont Graduate University. She also serves as the Director of Multicultural Education for the National Science Teaching Association (NSTA). Leena is a sought-after international keynote speaker, global education consultant, and advisor to schools, districts, charter school, and nonprofit organizations. She is a former county- and state-level administrator and mathematics, science and health teacher. Leena is also the host of the *Teaching STEM, #4Real* podcast. She leads research on the intersection of equity, justice, and science/STEM education and how we can create access and opportunities for each student regardless of race, ethnicity, religion, or socioeconomic status. You can learn more about STEM4Real at **www.STEM4Real.org**.

Acknowledgments

I am the granddaughter of Dr. Prafulla Chandra Bakshi, Sujata Bakshi, Kollegal Lakshminarasimha Garudachar, and Lalitha Garudachar. My dad was one of three children and the only son. Thus, he was the only one sent to an English school while my aunts went to the local school in town. His education led him to Mumbai, where my mother was working as a school teacher (the apple doesn't fall far from the tree). They eventually landed on 3rd Street of downtown Los Angeles. After my grandfather (Dr. Bakshi) passed away, my dad had to immediately fly to India, compromising his visa, and leaving his family alone for six months. I wasn't yet born, but during that time, my mother and sister, who was five years old, experienced a terrifying home invasion, but my mother, strong as ever, screamed "Get out!" and the intruder did. By the time I arrived into this world, my parents were nestled in the suburbs of Los Angeles County. I want to acknowledge the journey, strife, and triumph that my parents have been through in seeking out greater opportunities.

My parents were convinced that I would carry on my grandfather's spirit by becoming a doctor. That dream existed until I received my MCAT scores (although I did get a perfect score on the writing section, go figure). I took my mother's advice to get my teaching credentials and soon after that my mother alerted me that there was an open position for an eighth-grade math and science teacher. I was hired immediately to start teaching with three weeks of school left in the year. At the time I was hired, I thought they were impressed with my powerful educational quotes of Paulo Friere and Lev Vygotsky. When I entered the classroom on my first day, I knew they were simply grateful to have a warm body to take over. The substitute who was in place briefed me on how the students had a rotation of substitutes and it has been a party all year. Some students were playing slip-and-slide using soap and water from the sink. I came home in tears. My mother said, "You better march right back in that classroom and let them know who the adult is. Call the parents. Call each and every parent and introduce yourself!" I did just that and the rest was history. After my first year of teaching at the district of my alma mater, I knew I had found my jam. It was the most magical year of growth, hardship, and celebration, and then I was laid off. The educational system can be unstable, and we lose many great educators. Somehow, I have been able to carve out a place for myself in the education spaces and I am grateful for all of my students and colleagues. I want to thank every single one of my students, who have shared their learning journeys with me and taught me something about myself each and every school year.

I also want to thank the STEM4Real team for unapologetically implementing a vision for STEM for ALL. I want to acknowledge every single STEM4Real Educator, or how we like to call them, STEM4Real Netties. Every single Netty is a proud member of the STEM4Real network of schools, districts, and charters that have engaged in professional learning. STEM4Real is not just more professional development; this is an educational movement. In this book, you will find what I call "Netty Spotlights," which shine a light on the impact of the #4Real educators that have paved pathways for their students in STEM. The National Education Association defines a co-conspirator as someone who is compelled to take action against racism and oppression, regardless of the consequences. They sacrifice their own privilege and power in the daily battle for equity. My colleagues have served as my fellow co-conspirators. My mentor Marie Bobias Bacher put it best: "I was so quiet the first time I was in these spaces. I didn't think I belonged. I had amazing allies who helped me gain my confidence and help me grow as a leader in STEM." I want to acknowledge all of the administrators and leaders in education that have partnered and continue to partner with STEM4Real. It started out as a wild idea of teaching the Next Generation Science Standards (NGSS) through an equity and justice-centered lens. It has now been cemented as our motto: Standards + justice, you never have to choose!

I want to acknowledge my husband and his journey of making it. When my husband was in high school, he was labeled as "not a math person." He was encouraged to take on labor jobs and was laughed at when he started to think about pursuing college courses in engineering. Despite the naysayers and formidable circumstances, he went on to graduate magna cum laude with a bachelor's degree in mechanical engineering, followed by a master's degree, and he is now pursuing his Ph.D. But here is my question: What if we had a system of education that supported and encouraged students like my husband in their pathways to STEM? He may not have understood mathematics then; however, now he's doing graduate-level mathematics (I personally never made it passed Calculus II). Our power as educators is formidable. This is why I want to acknowledge Dr. Tyrone B. Hayes, world renowned endocrinologist from UC Berkeley and my endocrinology professor. He also serves on the STEM4Real advisory board. When I was in class one day, he posed this question: "If you want a male birth control, get more female researchers. If you want a cure for sickle-cell anemia, get more Black scientists." That quote immediately came back to me when I saw the lack of diversity in our science and STEM curricula. If our students want to get into STEM, they need to see #4Real STEM professionals that look like them. Thus, STEM4Real was born, and we wrote the first children's book, *There's Something in the Water*, which showcases the life of little Tyrone, the frog scientist. I'm grateful for my college roommate and dear friend Dr. Crystal Bray, who normalized Black in STEM and redefined the narrative against Black women. In fact, her mom also wanted to see her as a doctor. She said, "Given my background and upbringing, I realized that the physics I studied wouldn't be immediately useful to my family or friends. So, when I started my career, I wanted to make science serviceable—to my community, family, and friends. This was to ensure that I gave back to all those who gave to me. Benefiting them with the knowledge they had sacrificed for. Although my mom wanted me to be a medical doctor, I feel like she would have been proud of me being a physicist as well." Crystal serves on the STEM4Real Advisory Board.

This is going to sound wild, but I want to thank the few reviewers who provided their negative feedback and said that they would not recommend the publication as presented. Amidst all the positive feedback from the field, these few reviews reminded me that if achieving STEM for ALL were easy, we would be doing it already. There will be naysayers. However, when we have a broken system, we must be the curators and builders of multiple pathways to STEM. This means that we might have to completely change our mindsets on who we think belongs in STEM. If the answer is everyone, then we must build pathways where everyone has an opportunity to access STEM. I want to acknowledge my editor, Ashante Thomas, and the team at Jossey-Bass. The universe brought us together and it was no accident. I was determined to write a book on equity and STEM and, in a world full of book bans, she advocated for this work and made it happen. Miraculously, in a childcare crisis, the words came onto paper while I was juggling an infant and a toddler. Shout out to all the mamas and dadas out there! My children are the great grandchildren of a Native Hawaiian who was born with a birth certificate that displays Hawaii as a self-governing US territory and went on to become a mechanical engineer at Lockheed and taught programming courses in his spare time. It is a reminder that through the brutal histories that our ancestors experience, we can empower ourselves by leveraging STEM to create a just society.

In STEM education, an opportunity refers to any situation, program, initiative, resource, or experience that enhances learning, engagement, and achievement in STEM-related subjects and disciplines. As American economist and attorney, Roger W. Ferguson Jr. states, "When we limit the diversity in STEM, we limit the potential for discovery and advancement. Everyone should have the opportunity to contribute and excel." This book is the result of all the opportunities and platforms I have had thanks to the footsteps of our ancestors. As I traversed from teacher to instructional coach to administrator to university professor to nonprofit founder, I have been privileged to see education from multiple seats. I'm still growing and reflecting on my own journey, and I thank you for joining me in this critical reflection of our education system, particularly in STEM. I'm grateful for the opportunity to lead implementation of the NGSS at the county and state levels. I have learned so much from the teachers, coaches, and administrators as we have collaborated on instructional planning, professional learning, decision-making, and advocacy. I've been honored to serve on the boards of directors for the California Association of Science Educators and the National Science Teaching Association. Sometimes I find myself with a seat at the table and sometimes I do not. Congresswoman Shirley Chisholm famously said, "If they don't give you a seat at the table, bring a folding chair." My dream is that this book is everyone's folding chair. This book is your invitation to speak up, step up, and advocate for systems that support STEM for ALL, #4Real!

Foreword by Dr. Tyrone B. Hayes

I am honored to write the foreword for this extremely important and timely book, *STEM for All* by Dr. Leena Bakshi McLean. I was trained in biology at Harvard (B.A.) and at the University of California (Ph.D.) and I have served as a teacher in my capacity as a graduate student instructor and then professor at UC Berkeley for the last 35 years. My main course has been in human endocrinology for advanced undergraduate and new graduate students, but I have also taught courses for non-majors and lectured extensively in many venues for the public both nationally and internationally. I met Dr. Bakshi McLean when she was an undergraduate student in my course and we connected professionally several years later, through a common interest in STEM training and a shared concern for inequities that still exist in our education systems at all levels.

Dr. Bakshi McLean's motivation and insight stem from her experience as a teacher. Her experiences are real and reflect common experiences of teachers and widespread concerns about our current education system. In our early conversations about STEM education, Dr. Bakshi McLean and I quickly realized that problems in early education often continue through high school and college and even through professional schools. Realizing this path, Dr. Bakshi McLean originally approached me about her children's book, *There's Something in the Water* and how it would serve to bring a role model in STEM to low-income students of color who shared a background like mine. Having produced a very successful children's book, Dr. Bakshi McLean now moves forward with this critical treatment that will serve and train educators in numerous ways.

Many of the scenarios that Dr. Bakshi McLean describes in her work resonate with experiences that I have had as a Black student and with experiences that I have witnessed with students that I have trained as a Black professor. The importance of utilizing CRT (of all three types named in Dr. Bakshi McLean's work) is clearly explained in her examples along with reasons why all students (not just those from marginalized or minoritized backgrounds) must be taught with this framework in mind. Dr. Bakshi McLean also points out the importance of getting to know students as individuals and in Chapter 3 asks the important question of her students: "How is their overall mental health? How have they been feeling lately?" This consideration is even more critical today in this current environment where many people face mental health and social crises because of the isolation and loss of life associated with the pandemic. The learning gap experienced by many students and its differential impact on those with low incomes, first-generation Americans, immigrants, people of color, and other minoritized groups makes Dr. Bakshi McLean's work even more timely. The adaptation to learning styles post-pandemic is also important as students (and teachers) switch from online learning to socializing again in the classroom.

In Chapter 4, Dr. Bakshi McLean talks about the history of racism and cross-burning in San Leandro in 1985. Being knowledgeable about the temporal proximity of blatant racism and segregation is important in how we structure our teaching and approach our students, and this awareness is also important because in many places change has not happened as quickly as we would like.

Although adapting new and flexible teaching styles is critically important, Dr. Bakshi McLean also points out the importance of equitable grading and adjusting our evaluations of students suitably. For example, home life and environment may be a barrier to completing homework. Homework may be especially challenging for unhoused students at all levels, even at college level where housing security is a challenge for many (20-30 percent of students at UC Berkeley report housing and food insecurity, for example).

We also have to be aware of how we interpret students' efforts. Students who already feel that they are viewed negatively (in many cases because of implicit and ingrained biases in many educators; see below) might not want to ask for help. Tutoring, office hours, or discussion sections may be viewed as an "admission" that they are not qualified and enhance feelings that they might be judged by their teachers and their peers. To the teacher, however, the absence of a student from tutoring or office hours or discussion sessions may be viewed as the student not taking advantage of resources. Our perceptions and biases are critical in this regard. For example, in Chapter 12, Dr. Bakshi McLean talks about a survey "What have you heard about working with these groups of students and/or their families?" These types of biases described therein travel with students from grade school to high school to college, and even beyond. Even as a faculty member, I have been described as "grumpy" or "angry" simply for being a Black man speaking up, a situation that basically means that my concerns are dismissed, similar to what I experienced as a student and to what many students from minoritized backgrounds experience. In fact, many times during my career, I was directed to "lay low, and you will eventually get another promotion." So these biases travel with us, giving even more reasons why we should confront ourselves and work toward removing them.

Dr. Bakshi McLean's work is even more important because of the timeliness in its release. The pandemic intensified the already large disparity in education and preparedness for first generation, immigrant, people of color, and other marginalized groups. Although schools were closed for everyone, families with means could afford to hire private teachers/tutors and provide the computer resources that enhanced at home and Zoom schooling, whereas these tools and finances were not accessible by many. The learning gap created by the pandemic is much larger for students from marginalized communities. Without funding to address these disparities, sensitivity and efforts by educators to adjust on the fly in the classroom are critical. Dr. Bakshi McLean's work will be critical in assisting teachers, educators and administrators in understanding and responding to the difficult task ahead.

STEM for All is important for everyone for many reasons. Teachers and administrators need to be trained, students are trying to pursue STEM education, and everybody needs STEM literacy in their daily life to make decisions and to control their own fate. The pandemic forced everyone to watch science unfold in real time: from debates about the origins of the virus, the new RNA vaccines, the recommendations for health and safety, which were all argued in public. Many did not trust the science or questioned the process, illustrating the inadequate job that we have done to create and sustain STEM literacy. The mistrust was especially prevalent in minoritized communities. *STEM for All* is not only important for training a diverse group of people who will enter STEM fields, but also for generating the literacy that will be important for people to make decisions in their daily lives and for institutions to make policy decisions about stem cell research, climate change, vaccines, agriculture and pharmacology, gene editing, genetically modified foods, artificial intelligence, and many other areas that will impact a population that is headed toward a majority minority in the next generation. My congratulations to Dr. Bakshi McLean for this scholarly and timely work. It is an enormous step forward, and I am honored to have played some small role.

Introduction

Her name was Bridget Kyermateng, a young Black girl who was transferred to my eighth-grade Honors Algebra 1 class. The teacher stated that she was "too advanced for her class and needed to be challenged by Honors." As a first-year teacher, I was still figuring out the difference between Honors Algebra 1 and College Prep Algebra 1. I did not have the time or capacity to research or investigate how each student is labeled as an "honors student" or how they are tracked. My primary goal was to survive each day. Nonetheless, I welcomed Bridget into the class, and we began our discussion on simplifying quadratic polynomial expressions. Bridget was pleased to see another young Black girl, Brittney, in the honors class. She naturally gravitated to her.

One day, Brittney received her quiz grade and was in tears after seeing a very unfamiliar grade: a C. She had never received a grade like this before and knew that she had to seek out help. Bridget also wanted to inquire about meeting with me after school to best prepare for her new placement in Honors Algebra 1. What started off as a tutoring request turned to the girls' new favorite pastime: after-school algebra with Ms. Bakshi. Every day, Bridget and Brittney would sit with me as we discussed the methods for tackling the next mathematical strategies for the chapter. In between mathematical concepts, the two girls talked about their Guyanese and Nigerian upbringings, the commonality they had with their parents, the foods they ate, and their family life. They would also discuss the latest trends and dances just to make sure that their teacher was staying ahead of the curve.

These moments with Bridget and Brittney were priceless. I had the opportunity to get to know them on a deeper and more personal level. When it came time for class, they were my top students, always vying for the highest grade. As I recount the experiences of Bridget and Brittney, their narratives did not align with the overarching research on the invisibility of Black girls in mathematics. Dr. Nicole Joseph from Vanderbilt University researches the factors that contribute to building strong and robust mathematical identities for Black girls and the significance of these experiences in the national conversation about the underrepresentation of racialized minority students in STEM fields. In her work on how the role of socialization shapes Black girls' mathematics identity, she explores how Black girls, like other minority girls of color, struggle with participation and face challenges related to mathematics achievement:

1. Black girls encounter stereotypes, low expectations, adultification, marginalization, and various negative experiences both within and outside of school.
2. Black girls are frequently discouraged by counselors from enrolling in science, technology, engineering, and mathematics (STEM) classes, not due to a lack of ability, but largely because of the stereotypes they face in educational settings.
3. Black girls often have limited access to rigorous and high quality advanced mathematics and STEM courses in their schools.

Based on her research, Joseph states, "these findings suggest that Black girls perceive that their mathematics teachers and other school personnel do not believe they will succeed in STEM fields." My experience with Bridget and Brittney flipped that narrative.

The privilege of having them as students shows how much can change when students have access to high-quality STEM instruction and teachers who believe in their abilities.

As a first-year teacher, my primary goal was just to survive my first year. However, as I got settled and began learning more and more about the education system, I started asking some questions. Here are a few that came to my mind:

- What if I took the time to get to know every single student?
- Why was Bridget placed in a non-honors class in the first place?
- What if the other math teacher had never recommended Bridget into my class?
- Why does an Honors Algebra 1 class even exist?
- How are students designated into honors and non-honors classes?
- What sustained the motivation for Bridget and Brittney to spend extra time learning math?
- How did Bridget and Brittney feel a sense of belonging in my classroom?

I had the opportunity to catch up with both girls later, in their college years. I was so excited to see my very first students all grown up. Bridget went on to graduate from UC Santa Barbara, and Brittney graduated from my alma mater, UC Berkeley. I was sure they both would end up in some sort of STEM field. Unfortunately, when both of my students went on to high school, they had terrible mathematics experiences. Bridget was labeled "not a math person" and quickly assumed this identity.

Dr. Joseph was right: Their high school experiences had shaped their higher education success. Bridget and Brittney both steered clear of any STEM majors that involved mathematics prerequisites. We officially lost two Black women in STEM. What happened to the school-to-STEM career pipeline, and where was the broken crack? How did the education system go wrong with my students who had so much potential to be STEM professionals? How did our system let them conclude that they weren't math people?

I wanted to understand what happened. Why had they succeeded in my Algebra class only to fall off later on in their educational pathway? Upon reflection, several factors contributed to Bridget and Brittney's success in eighth-grade math:

1. I got to know the students outside of the classroom and I got to know their families. We spent an extensive amount of time getting to know each other, their likes, their dislikes, and who they are as humans.
2. I created content and standards in an environment that allowed them to learn and apply those lessons to their own lives. I gave them time to make mistakes, learn, and relearn the material in a non-evaluative environment. It became a routine where they would come after school and learn math in a context filled with laughter and socializing.
3. The girls felt a sense of belonging with me and, most importantly, with each other. Bridget saw another girl that looked like her and the two girls both saw another woman of color teaching them mathematics. They saw a little bit of themselves in me.

There are a lot of factors that went into creating this environment that were beyond my control. However, is it possible that these chance events can actually be quantified, researched, tracked, and normalized? How can we make the story of eighth-grade Bridget and Brittney the norm from kindergarten through college and beyond?

Dr. Bettina Love recounts a similar experience when she was in fourth grade in her book, *We Need to Do More Than Survive*. She said that her teacher "was keenly aware that school had to matter to us beyond our grades. She genuinely listened to us, took up our concerns in her teaching, and made sure each voice in the classroom was heard. She allowed me to see why I mattered to myself." As a teacher, I did not come in and "save" Bridget and Brittney. Together, Bridget, Brittney, and I collectively created a human-centric environment that allowed both girls and me to be our whole selves. As it turns out, what happened by chance is actually a formula that can be replicated.

Building a culture of STEM for all leverages those three steps that marked Bridget and Brittney's success. This body of work is based on the STEM4Real Connect-Create-Cultivate Framework that is built on three pillars. This framework challenges the notion that as STEM teachers, we are solely focused on STEM content knowledge. To ensure STEM for all, our instructional practices must encompass the whole child. After teaching for over four decades, Kevin Hewitson from the United Kingdom boldly stated in his book title *If you can't reach them you can't teach them* In this spirit, the STEM4Real Framework is based on the philosophy that as STEM educators, we are educators of students first; the academic content is secondary. This humanizes the STEM education system and allows for a comprehensive view of the student, family, school, community, and society. The three pillars of the STEM4Real Framework are: 1) getting to know students beyond the classroom, 2) creating relevant content and standards, and 3) fostering a sense of belonging. With Bridget and Brittney, I did a number of things to address these pillars.

Pillar 1: ***I got to know the students outside of the classroom and I got to know their families.*** We call this the connect phase. During the connect phase, we encourage teachers to get to know their students beyond the classroom. They choose one to two case-study students and ask them the following:

- What's their story?
- What are they passionate about?
- What interests do they have?
- What goals do they have?

Whenever we face a challenging relationship, especially with a student, we as educators must find the counternarrative and seek out resources to help the child.

Pillar 2: ***We created content and standards in an environment that allowed them to learn and apply the material to their own lives.*** The girls knew that they had to learn math in order to achieve, and the act of persisting through the algorithms was enough for them to gamify the process together in problem solving. Moreover, they saw the importance of applying the concepts to their own lives. This is the create phase, where we create standards-based, culturally responsive content that is aligned to the lived experiences and identities of our students.

Pillar 3: ***The girls felt a sense of belonging with me and, most importantly, with each other***. Together, we were able to cultivate a sense of belonging where the girls knew that

I would hold them accountable to the highest standards and expectations in mathematics. They would never feel like they did not belong in my classroom. They would never feel like they were "not math people." Cultivating a culture of anti-bias means addressing stereotypes and implicit biases head on and actively changing the narrative.

Educational equity is more than just a trendy term. Educational equity means digging deep into the archaeological foundations and artifacts of our current education system and understanding the historical context. Our system has been built on the rocky atrocities of the Jim Crow era and the tumult of the civil rights movement and a history of tracking children to be either scholars or laborers. From significant events such as Ruby Bridges's first day in a desegregated school to the current systems of special education classification, it is vital that education leaders recognize the student inequities that persist as a result of the systematically racist policies. Once we recognize these inequities, we must dismantle the practices and systems in place that allow them to persist. Finally, we must rebuild a system that allows students like Bridget and Brittney to have experiences of belonging and achievement in STEM throughout their entire education career.

At this time, I want to recognize the heavy lift of connecting with each of our students, their families, and the overarching community. For elementary teachers, that is 20 to 35 students, and for secondary teachers, that can be over 150 students. As a secondary teacher myself, I had 178 students in four different preparatory periods during my first year of teaching. When I attended a conference session on family engagement, the presenter was a Black teacher discussing his family engagement strategies. One participant said, "This is all great but I just do not have time to call all these parents." The presenter responded, "You don't have time NOT to call." I wish I could remember this person's name because he set the tone for my entire teaching career. The more I engaged with parents and families, the more support I had at home to foster these critical school-to-home connections. As STEM educators, we do not have to choose between connection and content.

In this book, we will continue to dissect the STEM4Real Framework and apply this to every context in STEM teaching, thus building comprehensive access to STEM for all, #4Real. As prominent, culturally responsive pedagogy expert and author Zaretta Hammond states, "all teaching is culturally responsive teaching." Whether we are teaching the second law of thermodynamics, biodiversity, polynomial factoring, or implementing computer science principles and coding sequences, STEM content is not exempt from addressing students' cultures and the whole selves that they bring into our classrooms.

CRT, CRT, or CRT? Culturally Responsive Teaching versus Culturally Relevant Teaching versus Critical Race Theory

In all the discussions of CRT that we hear and the politicization of CRT, it is best to define each of these terms to not only understand but also to build a culture of STEM that is not weaponized. *Culturally responsive teaching*, as defined by Gloria Ladson-Billings, is an approach to education that takes into account the cultural backgrounds, experiences, and perspectives of students in the learning process. Ladson-Billings, a renowned educational scholar, introduced the concept in her work to address the educational disparities faced by students from diverse cultural backgrounds, particularly African American students. In order to do this effectively, educators must take the time to get to know their students through an ethnographic lens that allows for learning about the student, their family, and their community.

Culturally relevant teaching, as popularized by educator and scholar Geneva Gay, goes a step further by not only responding to students' cultures but also making the curriculum and instruction directly relevant to students' cultural experiences. Educators can create instructional learning sequences that inspire students, are relevant to their lived experiences, and tap into their natural curiosity and engagement.

The final CRT is *critical race theory*, an intellectual framework that emerged in the field of legal studies in the late 20th century but has since been applied and expanded upon in various disciplines, including education. I first learned about critical race theory in my master's program to obtain my teaching credential. That is why I was quite confused when school boards across the nation were attempting to eliminate teaching it from our schools. The theory itself is not taught to students, but as critical educators, we must analyze the power structures and how they intersect with race, ethnicity, and disability status. This means questioning the suspension rates of Black students versus students of other races, or analyzing enrollment in advanced placement courses for Black and Latino populations versus white and Asian populations. With a stark connection to race and ethnicity, educational leaders would be remiss to not challenge the dominant narratives and critically examine historical perspectives, curriculum content, and pedagogical practices that may marginalize certain racial or ethnic groups. For example, when I was coaching a teacher, she took a moment to look at her behavior grades and noticed that each of the Black boys in her class received an "Unsatisfactory" for behavior. She could have concluded that "Black boys do not behave well in her class." However, she used this experience as an opportunity to meet with each student individually and get to know their best learning environment. She asked each of them how they learn best. She reported that the students immediately connected with her and her class and felt like they were asked to be part of building the class culture. It was not about managing her students' behaviors; it was about building her classroom environment to create a sense of belonging.

When you ask our team at STEM4Real the question of whether we use CRT, CRT, or CRT, the answer is, "Yes! We use all three." The first pillar of our framework allows us to connect with our case-study students, get to know them on a deeper level, and in turn, be culturally responsive to their specific learning needs. The second pillar, the create phase, enables us to think about instruction that is culturally relevant and meaningful to students' lives and community. Using the processes that you will see in this book, we encourage teachers to choose their standards, present the engaging hook, and discuss the implications for society. Finally, the third pillar, the cultivate phase, allows educators and leaders to recognize student inequities, dismantle systemic barriers in STEM, and rebuild policies and structures that support all standards for all students. A culture must be cultivated because we are sharing stories and narratives that challenge mainstream thought patterns and highlight the lived experiences of marginalized groups. This involves a critical perspective that amplifies the voices of students who have been historically marginalized and allows their stories to shape a new educational discourse. Moreover, we also ensure that students feel like they belong in the classroom. Students are able to bring their whole selves into the classroom and embrace their identities without having to check their culture at the door. We are able to build, restore, and foster our culture of STEM.

The STEM Equity Odometer

We created the STEM4Real Equity Odometer as a way to reflect on equity in our classrooms, schools, and districts. It is a survey with questions designed to highlight a school's vision and commitment to STEM education and equity by encouraging leaders to take a critical look at each facet of their leadership, curriculum, and instructional practices. This serves as a school system's launching pad for auditing and diagnosing the components of an equitable STEM program. Each of the following sections explore one component of the STEM4Real Equity Odometer.

A Clear Mission Statement Regarding Equity in STEM

The presence of a clear mission statement regarding equity and social justice in a school's STEM program not only indicates their commitment to these values but also serves as a guiding principle for all facets of the STEM education experience. It sets a high standard for inclusivity, diversity, and equal opportunities for all students, regardless of their background or abilities. This mission statement serves as a beacon, aligning actions and decisions with the overarching goal of fostering an equitable and just STEM learning environment. While some organizations may have a STEM mission statement or an equity mission statement, not all organizations explicitly address the intersection of equity and STEM. Creating a mission and vision statement specifically for equity in STEM allows organizations to recognize the systemic barriers that have historically excluded and marginalized certain groups from pursuing STEM education and careers. By explicitly articulating their commitment to equity in STEM, organizations can hold themselves accountable for dismantling these barriers and fostering an environment where all students have the opportunity to thrive in STEM fields.

The broken school-to-STEM pipeline, characterized by unequal access to resources, opportunities, and support, has resulted in a significant underrepresentation of minority groups in STEM fields. As educators, we have a responsibility to address this inequity by creating transformational change in our classrooms, schools, and communities. By embracing equity as a core value in STEM education, we can work toward a future where STEM fields are truly inclusive and reflective of the diversity of our society. This starts with developing a clear and comprehensive mission and vision statement for equity in STEM, one that guides our actions and decisions and inspires us to create a more accessible STEM learning experience for all students. Below are examples of mission or vision statements that illustrate the connection between STEM and equity:

- Cultivating an inclusive STEM learning environment where all students feel empowered, supported, and prepared to thrive in STEM fields.

- Eliminating systemic barriers in STEM education to ensure that all students have equal access to opportunities and resources, regardless of their background or identity.
- Fostering a culture of equity and social justice in STEM, where diverse perspectives are valued, celebrated, and reflected in our curriculum, instruction, and school community.

Systems, Policies, and Procedures in STEM

The existence of policies and procedures in STEM classes that reflect equity practices is a tangible manifestation of the school's commitment to ensuring that all students have the opportunity to succeed in STEM. These policies and procedures go beyond mere words on paper; they translate into concrete actions that level the playing field and create a supportive environment for all learners. By embedding equity practices into its day-to-day operations, the school demonstrates its dedication to removing barriers and fostering a STEM program that is truly inclusive and accessible. While we often focus on behavioral and social emotional growth in mathematics and English language arts (ELA), STEM (including computer science) is often forgotten. According to the Kapor Center's Leaky Tech Pipeline Initative, "Low-income students and students of color are 12X less likely to have access to computer science courses in their high schools." This disparity is even greater in honors and advanced STEM courses and electives. Additionally, the report states, "Just 1 in 10 employees across some of the largest and top-grossing tech companies are Black and Latinx," providing further evidence for the broken school to STEM pathways. It is crucial to constantly ask ourselves who has access to these opportunities and what barriers may be preventing certain groups of students from participating. By examining access to honors STEM courses, electives, and other STEM opportunities, we can identify and address the root causes of inequity in STEM education. Here are some specific examples of policies and procedures that can reflect equity practices in STEM classes:

- Grading policies that are fair and unbiased
- Attendance policies that are flexible and accommodating
- Inclusive extracurricular activities that cater to a variety of interests
- Discipline policies that promote restorative practices
- Professional development opportunities for teachers on culturally responsive pedagogy

STEM Advisory Committee in STEM

The members of this committee should receive training in equity and social justice in STEM. The presence of such a committee demonstrates the school's willingness to seek expert guidance on how best to serve all students in its STEM program. This committee, composed of individuals with specialized knowledge and experience, provides valuable insights and recommendations to inform policies, curricula, and instructional practices. Their expertise helps the school navigate the complexities of equity and social justice in STEM education, ensuring that all students have the opportunity to thrive. In addition to its role in promoting equity and social justice, a STEM advisory committee can also play a crucial role in ensuring that the school's STEM curriculum is aligned with the Next Generation Science Standards (NGSS) and Universal Design for Learning (UDL). The

Next Generation Science Standards are a set of K–12 science content standards that set the expectations for what students should know and be able to do. They provide a framework for K–12 science education that emphasizes inquiry-based learning, hands-on experiences, and the integration of science, technology, engineering, and mathematics (STEM). UDL is a framework for designing learning environments that are accessible and inclusive for all learners, regardless of their individual differences. A STEM advisory committee can help the school stay up-to-date on the latest advancements in STEM fields, such as computer science, artificial intelligence, environmental justice, and engineering design. This is especially important at the elementary level, where students are developing foundational skills that will be essential for success in STEM fields later in their lives. By having access to expert guidance, schools can ensure that their STEM programs are preparing students for the challenges and opportunities of the 21st century.

Another critical component of ensuring an equitable and inclusive STEM education is analyzing the existing STEM curriculum using the Toolkit for Instructional Materials Evaluation (TIME). TIME is a comprehensive framework that can be used to evaluate the alignment of instructional materials with the NGSS and UDL principles. By carefully examining the curriculum through the lens of TIME, schools can identify areas of strength and weakness, and make necessary adjustments to ensure that all students have access to high-quality, culturally relevant STEM learning experiences. Here are some specific examples of how a STEM advisory committee can support professional development, alignment to the NGSS, and the implementation of UDL:

- Providing workshops and training for teachers on NGSS-aligned teaching methods
- Developing curriculum resources that are aligned with the NGSS and UDL principles
- Assessing the school's STEM program to identify areas for improvement
- Recommending strategies for recruiting and retaining underrepresented students in STEM

A Supportive Administrative Team that Prioritizes STEM

The ability of the administrative team to identify equity issues in STEM and provide guidance to staff is a crucial indicator of the school's commitment to addressing these issues. This ability demonstrates a proactive approach to equity, recognizing that challenges may arise and requiring ongoing vigilance and attention. By equipping the administrative team with the necessary expertise, the school empowers them to lead with understanding and foster a culture of continuous improvement in STEM education equity. In addition to addressing the academic aspects of STEM education, a supportive administrative team also prioritizes the holistic development of students, recognizing that STEM education should not come at the expense of other essential areas of learning. This means moving beyond the hyperfocus on mathematics and ELA to embrace a more comprehensive approach to education that addresses the whole child. This includes creating multi-tiered system of supports (MTSS) plans that actively involve science and STEM, ensuring that all students have access to the support they need to succeed. Moreover, the administrative team should invest in professional development opportunities for teachers, particularly those at the elementary level, to ensure they have the skills and knowledge to effectively teach science and STEM concepts. By prioritizing the whole child and ensuring teachers are equipped to teach science and STEM, the administrative team can foster a truly equitable and inclusive STEM learning environment for all students. Here are some specific examples of how a supportive administrative team can address equity issues in STEM education:

- Conducting regular data analysis to identify and address disparities in STEM achievement among different student groups
- Providing professional development for teachers on culturally responsive pedagogy and inclusive teaching practices in STEM
- Developing and implementing policies and procedures that promote equity in STEM education, such as grading policies that are fair and unbiased
- Creating a supportive and inclusive school climate that values diversity and celebrates the contributions of all students in STEM
- Investing in resources and infrastructure to support STEM education, such as providing access to technology and STEM labs for all students

Translation Services and a Welcoming Environment for Non-English–Speaking Families The provision of interpretation services to support non-English–speaking parents ensures that all parents have access to information about their child's progress, curriculum, and opportunities in STEM. This commitment to multilingual communication breaks down language barriers and empowers families to actively participate in their child's STEM learning journey. By removing linguistic obstacles, the school fosters stronger family-school partnerships and ensures that all families feel welcomed and included in the STEM education experience. Historically, families of color have often felt excluded from school communities, leading to a sense of disconnection and a lack of engagement in their children's education. By creating welcoming and inclusive environments for non-English speaking parents, schools can begin to reframe this narrative and foster more meaningful partnerships.

Moreover, we can dismantle the narrative that "parents of language learners do not care." Because the history of the educational system is built on excluding certain cultures and languages, there exists a sense of exclusion among some families that persists to this day. Therefore, establishing language services and a welcoming environment that goes beyond robo-calls can allow for leaders to rebuild and reintroduce the school-to-family relationships. This open communication empowers families to support their children's STEM learning at home and actively participate in school events and decision-making processes. It can be done by:

- Ensuring non-English–speaking parents have equal access to information about their child's STEM education
- Fostering stronger family-school partnerships by removing linguistic obstacles
- Creating a welcoming and inclusive environment to address historical feelings of exclusion among families of color
- Re-framing the narrative around family-school relationships through meaningful partnerships
- Facilitating active participation in decision-making processes related to STEM education

In-service and STEM-focused Professional Learning

The inclusion of in-service opportunities that focus on equity and social justice in STEM in the annual professional development plan indicates that the school is committed to providing its staff with the training they need to effectively serve all students. This commitment to ongoing professional development demonstrates the school's recognition that equity work is an evolving process that requires continuous learning and growth. By investing in their staff's knowledge and skills, the school empowers them to implement effective and culturally responsive teaching practices that promote equity and social justice in STEM classrooms. In addition to prioritizing in-service opportunities that center on equity and social justice in STEM, it's crucial to acknowledge the systemic challenges that can hinder the effective implementation of such professional development initiatives.

The lack of substitute teachers to cover classroom responsibilities for educators participating in professional learning can be a significant barrier. Addressing this challenge requires a comprehensive approach, possibly involving the allocation of additional resources to ensure adequate coverage and minimize disruptions to students' learning experiences. Furthermore, recognizing the time and effort invested by teachers and school leaders in advancing their skills, it is essential to consider providing additional compensation for their commitment to ongoing professional learning. Systematizing professional development into the bell schedules and school calendar can help integrate these learning opportunities seamlessly into the school's routine, making them a consistent and integral aspect of educators' continuous growth. By addressing these practical challenges, schools can create an environment where professional learning becomes not only a commitment but also an accessible and sustainable part of the educational ecosystem, contributing to lasting improvements in equity and social justice in STEM education. Creating a focus on in-service and systematized professional development can look like this:

- Incorporating collaborative lesson planning sessions into professional development activities, enabling educators to collectively design and implement culturally responsive STEM lessons
- Creating mechanisms for ongoing feedback and evaluation of professional development programs to continuously assess their effectiveness and make necessary adjustments to meet evolving needs
- Establishing a culture of peer observation, where educators observe each other's STEM classes to gain insights into diverse teaching approaches, strategies, and the implementation of equity-focused practices
- Encouraging collaborative analysis of student work during dedicated sessions, providing a platform for educators to collectively assess the impact of their teaching methods on student understanding and engagement
- Implementing a structured method for sharing best practices derived from peer observations and student work analyses, fostering a community of continuous improvement and knowledge exchange among educators

Diverse Curriculum with Contributions from People of Color and Underrepresented Groups

The examination of contributions of people of color and underrepresented groups in STEM in the school curriculum helps to ensure that students from all backgrounds see themselves reflected in the STEM curriculum and school promotes a more inclusive and representative STEM environment overall that inspires and engages all learners. This intentional inclusion of diverse perspectives and role models challenges stereotypes, broadens students' understanding of STEM, and fosters a sense of belonging and connection.

In fact, the entire STEM4Real movement started with the children's book *There's Something in the Water*, which features the story of Dr. Tyrone Hayes from UC Berkeley, and further solidifies our commitment to diversity and representation in STEM education. Stemming from our mission to showcase and amplify leaders of color in STEM, the book serves as a tangible representation of our dedication to bridging the gap in the school-to-STEM pathway. By creating such resources, we aim to provide young learners with relatable role models, fostering a connection between their aspirations and the diverse faces of success in STEM. *There's Something in the Water* not only contributes to a more inclusive curriculum but also acts as a catalyst for sparking interest and curiosity among students about the myriad possibilities within STEM fields. This personalized approach helps repair and augment the school-to-STEM pathway by ensuring that students, regardless of their background, can envision themselves as active participants in the exciting and diverse world of STEM. Through initiatives like this, we actively contribute to breaking down barriers and inspiring the next generation of leaders in science, technology, engineering, and mathematics. We can continue to foster this by:

- Establishing a curriculum that reflects the true diversity of the STEM community and promotes a more equitable representation of achievement and innovation
- Fostering a sense of belonging and connection among students by showcasing role models who share similar backgrounds
- Ensuring that the contributions of people of color and underrepresented groups are not only acknowledged but also integrated intentionally
- Challenging stereotypes by showcasing diverse narratives and success stories in STEM fields

Implementation of Culturally Responsive Teaching Strategies

The use of culturally responsive strategies in teachers' lessons helps to dismantle barriers to learning for all students. These strategies, rooted in an understanding of diverse cultures and learning styles, create a more inclusive and accessible classroom environment. By adapting their teaching approaches to the needs of their students, teachers foster a sense of belonging and engagement, empowering all students to reach their full potential in STEM.

In addition to our commitment to diverse STEM content, we recognize the paramount importance of incorporating culturally responsive teaching practices into STEM education that extends beyond the confines of history and social science classrooms. It is a collective movement to ensure that student identities, cultures, and their entire selves are integrated into the fabric of instruction. Understanding that disparities in enrollment and achievement persist, especially in courses like chemistry and physics for Black and Brown students, prompts us to critically examine and reform the systemic aspects that contribute to these divisions.

By embracing culturally responsive teaching in STEM, we strive to create equitable pathways that allow for the success of all students. This involves acknowledging and valuing the diverse ways in which students learn, tailoring instruction to be inclusive and reflective of their cultural backgrounds and fostering an environment where every student feels seen, heard, and capable in the pursuit of STEM knowledge. Through this approach, we aim to break down barriers, dismantle systemic inequalities, and cultivate a learning environment that empowers every student to thrive in STEM disciplines. It can look like the following:

- Designing projects and assignments that allow students to explore STEM concepts within the context of their own cultural backgrounds
- Ensuring that teaching materials, examples, and case studies used in STEM classes reflect a diversity of cultural perspectives and contributions
- Incorporating real-world examples and applications that resonate with the lived experiences of students from various backgrounds (e.g., STEM4Real's SHS method of Standard-Hook-Society, as explored in Chapter 5)
- Encouraging collaborative learning and peer-to-peer interactions to create a supportive and inclusive classroom dynamic

Rejection of Early Tracking Based on Mathematics and Reading Levels

The avoidance of tracking students based on mathematics and reading levels underscores the school's commitment to equity in STEM education. Tracking, a practice often rooted in standardized test scores, can inadvertently create a hierarchy of classes, limiting opportunities for students who may not initially demonstrate high proficiency in math or reading. By rejecting early tracking, the school creates a space where all students are emboldened to explore and nurture their STEM potential.

This approach recognizes that STEM talent and aptitude can manifest in diverse ways and that students should not be prematurely labeled or restricted based on limited assessments. However, the challenges of early tracking persist, dictating the future of a student based on their fifth-grade mathematics and reading scores. This reliance on arbitrary assessments becomes particularly problematic when determining placement in science and engineering courses or honors levels. The tracks, shaped by teacher recommendations and student behavior marks, risk perpetuating inequities by basing educational trajectories on subjective evaluations. Such early tracking can set the groundwork for inequitable science tracks that lack a genuine foundation in scientific merit. This concern is exacerbated by the fact that many students do not receive daily elementary science education, compounding disparities in exposure and preparation. Advocating for a shift toward holistic evaluation methods and reforms in the track creation process becomes imperative to ensure that all students have equal access to a robust and inclusive STEM curriculum, unburdened by premature labels or arbitrary restrictions. You can address challenges in tracking practices by doing the following:

- Advocating for the adoption of comprehensive evaluation criteria that extend beyond standardized test scores, considering students' interests, problem-solving abilities, and potential for growth in STEM fields

- Involving parents and students in the decision-making process regarding track placement, fostering collaboration and a shared understanding of the criteria used to determine educational trajectories
- Implementing periodic reviews of tracking policies to assess their impact on equity, making adjustments based on evidence and feedback to continually improve the fairness and inclusivity of the educational system
- Establishing transparent and well-defined criteria for placement in science and engineering courses, eliminating ambiguity and ensuring fairness in the track creation process

Inclusion of Students with Disabilities in STEM

The school's commitment to ensuring that students with disabilities have access to and opportunity in STEM classes reflects its unwavering dedication to inclusivity and equity. By breaking down barriers and providing necessary accommodations, the school empowers students with disabilities to pursue their STEM interests and aspirations. This commitment extends beyond simply providing access to classes; it also encompasses creating a supportive and inclusive STEM learning environment where students with disabilities feel valued, respected, and fully capable of achieving their goals. By embracing diversity and recognizing the unique strengths and perspectives of students with disabilities, the school fosters a truly equitable and inclusive STEM learning community.

However, it is crucial to address existing challenges that may inadvertently exclude students with disabilities from fully participating in STEM education. There is a notable gap in the representation of science in individualized education programs (IEP) and 504 plans, indicating a potential lapse in accommodating the unique needs of students with disabilities in science courses. Additionally, the absence of co-teaching models in science classrooms can create barriers to inclusive learning experiences. To address these gaps, STEM4Real has taken proactive steps by incorporating special education teachers into science content professional learning initiatives. This approach ensures that the work toward equity and inclusion in STEM education is comprehensive and reaches all teachers, creating an environment where every student, regardless of ability, feels supported, valued, and capable of thriving in STEM fields. By recognizing and actively addressing these challenges, the school continues to strengthen its commitment to cultivating a truly equitable and inclusive STEM learning community for all students. You can include the following practices:

- Conduct a comprehensive review of Individualized Education Program (IEP) and 504 plans to ensure the explicit inclusion of science-related accommodations and support for students with disabilities.
- Provide ongoing professional development opportunities for all educators, including special education teachers, focused on implementing inclusive practices in STEM education.
- Establish a system for regular evaluation and assessment of the effectiveness of inclusive practices in STEM education, with a particular focus on the experiences of students with disabilities. Later in this book, we will refer to the STEM + SPED Toolkit.

- Develop a co-teaching model and implement strategies to create a supportive and inclusive STEM learning environment where students with disabilities feel not only accommodated but valued, respected, and fully capable of achieving their STEM goals.

An Open Invitation to Reflect on Anti-Racism in STEM

There has been a push to ban words like *equity* and *anti-racism*. The Boston University Community Service Center defines anti-racism as the practice of actively identifying and opposing racism. The goal of anti-racism is to actively change policies, behaviors, and beliefs that perpetuate racist ideas and actions. Who wouldn't want to be anti-racist? The word *anti-racist* is not meant to shut anyone out or land us on a list of banned books. The spirit of this work is to call people in on a collective mission to create inclusive pathways in STEM, for real. I am personally inviting readers to join me on a journey that captures the history and foundations of the school to STEM pathways, and our critical role in ensuring that STEM education is truly accessible to all students. In this journey, it is essential to recognize that the legacy of systemic racism persists within our educational structures. However, there is a discomfort and avoidance of addressing issues of race and racism. According to author Beverly Daniel Tatum of *Why Are All the Black Kids Sitting Together in the Cafeteria?*, "Most of the White people I talk to either have not thought about their race and so don't feel anything, or have thought about it and felt guilt and shame. These feelings of guilt and shame are part of the hidden costs of racism." If you feel defensive, it's normal. Robin DiAngelo, author of *White Fragility: Why It's So Hard for White People to Talk About Racism*, states, "The simplistic idea that racism is limited to individual intentional acts committed by unkind people is at the root of virtually all white defensiveness on this topic." While some may perceive racism solely in extreme manifestations such as the burning of Black churches, racism continues to persist in the form of extreme educational inequities. When I see our Black students are not reading at grade level and are not graduating at the same rate as white students, that signals that we have a problem rooted in systemic racism and, as the educators who make up this system, we have a moral call to action to ensure that STEM is for all, regardless of race or background. Achieving pathways to STEM for all requires a transformative approach. It does not necessarily mean that we throw everything out and start over. Our call to action is to repair the broken pathway. This process can be unyielding. This is why I see this book as an active companion and collaborator. Each chapter ends with a series of questions and discussion prompts. The goal of these prompts is to serve as individual and collective opportunities for reflection and to apply each chapter to your own pedagogy and leadership. As we break down the walls and reimagine STEM through a justice-centered lens, there might be some initial thoughts and reactions. At times, you may cheer in solidarity, vehemently disagree, feel overwhelmed, or you may feel validated in the work that you are already doing. I am going to walk you through some common oppositional reactions as we embark on this exploration together:

- **"This text needs to be less confrontational and accusatory about prior or current science teaching."** The intention behind this text is not to cast blame or point fingers at individual educators, but rather to engage in a critical examination of systemic inequities within STEM education. Like many in the STEM4Real movement, I am learning and reflecting on how I can learn better and teach better. My aim is not to single out educators or assign fault, but rather to collectively confront the structural barriers that hinder equitable access to STEM education for all students.
- **"Every class needs to include cultural projects and lessons. STEM needs to include all students but you cannot throw out traditional science and start over."** Culture goes beyond the typical celebration of tasting foods from other countries. Dionne Champion, research scientist from the education nonprofit organization TERC, was part of a collective study called "Designing for Learning Computational STEM and Arts Integration in Culturally Sustaining Learning Ecologies." In the study, they stated that their use of culture as a construct refers to the historical and socially shared practices in which communities or groups of people engage. Culture is created, re-created, and remixed every day. Principal investigator Eli-Tucker Raymond states, "Our findings indicate that computing is deeply cultural, and the cultural dimensions should be heavily engaged with when working with people who come from demographic groups historically and currently marginalized in STEM and computing, such as Black women. The idea is to not throw out traditional science. It is about expanding the scope of STEM pedagogy to be more inclusive and reflective of the diverse backgrounds and experiences of all students."
- **"The book is written from the viewpoint that all current science teachers are racist, uncaring, and are not concerned about making science more inclusive."** First, I want to honor and recognize the dedication and passion of educators across the board, including my very own high school science teacher. (Hi, Mr. Peterson!) While acknowledging the existence of systemic barriers that may inadvertently perpetuate inequities in STEM, the book does not attribute individual malice or intent to any educator. This is not the proverbial "witch hunt" that accuses anyone of being racist. It is meant to invite reflection on the ways in which implicit biases, microaggressions, and systemic structures may impact teaching practices and student outcomes in STEM. One of my student teachers, Ernesto, recalled an experience where he felt like his high school chemistry teacher did not give him a fair chance. He tried to ask for help after school and it was clear that she did not want to help him. He ended up giving up and not passing the class. He eventually retook the class and she expressed to another teacher that she was not excited to have him in her class again. Fast forward, Ernesto is a high school biology teacher and now leads the science bilingual education program as a high school science teacher. I do not think Ernesto's teacher had malicious intentions. This profession can be exhausting and extremely difficult. However, the impact on Ernesto could have been detrimental in his STEM journey. Luckily, he found a way to use this experience to become the teacher that he wanted as a student. That is what makes STEM inclusive.
- **"The sentence 'Because the history of the educational system is built on excluding certain cultures and languages,' is not useful."** While I understand

that this statement may be challenging for some readers, I believe it is important to confront uncomfortable truths in order to facilitate meaningful change. My intention is not to dwell on past injustices, but rather to use this knowledge as a catalyst for positive action and transformation within our educational institutions. It is essential to recognize and confront the historical realities that have shaped our educational system. The acknowledgment that our educational system has historically excluded certain cultures and languages is not only factual but also serves as a foundation for understanding the systemic barriers that continue to impact marginalized communities today. For example, I am struggling to find resources for the Hawaiian language because it was historically outlawed and is now an endangered language. By acknowledging this history, we can begin to address the root causes of inequities within our educational system and work toward creating more inclusive and culturally responsive learning environments. While this statement may be challenging for some readers, it is important to confront uncomfortable truths in order to facilitate meaningful change. The intention is to use these historical contexts as a catalyst for positive action and transformation within our educational institutions.

- **"You expect me to dump the lecture? One of the 'new' things in education is to 'dump the lecture' and allow students to teach themselves. Students being forced to teach themselves when they are struggling learners is absurd."** The aim is not to disregard the valuable role of teachers in guiding and supporting students through their learning journey. Instead, it's about redefining the teacher's role as a facilitator of learning. It is understandable that the notion of moving away from traditional lecture-based teaching methods may raise concerns, particularly for educators committed to supporting struggling learners. As you will see in the create phase, it is not about "dumping" the lecture, but moving the lecture to allow for exploration and inquiry first. Strategies that we will discuss in the book such as collaborative group work, hands-on activities, and problem-solving tasks, empower educators to create dynamic learning environments where students are actively involved in constructing their knowledge. These methods not only enhance retention and comprehension but also cater to diverse learning styles and abilities.
- **"This book has a 'holier than thou' attitude, where they think they are above the rest of us."** I want to take this time to thank every single educator that I have worked with, quoted, interviewed, and amplified in this book. I personally am learning every day and I have the privilege to walk alongside STEM educators around the world that are committed to creating equity in STEM for all. I also want to thank my students for teaching me just as much as I taught them. This book is an account of all of the successes, failures, risks, fumbles, and triumphs in STEM education. One of the first teachers I worked with as a coach was Deja. She told me that a student that she had in fifth grade, a Latino male student named Edward, walked into her classroom as a high school senior to visit. He said that science started for him in her classroom. This was the first time he ran investigations with independent variables. He has now been accepted to multiple universities in the University of California and California State University systems for civil engineering. These stories are meant to inspire and create a viral sensation of redefining a new norm in STEM access for all. This book is here to

serve as a guide for opening more doors for students like Edward, Ernesto, Brittney, and Bridget. If there is a pontifical tone, it is only my pure admiration for the educators who are doing this work and making it look seamless. As I always say, you are never "just a teacher." Teachers are innovators and the educators of innovators.

- **"STEM is upper level, higher thinking, synthesis of ideas to create new things. This means that struggling learners will also struggle with the rigor of the content."** Out of all of the thoughts that you can have while reading this book, this one is the most dangerous to our children. As STEM educators, we cannot be gatekeepers on who gets access to STEM and who does not based on a perception of students' thinking and whether their thinking is "higher-level" or not. It is crucial to reject the assumption that "struggling learners" are inherently incapable of engaging with and excelling in STEM subjects. In fact, research and experiences found in this book have shown that with the right support and resources, all students, regardless of their academic background, can thrive in STEM. Rather than viewing struggling learners as inherently disadvantaged in STEM education, it is vital to recognize the diverse strengths and abilities that students bring to the learning environment. We, as STEM educators, should not get to decide who has "upper-level and higher thinking."

Now that I have dissected some common thoughts that you may experience throughout the book, there is one very important prerequisite to ensuring STEM for all that actually supersedes reading this book. The very first step is to have the unconditional belief that STEM is truly and absolutely for *all* and that every student belongs in STEM. Then and only then can we proceed to the next step, and that is reading this book and using it as your guide. The reason why I share these common reactions is because I, too, have also expressed these similar thoughts. It is easy to control the class when I have a clipboard and class roster with points taken off due to behavior. It is easy to blame the parents, families, school, and the rain when students are not performing. However, do we want easy or do we want equitable? That is when I knew that I needed to reflect, refract, and rethink my STEM teaching. As Robin DiAngelo says, "If I believe that only bad people are racist, I will feel hurt, offended, and shamed when an unaware racist assumption of mine is pointed out. If I instead believe that having racist assumptions is inevitable (but possible to change), I will feel gratitude when an unaware racist assumption is pointed out; now I am aware of and can change that assumption."

When I made the transition from teacher to administrator, I supported educators in implementing the new science standards and science teaching reform. As I was conducting these professional development sessions, I had colleagues attend various workshops on equity, implicit bias, systemic racism, and social justice. I wanted the science and STEM education community to participate in these same conversations. Simultaneously, I wanted the attendees in the equity workshops to attend the NGSS workshops. I realized I wanted to break down the walls between STEM content and equity, and thus STEM4Real was born. STEM4Real centers STEM professional development on the foundation of anti-racism, anti-bias and justice-centered pedagogy: Standards + justice, you never have to choose.

This book serves to illuminate the critical intersection of culturally responsive teaching and STEM education. Our goal is to rebuild the school-to-STEM pathways. The narratives of Bridget and Brittney, their journey from my Honors Algebra 1 class to their respective college graduations underscored the long-lasting impact educators can have on students' lives. It became evident that the leak in the school-to-STEM pipeline occurred during high school, where Bridget's mathematical identities were unfairly molded. Recognizing these moments can help us repair and rebuild a sense of belonging in STEM. If at any moment in the book you feel overwhelmed, take a deep breath and remember that a series of incremental shifts can make a huge impact. For example, when connecting with students and their families, it does not have to be all 178 students at once. You can start with one or two. It just takes one student connection or one culturally relevant STEM lesson. We may not know which door a student enters; however, it is our job to open every door we see closed.

Let's make STEM for *all*.

PART 1

Connect

CHAPTER 1

What Is Your *Why*? Our Vision 4 Justice in STEM Education

'I don't believe that there are many systems that serve ALL students. Some systems probably hurt our students. In order to better serve ALL students, we must break these systems and make adjustments in order to fight for social justice and an anti-racist agenda. Does a growth mindset hurt our students?'

—Frank Gonzalez, Leadership 4 Justice graduate, 2020

Within the hustle and bustle of lesson plans, standardized tests, standards, initiatives, and formative assessments, it is important to ask the following question: What propels you forward? What fuels your unwavering commitment to your classroom, school, or institution? What is the spark that lights the path for every student in your jurisdiction? It's in that sacred space, where passion meets purpose, that we find our why. This question transcends the daily routines; it encapsulates the essence of our journey as educators. So, as we embark on a chapter dedicated to creating a Vision 4 Justice in STEM education, let's begin by reflecting on our individual and collective whys. Why do we tirelessly advocate for an inclusive and equitable educational experience? Do we inherently believe in the transformative power of STEM for all students, regardless of their background or circumstances? Our answers will be the compass guiding us through the complexities that lie ahead, steering us toward a future where every student's potential is not just recognized but actively cultivated. At the end of this chapter, we will revisit this question: What is your why?

Along the way, we will discuss the components of a solid Vision 4 Justice and how they are fueled by our why. This will help us build our overarching Vision 4 Justice in STEM education. But we can't build a comprehensive, equitable vision without first recognizing the factors that influence student equity. An equitable classroom will have all of the following six key pillars of educational equity in STEM. In inequitable classrooms, at least one pillar will be missing or poorly constructed, which throws off the foundation. They include:

- **Equal Access:** Ensuring that all students, regardless of their gender, race, ethnicity, socioeconomic status, or other factors, have equal access to STEM courses, resources, and extracurricular activities.
- **Family and Community Engagement:** Involving families, communities, and stakeholders in the educational process to create a collaborative and supportive network that promotes equity in STEM education.
- **Inclusive Curriculum:** Developing and implementing a curriculum that reflects diverse perspectives, cultures, and contributions in STEM fields. This helps students see themselves represented and engaged in the material.
- **Equitable Teaching Practices:** Using teaching strategies that recognize and accommodate different learning styles, backgrounds, and abilities. It involves avoiding biases and stereotypes that may limit certain groups of students in their pursuit of STEM education.
- **Anti -Bias Professional Development:** Providing ongoing professional development for educators to enhance their understanding of equity issues, unconscious bias, culturally responsive teaching practices, and strategies for creating an inclusive STEM learning environment.
- **Supportive Learning Environment:** Creating a classroom and school culture that values belonging and diversity, promotes inclusivity, and supports the diverse learning needs of students. This includes providing appropriate accommodations and support for students with disabilities.

Ideally, the education system that we would like to think we are part of is an inclusive and equitable system that allows every single student the opportunity to receive a rigorous, relevant, and applicable education that will create informed members of society who are prepared for college or their respective careers. We would like to think that all six of these components are firing equally like cylinders in a vehicle. However, data indicates female students and underrepresented groups (including rural students) are less likely to have access to high-quality computer science content. The U.S. Bureau of Labor Statistics (BLS) estimates that in 2023, 27.7 percent of people employed in computer and mathematical occupations were women, 9.2 percent were Black or African American, and 8.9 percent were Hispanic or Latino. Black, Latino, and Indigenous individuals represent approximately 30 percent of the overall U.S. population but are only 23 percent of the STEM workforce due to underrepresentation among those with a bachelor's degree or higher. Now, not everyone may dream of being a STEM professional, but STEM has the potential to open doors for many of our students of color. According to the Bureau of Labor Statistics, in 2021, STEM professionals earned a higher median salary ($95,420) compared to non-STEM professionals ($40,120) All students, regardless of their background, should have the choice to set themselves up for a financially secure future in STEM. Here are some more stark statistics that highlight the disparities in STEM education and workforce representation:

- According to the College Board's "AP Computer Science Principles Course and Exam Description" (2019), female students and underrepresented minority students, including Black and Hispanic students, are significantly underrepresented in AP Computer Science courses compared to their white and male counterparts.
- A report by the National Center for Education Statistics (NCES) in 2020 found that students in high-poverty schools have less access to advanced STEM courses, limiting their exposure to rigorous STEM content compared to students in low-poverty schools.
- The American Society for Engineering Education (ASEE) reported in 2021 that women and underrepresented minority students continue to be underrepresented in engineering degree programs, hindering diversity in the STEM workforce.
- Data from the National Science Foundation (NSF) Science and Engineering Indicators 2022 show that underrepresented minority groups, including Black, Hispanic, and Native American individuals, are significantly underrepresented among those earning doctoral degrees in STEM fields.
- The gender pay gap persists in STEM fields, with women earning less than their male counterparts. The American Association of University Women (AAUW) reported in 2021 that women in STEM occupations earn only 82 cents for every dollar earned by men in STEM occupations.

These statistics underscore the need for concerted efforts to address systemic barriers and promote inclusivity in STEM education and careers. They highlight the importance of creating equitable opportunities for all students, regardless of their gender, race, or socioeconomic background, to pursue and succeed in STEM fields. In order to create these opportunities within our schools and classrooms, we need a Vision 4 Justice. But creating that Vision 4 Justice requires us to undergo inner reflection about ourselves, our surroundings, and our overarching community. We call this system the RDR Process, which stands for Recognize-Dismantle-Rebuild. As we look inward, we will be able to truly assess our education system and recognize the student inequities that exist, dismantle the systems and processes that perpetuate these inequities, and rebuild an educational foundation that is equitable, just, and student-centered in STEM.

Recognize

In order to understand our *why*, we must first understand the history of the education system to serve as a guide for how we want to rebuild the future of our education system. The harsh reality is that the foundations of our school systems have been built on inequity. In 1779, Thomas Jefferson proposed a two-track educational system, one for "the laboring" and one for "the learned." Almost 245 years later, our current system is still divided into tracks, labels, and cohorts that mirror the same student inequities that this very system was built upon.

This is the first step in deciphering the student inequities that are manifested within the walls of our system: to recognize. Where can you recognize tracks, labels, and cohorts that create an inequitable education for a student? Revisiting Mr. Gonzalez's observation at the opening of this chapter, is there a system that has been built whereby each student receives equitable access to a high-quality education? How about a high-quality STEM education? As educators, I believe it is our duty to take full responsibility for these statistics mentioned. As we frame our why, we should think about our place within the system and our sphere of influence. What gets educators like us out of our seats and in front of our students, staff, colleagues, and faculty every single day? Is it to educate some students? Is it to leave a mark? Is it to educate all students?

As we define our why, we can use this time to define educational equity in STEM. STEM4Real defines educational equity as follows:

> Educational equity in STEM refers to the just distribution of resources, opportunities, and support to ensure that all students, regardless of their background, identity, or circumstances, have equal access to a high-quality STEM education. It involves creating an inclusive learning environment of belonging that addresses systemic barriers and provides every student with the tools and opportunities needed to succeed in STEM, #4Real.

In order to truly connect with our students, we must build a relationship with them. This step is called **building resilient relationships.** At STEM4Real, we posed the following questions to our participants: How do you get along with your colleagues, staff, and administrators? How did you work through a rocky or recalcitrant relationship at school (either with staff, students, parents, or any other stakeholder?) Here is an example response from a teacher participating in a training where these types of reflection questions were asked:

> *Conflicts arose from a difference of work ethic between other colleagues. I overcame this by taking a step back to reflect on the type of work relationships I want with coworkers. In short, take a step back, reevaluate, and approach the situation in a different way.*

In this response, the educator recognized that there was a perceived difference in work ethic. Many of the conflicts we encounter with our students, colleagues, and administrators are oftentimes manifestations of the relationships we have in our own life. Just as we all have to work through conflict resolution in our personal lives, we encourage our educators to think about how they would resolve a professional conflict, especially considering the power dynamics involved between teachers, students, and administrators. The first exercise is called "The Struggle Is Real" Story. This identifies an educational dilemma that you are currently struggling with or have struggled with in the past. Now, retell this story through the lens of multiple stakeholders. This can be the student, teacher, principal, parent/family guardian, instructional coach, or district administrator.

Use this graphic as a guide to fill out each of the perspectives:

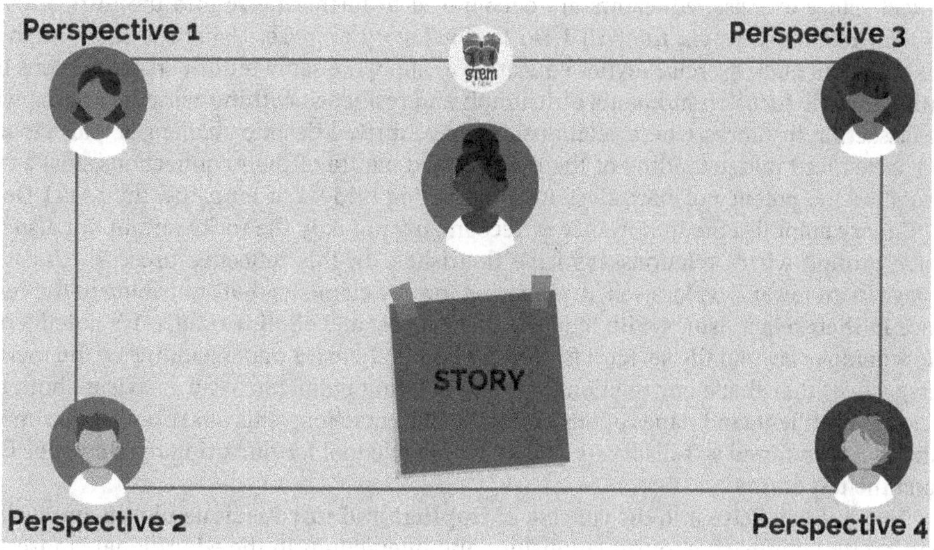

This exercise was modeled after the famous Ted Talk by Chimamanda Ngozi Adichie, "The Danger of a Single Story." Our acknowledgment of perceived differences in work ethic becomes a poignant reminder of the complexities that interlace our personal and professional lives. Often, the conflicts we navigate in educational settings echo the relational dynamics we grapple with in our own spheres. As architects of learning environments, it's imperative for educators to scrutinize these conflicts through a lens that captures the nuanced power dynamics existing between teachers, students, and administrators. "The Struggle Is Real" story exercise invites educators to delve into an educational dilemma and to unravel its complexities, not through a singular lens but through the varied perspectives of stakeholders—students, teachers, principals, parents/family guardians, instructional coaches, and district administrators. Just as Adichie cautioned against the dangers of a single story, we recognize the potency of multiple narratives in constructing bridges of empathy and connection. Tesha Irving-Sengupta, Associate Professor of Learning Sciences and STEM Education at UC Berkeley School of Education, urges us to go beyond the single story in STEM as well. She states, "As educators and school leaders, supporting youth to 'save the world' begins by replacing the single story of STEM as the solution with the reality that STEM also contributes to the world's problems. That single story of STEM as the solution dominates public discourse and public schooling. But we believe that educators must move beyond simplistic narratives of STEM to engage students in more complex analysis and action." Just as Adichie cautioned against the dangers of a single story, we recognize the potency of multiple narratives in constructing bridges of empathy and connection. In our collective work in education, this exercise serves as a powerful tool for cultivating resilient relationships, urging us to dismantle the confines of singular narratives and embrace the richness that emerges when we comprehend the myriad perspectives that shape our lived realities.

In tandem with the exploration of educational dilemmas through "The Struggle Is Real" story exercise, educators are encouraged to further delve into the intricacies of resilient relationships via the "All I Do Is Win" story exercise. Using the same method, this supplementary exercise invites educators to apply the same multi-perspective lens but with a specific focus on moments of triumph and resilience within their educational win. By dissecting instances where relationships have thrived despite challenges, participants gain a nuanced understanding of the multifaceted nature of their connections. Just as we recognize the potency of narratives in constructing bridges of empathy, the "All I Do Is Win" story amplifies the importance of recognizing not only the rocky terrain but also the fertile ground where relationships have flourished. In this reflective process, educators engage in an inward exploration, deciphering the key elements that contribute to the resilience in their relationships with students, colleagues, and administrators. It's a deliberate effort to move beyond the surface, fostering a comprehensive understanding of the myriad perspectives that shape our relationships and defining moments. As we navigate both the rocky and resilient landscapes of our professional interactions, this dual exercise becomes a catalyst for profound self-discovery and an invaluable tool for nurturing relationships that stand the test of time.

Now we will delve into the concept of **implicit and unconscious biases**, unraveling their profound impact on our relationships and interactions in the educational landscape. As Pamela Fuller, author of *The Leader's Guide to Unconscious Bias*, states Cultivating connection is a two-sided endeavor. It involves the skill of building connection with others and also the value of knowing that others are cultivating connection with you. Ultimately, both sides of this enterprise impact performance. This is why we take the time to truly understand the relationships we cultivate that build our sense of belongingThe first two exercises involved stories of struggle and triumph between a certain set of humans within the sphere of the story. As you go through each of your single stories, can you see if and how any of the themes of social injustice, racism, bias and inequity play out? What observations or inferences can you make?

As we navigate the landscape of relationships, Fuller's insight underscores the dual nature of connection-building—a reciprocal dance where individuals not only craft connections with others but also recognize the significance of being embraced in return. The profound interplay of these two dimensions significantly influences performance, making it imperative for educators to explore the multifaceted layers of their relationships. What subtle nuances can be discerned? What observations or inferences emerge as we unravel the threads of our individual narratives, bringing to light the complex interplay of race, identity, and belonging in our educational spaces?

Reflection on personal biases within the educational context is an essential facet of fostering equitable and inclusive learning environments. Often, biases manifest subtly, such as when a teacher articulates a perception that parents and families of emergent multilingual learners may not value education in the same way English-speaking students do, influencing the approach taken toward these students. I remember when my cousin was arbitrarily placed in the English Language Development (ELD) course because she used a Gujarati word dhakāṇ for lid. Many ELD courses involve tracks that remove students from the core content and create detrimental setbacks. Instances where students are redirected from core subjects like science for ELD preparation or are assigned alternative, potentially less challenging, tasks underscore the pervasiveness of biases. In these scenarios, the implicit biases of educators can impact instructional decisions and shape the opportunities provided to students. Examining personal experiences and encounters with bias in education allows for introspection and self-awareness, fostering a commitment to dismantling these biases and cultivating learning environments that truly honor the diversity and potential of all students.

As educational leaders, it is imperative to recognize and challenge damaging stereotypes that have long shaped the narrative around various student groups. Dr. Julia Aguirre's "Mathematics Methods" course exemplifies the importance of actively dismantling these stereotypes, which are particularly evident in deficit-framed messages about Black boys in mathematics. Stereotypes that perpetuate notions that some kinds of students have "low attention" or their "families don't support" education can have profound implications on students' self-perception and their educational journeys. To counteract this, educators must adopt a strength-based frame that emphasizes high expectations, successful graduates, a passion for learning, knowledge, maturity, college aspirations, and a love for the subject matter. By actively reframing stereotypes, we create a narrative that not only uplifts and empowers students but also contributes to a more inclusive and equitable educational landscape, creating an environment where every student is seen, valued, and provided with the opportunities they deserve, especially in STEM.

Another key component of recognizing inequities is by **measuring our potential impacts.** The county office of education was, at times, referred to as "the graveyard" of education. This is because people at the end of their education careers could retire at an easy desk job while drawing a higher salary. This is where we encourage people to ask themselves whether they are perpetuating the status quo or recognizing issues of inequity. Monitoring and measuring impact is crucial for educators at all levels to ensure they are not merely sitting in compliance but actively standing up for justice. It requires a multifaceted approach that encompasses various key performance indicators. Surveys play a pivotal role, including pre/post surveys to track teacher and student growth, professional development surveys to gauge the effectiveness of events, and interest surveys to tailor support to teachers' needs. Interviews provide a more qualitative dimension, involving feedback from teachers, administrators, and even students to obtain a holistic understanding of one's impact. Analyzing achievement data, especially focusing on specific student groups, offers valuable insights into overall effectiveness. Classroom implementation observation allows educators to note strategies implemented thanks to their support, creating a repository of effective practices that can be shared across the school and district.

The effectiveness of educational practices should be measured not just in compliance but in transformative impact. Educators must critically assess existing systems that either support or stratify student groups, such as tracking or tiered supports. Access to rigorous but scaffolded instruction is a key consideration, ensuring equitable opportunities for all students. Aligning district goals with the support provided to various student groups ensures a cohesive and purposeful approach, reinforcing the commitment to justice and equity in education. Regular reflection and data analysis are essential components of this ongoing process, fostering a culture of continuous improvement.

Dismantle

Now that we have recognized issues of inequity that can persist in many facets of education, and particularly in STEM education, we have to look at how these **inherently inequitable educational systems** can be dismantled. This involves taking a closer look at instructional planning and defining what equitable instructional practices look like.

Implementing equitable instructional practices in STEM involves creating a learning environment that ensures fairness, inclusivity, belonging, and opportunities for success for all students, regardless of their background, identity, or abilities. Establishing a culture of STEM education involves cultivating a culture of equity, where every student, regardless of their background, is provided with equitable opportunities to engage, excel, and find success in STEM fields. By embracing the principles of equity in STEM, educational institutions can break down barriers that historically hindered the participation of underrepresented groups. Creating such a culture involves not only offering inclusive and diverse STEM curricula but also fosters an environment where students feel valued, supported, and encouraged to pursue their interests in science, technology, engineering, and mathematics. It means dismantling stereotypes, challenging biases, and actively promoting an ethos that recognizes and celebrates the unique contributions of individuals from all walks of life to the STEM landscape. This also involves creating visibility for yourself, no matter where you are in the educational equation.

In this next exercise, we need to ask the question: "Do you even know my name?" If we are going to be dismantling inequitable systems, the first thing we must do is establish visibility. Visibility at both the school and district levels plays a pivotal role in promoting equity in STEM education. Actively engaging with various stakeholders, such as participating in presentations, attending board meetings, and collaborating with administrators, not only enhances visibility but also underscores a commitment to advancing equity in STEM. Regular interactions with a diverse range of individuals within the educational community contribute to building relationships and fostering a deeper understanding of the unique needs and challenges faced by different student groups. This visibility allows for meaningful advocacy and the dissemination of equitable practices, ensuring that the principles of equity are not only embraced within individual classrooms but are woven into the fabric of the entire educational ecosystem. As an educational leader, the impact of one's visibility extends beyond personal connections; it becomes a catalyst for systemic change, influencing policies and initiatives that further promote equity and inclusion in STEM education.

Dismantling education systems also requires a critical examination of the structures and practices that either serve or undermine the needs of all students. It involves scrutinizing systems such as behavior management, attendance policies, tracking, residential zoning, master scheduling, and hiring and recruiting practices. For instance, reevaluating tracking practices that can disproportionately impact certain student groups and examining the fairness of behavior management systems are critical steps. Tracking, in fact, is most likely due to the distribution of mathematics standardized test scores and achievement data. Additionally, addressing residential zoning policies that contribute to segregation and ensuring hiring practices prioritize diversity and inclusion are integral components of systemic change. Going beyond the school system allows for communities to see the inequities of police brutality, food deserts, air pollution, and water quality and how each of those has an impact on students' learning environments and educational achievements. By actively engaging in this process, educators can work toward creating systems that genuinely serve the needs of every student, dismantling these barriers to equity.

The next crucial step in dismantling inequitable systems in STEM involves **reimagining core instructional planning.** This is done through providing access to the core content, diversifying the curriculum, and amplifying counternarratives. To achieve this, educators can begin by cultivating a sense of curiosity through captivating phenomena relevant to students' lives. Linking these phenomena to content-based standards establishes a meaningful context for learning, which we will explore further in the "CREATE" phase of the framework. The key to promoting equity lies in telling counternarratives that present alternative perspectives and sides of the story, challenging stereotypes and providing a more inclusive understanding of the subject matter. Additionally, educators should explore local contexts that students can relate to, making the learning experience more engaging and relevant. By incorporating diverse perspectives and counternarratives into the curriculum, educators can create a learning environment that reflects the richness of different cultures and experiences.

Embracing anti-racist teaching involves a deliberate shift away from traditional, teacher-centric practices like rote memorization toward a more dynamic and student-centered approach. Anti-bias teaching seeks to dismantle systemic inequities by acknowledging the diverse backgrounds and experiences of students. It involves designing instruction that not only recognizes but also values the unique strengths and perspectives that each student brings to the learning space. Incorporating varied teaching methods that cater to different learning styles ensures that all students have equal access to the content. Furthermore, anti-bias teaching emphasizes critical thinking, problem-solving, and collaborative learning, giving students valuable skills that translate beyond the classroom.

As you are building your inclusive environment, think about the microaggressions that can take place. Dismantling microaggressions is a crucial step in building an environment where students and teachers feel seen, heard, and valued. Getting to know your students and colleagues on a personal level allows for more open and honest discourse, creating a space where microaggressions can be identified and addressed. By understanding the impact of certain phrases and behaviors, educators can actively work to eliminate them from their interactions. This commitment to dismantling microaggressions contributes significantly to building a sense of belonging in the classroom.

A microaggression is defined as a remark, behavior, or event seen as an example of indirect, discreet, or unintended prejudice against individuals belonging to a marginalized community, such as a racial or ethnic minority. A student or teacher who feels safe and supported, and that they truly belong in the educational setting is more likely to engage fully in the learning experience. When individuals are free from the burden of microaggressions, they can focus more on the core instructional content, leading to enhanced participation, collaboration, and overall academic success.

Rebuild

Now that we have dismantled the systems that perpetuated inequities in STEM education, the crucial next step is rebuilding with a steadfast commitment to the core principles of our Vision 4 Justice in STEM Education. **Family and Community Engagement** emerge as central pillars in this reconstruction process. To build trust and authentic relationships with parents and families, particularly after acknowledging the rocky and racist history within education, it is imperative to adopt a community-centered approach. Key elements of this include actively involving families in decision-making processes, valuing their insights, and recognizing their diverse perspectives. Establishing open lines of communication, hosting inclusive events, and fostering a sense of belonging within the school community contribute to rebuilding relationships. By nurturing partnerships with families, schools can tap into a wealth of cultural knowledge, ensuring that STEM education is not only inclusive but also relevant and responsive to the unique needs of each student. Rekindling the family and community relationship becomes foundational to our Vision 4 Justice, fostering an environment where collaboration and mutual respect thrive, ultimately promoting equity and excellence in STEM education. As one of our participants stated: *"Many parents are scared or do not know they can ask for resources and help. It is important to set up a relationship where you can easily talk to the parents, and they feel comfortable enough to talk and reach out to us."*

Challenging stereotypes and dismantling barriers is an integral part of rebuilding equitable family and community engagement. Statements like "These parents don't care" or "Students are a product of their home" perpetuate harmful assumptions that hinder authentic partnerships. Recognizing the common barriers to family engagement, such as language barriers, at-promise (at-risk) students, lack of time, necessity, and trust, is the first step towards creating strategies that break down these obstacles. By proactively addressing language barriers through translation services and creating inclusive spaces, schools can debunk the myth that learning English is the sole indicator of engagement. Moreover, acknowledging at-promise students as individuals with unique strengths and challenges opens avenues for tailored support. Providing flexible and accessible engagement opportunities, coupled with building a culture of trust and necessity, dismantles preconceived notions and encourages meaningful participation. Rebuilding family and community engagement requires a commitment to dispelling stereotypes, understanding barriers, and crafting inclusive practices that resonate with diverse realities. We will explore this more in Chapter 4 when understanding the family and community context of our systems.

In our continued process of rebuilding, we have to recognize that we either take a racist or anti-racist stance. We either take a biased or anti-biased stance. This means we must critically assess our current professional learning. **Rebuilding professional learning** with a keen focus on equity requires a transformative shift from acknowledging racism to actively promoting anti-racism. Understanding the educational landscape's impact on Black students is crucial, given the stark disparities they face. Shocking statistics reveal that Black high school students are twice as likely to be suspended as their white or Hispanic counterparts. A deeper examination illustrates that Black students are disproportionately represented in disciplinary actions and retention rates, underscoring the urgent need for anti-bias and anti-racist professional development. Researchers from Stanford University, Jason Okonofua and Jennifer Eberhardt discuss disciplinary measures that perpetuate the "Black Escalation Effect," where Black students are more likely to be labeled troublemakers than their white peers. This escalation directly contributes to the higher rates of suspension for Black students, hindering their classroom engagement and overall learning experiences. The imperative question arises: how can professional learning dismantle these punitive disciplinary practices and create environments that foster inclusivity?

Examining the disparities in access to Gifted and Talented Education (GATE) programs illuminates another layer of inequity. While Black students constitute nearly 17 percent of the total student population, less than 10 percent of students in GATE are Black. This raises critical questions about the criteria for selecting students into GATE courses and the referral process for special education classes. The existing underrepresentation of Black students in GATE points to systemic biases in identification and referral practices, necessitating a reevaluation and transformation of these processes. Furthermore, the tracking of students based on mathematics scores, teacher recommendations, or behavior as early as age 9 perpetuates disparities in educational trajectories. Nationwide studies highlight that Black and Hispanic students, particularly in seventh grade, are less likely to enroll in advanced math courses compared to their white counterparts. Prerequisite courses create barriers, limiting access to advanced placement opportunities for these students. An equitable professional learning plan must address and dismantle these early tracking practices, advocating for a more holistic evaluation method that ensures every student, regardless of background, has equal access to a robust STEM curriculum.

In your journey of recognizing, dismantling, and rebuilding educational systems with a dedicated focus on equity in STEM, I urge you to reconnect with your *why*. Why did you embark on this transformative path within the realm of science, technology, engineering, and mathematics? How has your *why* evolved throughout the process of acknowledging and challenging systemic inequities in STEM education? In the intricate landscape of recognizing biases, dismantling oppressive structures, and rebuilding with justice in mind, your initial motivations may have deepened, shifted, or crystallized, especially within the STEM framework. This introspective exploration is crucial, unveiling the profound connection between your personal mission and the broader quest for equitable STEM education. As you navigate the complexities of STEM educational systems, ask yourself: How has this journey enriched your understanding of equity in STEM, challenged your perspectives on inclusivity, and invigorated your passion for creating a STEM landscape that genuinely serves every student? Consider how this process has transformed your commitment to fostering diversity in STEM, dismantling bias, and cultivating resilient relationships within the STEM education sphere. Your *why* is a guiding force—a beacon that evolves in tandem with your dedication to transformative change in STEM education.

As science educators, we are not exempt from addressing systemic racism and culturally responsive teaching methods. While these topics can be difficult, it is necessary to actively address them and to not avoid these critical conversations. Sephali Thakkar, the former executive director for the National Science Education Leadership Association presented her work on the difficulties STEM educators face concerning diversity, equity, and inclusion. In this presentation, she shares a gut-wrenching experience where her son's white classmate called him "dirty" and her naive son scrubbed his skin for thirty minutes in the bathtub, attempting to remove the "dirt" that was his brown skin. Because we are responsible for teaching science and STEM content, teachers have an opportunity to respond to such incidents in ways that support student learning and culture. The why behind a lesson about melanin and cellular biology can inform our students and interrupt the detrimental thinking that has persisted through decades of societal discrimination. Our *why* can teach and transform. We do not have to choose.

Now, as you stand at the intersection of recognition, dismantling, and rebuilding within STEM education, what emerges is your Vision 4 Justice. The vision intricately braids equity, inclusivity, and transformative change, specifically tailored to justice in STEM. This Vision 4 Justice is a commitment to creating a STEM environment where every student, regardless of background or identity, has not only access but also genuine opportunities to thrive and excel within the classroom and throughout the overarching system. It is a vision that envisions STEM classrooms as crucibles of innovation, fueled by diverse perspectives and an unwavering determination to dismantling biases. Your Vision 4 Justice embraces the principles of anti-racism, challenges systemic inequities, and reconstructs STEM educational systems to be beacons of excellence for all. It recognizes the importance of resilient relationships, dismantling microaggressions, and actively engaging with families and communities. In essence, your Vision 4 Justice for STEM is a call to action, a roadmap, and a pledge to create an educational landscape where each student's potential can flourish unimpeded by systemic barriers. As you carry this vision forward, it becomes a catalyst for lasting change, propelling you to actively shape a future where STEM education is a vessel of empowerment and equity.

#4Real Reflection Prompts

What is your *why*? How did your *why* evolve as you engaged in this chapter?

Reflect on the fundamental motivations that drive your commitment to education and STEM. How have these motivations transformed or deepened throughout your journey of recognizing, dismantling, and rebuilding for equity in STEM? Consider the personal and professional experiences that influenced the evolution of your *why*.

What is your overarching Vision 4 Justice? How does it encompass educational equity in STEM?

Articulate your Vision 4 Justice, specifically tailored to the field of STEM education. Describe the key elements that make up this vision—from fostering inclusivity in STEM classrooms to challenging systemic biases. How does your vision align with the principles of justice, equity, and anti-racism within the STEM context? Explore the nuances of your Vision 4 Justice as a guide for transformative change in STEM education.

Think of something concrete you can implement in your STEM teaching or leadership role.

Identify a tangible action or initiative that you can implement in your role as an educator or STEM leader. This could range from incorporating diverse perspectives in your curriculum to actively engaging with families and communities. How does this specific action contribute to your overarching Vision 4 Justice? Reflect on the potential impact and challenges, considering how this implementation aligns with your commitment to equity in STEM.

CHAPTER 2

Creating Your Squad: The Professional Learning Squad

Is it possible to teach science every day?

Absolutely. And I'll tell you why. We have our associate superintendent who believes in it and our director of curriculum instruction believes in it, and we were all teachers 20 years ago in the same district. And we're now in these leadership positions where we know how important science is. And especially if you flip it and put science at the beginning of the day where all of a sudden your attendance improves, and your engagement improves and the discipline and challenges decline. And all of a sudden, you know, everyone is excited to be at school again.

—Will Franzel, Principal, Alisal Unified School District

One cannot create and transform a culture of STEM for all individually. Recall from the introduction, the STEM4Real Equity Odometer is a tool to audit and assess the current practices, policies, and systems that yield an equitable STEM education. In exploring the odometer of your own context, there are many systems and variables that impact this work. It is one thing to teach STEM and implement a few STEM initiatives here and there, but that is not what this book is about. In this book we seek to reform STEM education from the ground up, recognizing the students and cultures that we are leaving behind, dismantling the barriers that keep students sequestered into their specific labels, and rebuilding a vision that prioritizes equity in STEM.

Principal Franzel, quoted above, served as a county office of education coordinator before returning to his previous school district as a principal. From the county office perspective, one is able to receive a bird's-eye view of multiple schools and learn how district systems operate. Knowing the research behind STEM reform and creating dream school systems, Franzel returned to his district knowing that he had the support of his squad: a director and associate superintendent who supported his vision and encouraged him to implement daily science instruction at the elementary levels. Franzel didn't just care about introducing sporadic STEM initiatives; he introduced a strategic effort to rebuild the educational landscape from the ground up, ensuring that no students or cultures were left behind. The success of this venture underscored the power of collective action and the significance of cultivating a supportive team when striving for impactful change in STEM education.

Creating a culture of STEM goes beyond sporadic instances of hands-on activities, the adoption of the latest shiny ed-tech tools, or the establishment of after-school STEM clubs. While these initiatives have merit, a true culture of STEM involves the systematic integration of STEM education into the core curriculum, aligning it with the Next Generation Science Standards (NGSS). It extends beyond exciting projects to become a consistent and accessible part of every student's learning experience. A genuine culture of STEM prioritizes belonging and inclusion, ensuring that students with diverse needs, backgrounds, and abilities are not excluded or marginalized. This means that emergent multilingual learners, students with disabilities, and students from underrepresented groups should not face barriers but should be seamlessly integrated into the core content and structures of the school. Some of the best programming out there includes Black Girls Code, The Hidden Genius Project, Girls Who Code, and TechBridge Girls. While these are fantastic organizations, they mostly comprise expanded learning models that happen outside of the school day. In order to build STEM for all, the programming must infiltrate the school day. When STEM4Real partners with other nonprofit organizations that support schools, our first question is whether or not the program is built into the school day and if not, how can we create this model? As a county administrator, I was reviewing multi-tiered systems of support (MTSS) plans and there were three checkboxes at the top of the page: mathematics, literacy, and social-emotional learning. Science was not even an option to discuss. As Dr. Sharon Delesbore, a school administrator from Sugar Land Texas states, "Because science understanding is not measured and assessed as frequently as math and reading, the lack of importance to the science discipline has been woefully negated and our workforce is suffering from lack of qualified science-based candidates." This is why when we are in these leadership conversations, we have to be the proverbial Jiminy Cricket from the Disney movie Pinocchio and remind leaders' conscience of the presence of science and STEM.

The commitment to instruction within the core curriculum and aligned with Next Generation Science Standards (NGSS) ensures that STEM is not an add-on but an integral part of the educational experience. Exclusionary practices, such as the disproportionate suspension of Black students, erode instructional time and undermine the foundations of a true STEM culture. Therefore, the alignment of your squad's vision is paramount—it's about collectively understanding and committing to the principles that define a genuine culture of STEM, where every student, regardless of background or ability, has the opportunity to thrive in STEM education. As Elena Aguilar, author of *Coaching for Equity* states:

> My community helps. I'm selective about the people I spend time with. I've purged my social networks of people who are toxic or draining, or who aren't willing to examine their own biases. It's OK to draw boundaries and to find people who nourish you, with whom you can learn and grow, and who listen to you. I need to be around people of color—and specifically, around people of color who are on their own journey of awareness and healing. And I am intentional about finding white allies—those who are on their own journey of learning and healing.

Aguilar's insight highlights the critical importance of intentional and selective connections when building a squad for creating a culture of STEM for all. Her emphasis on surrounding oneself with supportive, nourishing, and growth-oriented individuals underscores the idea that the success of reshaping STEM education is intricately tied to the quality of relationships within one's professional network. The act of purging toxic or unexamined biases from one's social circles is a strategic move toward creating an environment that ignites positive change.

Everyone Has a Culture

In the context of building a culture of STEM, this mentality is vital for several reasons. First, STEM education reform requires a collective effort, a squad that is aligned in its vision, values, and commitment to equity. Collaborating with individuals who are willing to examine their biases and actively engage in their own learning journey ensures that the squad is attuned to the complexities and nuances of creating an inclusive STEM culture.

Second, the intentional inclusion of diverse perspectives, such as people of color, acknowledges the richness that diversity brings to the educational landscape. It allows for a more comprehensive understanding of the challenges and opportunities inherent in STEM education. Finally, the quest for white allies who are committed to learning and healing is crucial for dismantling systemic barriers and biases that may exist within educational structures. Aguilar's approach serves as a blueprint for assembling a squad that is not only supportive but also reflective of the values and principles necessary for the successful implementation of a transformative vision for STEM education. The intentional cultivation of such a squad is an essential step in ensuring that the journey toward a culture of STEM is collaborative, informed, and ultimately impactful.

Once the squad is assembled, the initial phase of constructing a culture of STEM for all involves a critical introspection to define one's own culture. Culture, often immediately associated with ethnicity and race, is a comprehensive mosaic from our entire identity and lived experiences. It extends beyond individual characteristics to encompass the broader context of local communities, societal norms, and the everyday occurrences that shape our worldview. This holistic understanding of culture also embraces elements like politics, civic engagement, and our role as global citizens. Recognizing and articulating the multifaceted dimensions of our culture lays the foundation for creating a robust and inclusive cultural identity.

To initiate this reflective journey, we begin by exploring the cultural nuances of self-expression without words. Dr. Jeremiah Sims introduced this activity at his book launch for *Revolutionary STEM Education: Critical-Reality Pedagogy and Social Justice in STEM for Black Males*. How would you introduce yourself in a cultural manner without saying anything about your job, title, or education? We are defining cultural in the broadest context (e.g., ethnicity, race, language, family, spiritual beliefs, religious affiliation, generation, gender identity, birth order, or any other self-identifying manner). What do you notice about this type of introduction?

This experiential activity can serve as a powerful tool for fostering cultural awareness. By engaging in nonverbal expressions tied to our unique cultural backgrounds, we can delve into the intricate layers of our identities. This may involve gestures, symbols, or artistic representations that hold personal or cultural significance. The aim is to uncover the subtleties that often escape verbal expression but contribute significantly to one's cultural identity. The impact of this exercise is profound in building an individual's cultural identity within the broader framework of a shared culture. It encourages everyone in the squad to introspect, articulate, and celebrate the intricacies of their cultural heritage. Through the exploration of nonverbal expressions, we become attuned to the richness of our unique cultural contributions. This heightened awareness not only strengthens one's connection to their roots but also lays the groundwork for appreciating and respecting the diverse cultural identities that will collectively shape the emerging culture within the group or community. In essence, this exercise becomes a pivotal step in the journey toward a more inclusive and culturally enriched environment.

In contrast, the next phase of our reflective journey involves a shift from non-work-related expressions to a more explicit introduction, including our job titles, roles, and experiences. This transition highlights the multifaceted layers of our identity, revealing the interplay between our cultural backgrounds and professional personas. Introducing oneself with a job title prompts us to navigate the intersectionality inherent in our identities. How we are perceived and how we perceive ourselves can undergo subtle or pronounced changes as we toggle between aspects of our cultural and professional spheres. Through this exercise, we are prompted to contemplate how we present ourselves in different spheres, providing a mirror to the intersectionality inherent in our being. It's an exploration of the dance between the personal and the professional, delving into the nuanced layers that contribute to our sense of self within diverse contexts. This intentional self-reflection invites us to acknowledge and appreciate the complexities that shape our identities, fostering a heightened awareness of the interconnections between cultural nuances and our roles in the professional realm. It serves as a tool for cultivating a more profound understanding of the mosaic that is our identity, painted with the brushstrokes of our lived experiences and cultural heritage.

Culture of Power Dynamics

Now, we ask the tough question: "Would you be willing to give up your title?" This serves as a powerful provocation, exposing the inherent challenge embedded in dismantling systemic inequities. Fear of repercussions on job security often acts as a formidable barrier, preventing individuals from initiating meaningful change within the systems they operate. The reluctance to challenge the status quo stems from the understandable anxiety about personal and professional consequences. Remodeling homes, supporting families, and maintaining stability are legitimate concerns that further entrench the reluctance to jeopardize one's career. This fear-driven inertia contributes to the perpetuation of systemic inequities, as individuals, whether consciously or not, prioritize personal stability over confronting deeply ingrained structural issues.

The imperative to reduce power dynamics and hierarchies is a critical step towards dismantling systemic injustices. By acknowledging the privilege embedded in existing structures, individuals can actively work to mitigate the perpetuation of inequities. Creating opportunities for historically marginalized individuals involves stepping back and making intentional space for diverse perspectives to flourish. However, the challenge lies not only in envisioning these changes but in overcoming the fears associated with potential professional repercussions. When I resigned from my position as a program director, I was surrounded with a squad of people who also resigned. However, there were people who also expressed dismay in the system. This exemplifies the real-world complexities individuals face. The inability to make drastic changes due to personal responsibilities underscores the broader systemic challenges that impede the transformation of existing power structures. I made the decision to resign from my position when I felt that the work was not aligned to my personal vision for equity. However, at the time of my resignation, I did not have a family of my own and as many of us navigate careers in education, we have to face the reality that it can be a privilege to quit.

While we fight for a seat at the table, many people seek to build their own table instead. That is what creating a squad is about. It is about building your own roundtable of colleagues who are aligned to your vision, whether you are operating within the system or not. Fostering environments that genuinely support individuals in taking risks without fearing professional consequences becomes paramount in dismantling systemic inequities.

Crafting Your Squad

Let's talk about crafting your squad. Here are the primary qualities to look for when creating your squad. As we delve into each of them, remember that your squad forms the backbone of your transformative journey in building your culture of STEM.

- **Commitment to equity work:** Crafting an effective squad for building an equity-focused culture of STEM begins with individuals who embody unwavering commitment to equity work. Seek out team members who recognize the inherent disparities within the educational system and are passionate about addressing them. Their commitment should extend beyond mere acknowledgment to active engagement in dismantling inequities.
- **Willingness to open up their classroom:** Willingness to open up their classroom is another crucial quality in squad members. Look for educators who are not only

dedicated to their own students' success but are also eager to share their practices openly. A squad member who welcomes others into their classroom ignites a collaborative and supportive environment, essential for collective growth and learning.

- **Vision alignment:** Alignment with the overarching Vision 4 Justice, as discussed in Chapter 1, is a nonnegotiable quality. Your squad members must share a common vision for equitable STEM education. Ensuring that everyone is on the same page regarding the goals and values of your initiative creates a unified front, amplifying the impact of your collective efforts.
- **Role, institution, and grade band:** Consider recruiting individuals in similar roles and grade bands. This alignment facilitates smoother collaboration and resource-sharing, as team members can directly relate to each other's challenges and triumphs. While vertical articulation is a great opportunity for collaboration, it is also great to collaborate closely with people in your grade band, school style, or same system such as a charter, district, university, or community college. If you're a leader, make sure you are able to collaborate with other leaders who are in your position. There are pros to job-alike groups and groups that have multiple levels of leadership within the system. Having a squad with diverse yet comparable roles ensures that your equity work is holistic and applicable across various educational contexts.

In the movie *A Million Miles Away*, Jose Hernandez, portrayed by the actor Michael Peña, is seen getting mistaken for the custodial staff when he reports for duty as a scientist and mechanical engineer. Many classroom teachers are encouraged to portray scientists and engineers of color in their classrooms. However, showing students pictures of successful STEM professionals only scratches the surface of truly ensuring STEM for all. Building a culture of STEM that goes beyond superficial representations demands an exploration of belonging—a theme we will delve into more deeply in Chapter 10. The story of Jose Hernandez in *A Million Miles Away* serves as a poignant reminder that portraying diverse scientists in classrooms is just a starting point. Mr. Hernandez submitted his application to NASA 12 times before he was accepted. This type of persistence, resilience, and grit has to be actively taught. Our students, the future architects of STEM, need to not only see representation but also understand the earned belonging of individuals like Mr. Hernandez. These students will grow up to be future members of someone's team or squad.

As we create our current squad of leaders doing this work, we also have to be mindful of the future squad and team members that we send into the workforce. How do we ensure that scientists like Mr. Hernandez not only deserve to belong, but they have earned the right to belong? This stems from cultivating a culture of belonging which we will continue to explore in Chapter 10. In order for us to cultivate this culture of belonging that we want for our students, we must experience belonging for ourselves first and what that looks like in the systems and environment that we create that transcends from the classroom to the cubicle.

As I got to know the organization more, I learned that the first Asian American woman they'd hired, Tina, who had been there for five years was passed up for promotion to the position of director of science—a position which was instead given to a newly hired white woman. Tina later expressed to me that she was not even considered, and no one asked about whether she was interested. The new director was an "appointment." Though the director was qualified for the job, the pathway to promotion was clearly without any consideration of the current voices of color on the team. This set the tone for our group meetings. Tina later resigned and moved on to a site-level leadership position. I quickly learned that ideas from non-white voices were not valued as much as ideas from white colleagues. I slowly began to retract in all of our team meetings. While white colleagues were creating programming and project designs, my role involved organizing the supply closets and shopping to ensure that we had all of the materials necessary for each professional development session. Do not get me wrong; I truly enjoyed using my time to go on a wild goose chase to purchase emergency dry ice. However, I had dreams of creating content that would help fellow science educators understand the Next Generation Science Standards and the spirit of reforming science education for all.

When I first started my position as a county office administrator in science education, I was the second Asian American woman hired. The first, Tina, ended up resigning as she did not see any further growth or pathway for promotion. I found myself being the token person of color in many science leadership spaces. Most of the speakers, facilitators, and panelists were white, with very few voices of color representing science education and leadership. This affected my confidence in these spaces, as I developed a sense of imposter syndrome. It was not until I attended a science event and found myself in a room full of white educators that I finally spotted a Brown Filipina American woman who looked just like me. She had no idea that we were going to become lifelong friends. Marie was a leader in her craft and succeeded quietly. She never felt the need to showcase her talents or highlight her successes. In fact, I wished she did more of that, especially as I witnessed mediocre colleagues who spoke highly of themselves. Marie's leadership spoke volumes, not through self-promotion but through quiet and impactful success. Reflecting on her approach, I found myself wishing for more visibility of her accomplishments, especially amid the cacophony of less noteworthy colleagues. As I grew into my leadership role and began to form allyships with leaders like Marie, I found myself growing in confidence and finding my voice. I was able to create meaningful content that helped fellow science educators understand the Next Generation Science Standards and the spirit of reforming science education for all. My supervisors and colleagues also saw this newfound confidence and started supporting my programming and leadership. I needed to create a sense of belonging for myself in a space that lacked diversity.

But this is not a crusade against white colleagues. In fact, white allies are pivotal in creating a movement against a rigged system. As Pete A'Hearn, former president of the California Association of Science Educators states, "As a white educator, I believe it is critical to have a community with whom we can explore ideas, reflect, and challenge beliefs and biases." Some ideas for establishing or growing that community include finding an anti-racist buddy or mentor, joining social media groups dedicated to anti-racist work, and reading works by anti-racist leaders. A commitment to anti-racism is more important than ever, particularly for white teachers, as it is the moral duty of all educators to use their platforms to overcome racism. Not only has Pete been on the frontlines for science advocacy and leadership, he has opened the doors for other leaders of color, like myself, to have a voice. I remember speaking at the CA State Board of Education meeting in front of the honorable Dr. Linda Darling-Hammond. Our organization was advocating for science to be included in the state accountability system. Pete not only made me feel like I had a seat at the table, but also ensured that my voice would be heard and known. I also met my next ally, Anna, a white woman from rural California and Texas. Her breadth of experience and commitment to students were unrivaled. Her allyship was crucial as I was building my career. There were moments when she advocated for my work and called upon colleagues to reflect on their airtime and actions. I was early in my career and did not realize that I was creating my squad as I met people like Marie, Pete, and Anna. My squad is a physical and human representation of the Vision 4 Justice that I have created. As I build my squad, I am thinking about all of the assets that we can collectively put together to ensure STEM for ALL.

Building Collective Definitions

When there is a collective realization that sees student inequities in STEM and also sees the stark mistreatment of BIPOC individuals and people with disabilities in the STEM workforce, then there can be a focal point where the squad can come together to solve this problem. When people in the squad do not recognize that there is a blatant issue of inequity, then it is difficult to stay committed to equity work. This is where the group should take the time to define what equity means to them. Some individuals think it is as simple as implementing "sentence frames." The mere task of adding a quick writing scaffold can make educators feel like they are doing equity work. Others think of equity as taking the time to address implicit biases and microaggressions. They think about the overarching system and how many policies lead to educational inequity. Take the time to sit with your squad and define the following terms: anti-racism, social justice, equity, and anti-bias. Getting on the same page for these terms is a great way to set the foundation for what your squad wants to achieve together. Here is how our team at STEM4Real defines these terms. Note that anti-bias and anti-racism are related concepts but have distinct focuses within the broader framework of promoting equity and justice.

Anti-bias education aims to create awareness and address prejudices, stereotypes, and biases that individuals may hold against people based on their race, ethnicity, gender, religion, or other characteristics. The goal is to foster an inclusive environment by challenging discriminatory attitudes and promoting empathy and understanding. Anti-bias education extends beyond race and can encompass various aspects of identity and ability, aiming to eliminate all forms of bias and discrimination.

Anti-racism, by contrast, specifically targets racism and systemic racial inequities. It goes beyond addressing individual biases to actively challenge and dismantle structures, policies, and practices that perpetuate racial injustice. Anti-racist efforts involve acknowledging historical and systemic oppression, advocating for policy changes, and actively working to eliminate racial disparities. Anti-racism is a more proactive stance that focuses on changing systems to ensure equity for all racial and ethnic groups. Team members should seek to understand the differences so that they can lean into their own experiences and be able to specifically name and address their story.

Social justice is a broad and comprehensive concept that encompasses the fair and just treatment of individuals and groups within a society. Because education plays a large part in society, we want to explore the role of justice-centered education and what foundational instruction in STEM could look like as we build the multiple school -to -STEM pathways. Social justice involves addressing and rectifying systemic inequalities and promoting the overall well-being of all members of society. It extends beyond issues of race and includes considerations of economic, political, and cultural dimensions. The goal of social justice is to create a society where all individuals have equal access to resources, opportunities, and rights. This is where tech companies, hospitals, and other business sectors can critically look at the culture they are building and how the culture of STEM plays out in the overarching society and community.

Equity and inequity focus specifically on fairness and justice concerning the distribution of resources, opportunities, and privileges. As a concept, equity recognizes that different individuals or groups may have different needs and aims to provide what is necessary for each person to have an equal chance of success. Equity acknowledges and seeks to address historical and systemic disadvantages that certain groups may face, ensuring that everyone has what they need to thrive. For example, as a student, I had the privilege to be involved in the Gifted and Talented Education (GATE) program and was taken on a variety of field trips to science centers, museums, and special events as a student. As a teacher, I remember working with another colleague that managed the GATE program and arranged for a show with Bill Nye the Science Guy. As exciting as the opportunity was, I often thought about how we could make this program accessible to all of our students. Who had the privilege of receiving this content and who did not? I am not suggesting that we remove the opportunity to see Bill Nye. What I am urging us to do is reflect on the programs, policies, and procedures that are currently in place and to ask the question of who has access, who does not, and why. More often than not, this process will unveil the many inequities that are both implicitly and explicitly exclusionary.

Finding a Seat at the Table

After my previous organization had a few changes, I noticed that my team, where I was the lone token voice of color, had slowly transitioned and I was now surrounded by fellow colleagues of color. There were two colleagues in particular: an Asian American in mathematics, Christina, and a Latino American in technology, Fernando. These two individuals revamped my entire thinking processes in STEM. Christina ran a "Social Justice in Mathematics" community of practice. I was running a Science Community of Practice; however, when I saw that her focus was on issues of social justice, I felt like the science education community also had issues of social injustice to address as well.

When I first created the community of practice, I was surrounded by white colleagues. When the people around me shifted, and I had diverse perspectives to bounce ideas off of, my vision for science changed. This is why the squad is so vital. As you frame your definitions with others, these definitions can mean something completely different depending on the squad you have created. I proceeded to create my "Social Justice in Science" series, and it was a hit. I remember when I first pitched this to my team, the first response was, "Can we call it 'All Standards, All Students' instead of 'Social Justice in Science'?" The excuse to veer away from social justice was that we should use the wording of the K–12 Framework for Science Education. This also shows that language can be triggering. For example, social justice, equity, and the abbreviation CRT have been used as political weapons in the politics of education. Nonetheless, shifting my squad allowed me to hear and see other words, languages, and phrases that I would have never thought of. The "Social Justice in Science" series would eventually serve as the foundation for STEM4Real's vision for social justice in STEM.

Later that year, Fernando was creating a computer science fair and one of the critical components of the fair was to reach students from the court and community schools and teach them how to code. Fernando was a master teacher, storyteller, and visionary. He spent weeks working with the site leaders and creating curriculum and content. The computer science fair was set to take stage at the local university. Our team had arranged for all of the logistics, materials, volunteers, advisors, everything. Approximately two weeks before the event, our supervisor informed us that the students from the court and community schools were uninvited because there was not enough security for "those kids." Fernando was devastated. I saw him speak up at the meeting to talk about how inequitable this was for students. It was at this moment that I faced a career crossroads. I had survived a career in administration by keeping quiet, following the rules, and playing the game. This was the first time where speaking up involved clear dissent against upper management, the chief of curriculum and instruction, and the assistant superintendent of educational services. I knew speaking up was the right thing to do and I joined Fernando in expressing my utter disagreement with this decision. The other members of our team also expressed their disagreement. As a unified front, we spoke up and saw that the decision was reversed. We were ecstatic. Until the aftermath.

Despite a successful event, it was the last time that the organization would ever see a computer science fair again. We were asked to submit our thoughts in an employee survey, and we all discussed how inequitable the situation was about uninviting the students from the court and community schools. After our collective (and anonymous) feedback was tabulated, there were a series of individual meetings with leadership and our physical cubicles were separated from each other. Other team members were passed up for promotion and the culture was crushed. After one person resigned, two other people also resigned, myself included. I had to ask myself whether I was going to continue to sit down in compliance or take a stand for justice. I wanted to make sure that if I was going to take on equity- and justice-centered work, that I would be backed by an organization and squad that felt the same way, collectively. I had worked so hard to find a seat at the table, but what was the point when I did not have a squad that was committed to the vision for justice in STEM? It was time to build my own table and thus, build my own squad.

Building My Own Table, through STEM4Real

In the wake of resignations and a realization about the need for a squad committed to justice in STEM, the transition highlighted the moment of introspection that was prompted by a stark choice between compliance and justice, and it marked the juncture where personal commitment converged with a broader understanding of equity work. I could have joined another organization that had a justice-centered vision, or I could create my own organization, with my own squad. The latter option would be much riskier, but I decided to try it. Not every person has the opportunity to resign and create something from scratch, but I did. This was my time to build a table that was inclusive and committed. If adults do not have a sense of belonging, how can we begin to help our students experience a sense of belonging?

To meet our students where they are, we must look at the teams we have in place to support them. Meeting students where they are involves having a team that recognizes the systemic barriers that contribute to inequitable student outcomes. Creating an inclusive working environment that values diversity, authenticity, and belonging was our vision for creating a squad. Because our students come from diverse backgrounds, it is important they are able to thrive in a place where their own identities are valued while we, as the adults teaching them, are also able to thrive in those same spaces.

In the landscape of equity work, we must remember and bring our authentic identities into the forefront of our efforts. Embracing our individual identities enables us to lead with our whole selves, fostering genuine connections and understanding within our squad and broader community. It prompts us to reflect on our values, experiences, and perspectives, grounding our commitment to equity that encompasses our lived realities. Leading with our whole selves is an act of vulnerability and strength, allowing us to forge connections based on authenticity. It compels us to question whether we are truly willing to take a stand and push back against systems and practices that perpetuate inequities.

This introspective approach not only strengthens our resolve but also reinforces the collective power of our squad as we navigate the complexities of building an inclusive culture of STEM for all. Building a squad and team committed to diversity, equity, and inclusion is a nuanced process that demands intentional steps. Firstly, **surveying your team** becomes imperative, posing questions that not only probe the current sentiments but also lay the foundation for vital leadership changes. The survey should create a safe space where team members feel empowered to share their authentic experiences, uncovering the unfiltered truth. Upon reading the results, a critical juncture emerges where the distinction between the desire for genuine change and a quest for power becomes apparent. Reflecting on these findings is pivotal to ensuring every team member feels integral to the collective.

Take the time to **build community** and get to know each other. Lean into one another's narratives, stories, and backgrounds. Allow each individual to embrace their whole identity. We will explore this more in the next chapter as we discuss code switching. Discuss examples of when group work and teamwork had a negative impact and discuss examples that hinder the cultivation of a supportive work atmosphere. Building a team of belonging emphasizes breaking free from a single story, **fostering empathy** by embracing multiple perspectives. This process involves addressing power dynamics, pay structures, and flexibility, and humanizing the work environment. Conduct a **root-cause analysis** to understand the reasons behind team success or failure and uncover the critical factors. Adopt a student-first commitment that creates a culture where safety and bravery in speaking up are encouraged. Other essential elements include an intolerance for mediocrity and an environment where team members feel valued. Philip Bell, professor of Learning Sciences and Human Development at the University of Washington discusses the need to work together on a learning infrastructure for STEM teachers. He states, "Our individual efforts are important and useful, but systemic transformation benefits from packaging collections of such work that can support longer timescales of multi-faceted capacity building within and across systems. We might decide to collaborate on developing networked justice improvement communities—social movements that use science teaching as a key lever for equity and justice." With support from the National Science Foundation, The STEM Teaching Tools initiative was born to provide a curated set of research and practice briefs that can support equity-centered STEM educators (http://stemteachingtools.org). As you are building your own team, there are resources grounded in equity and justice that can support each team member. In the quest for creating an inclusive team, team researcher, Dr. Tanya Vacharkulksemsuk's words resonate—acknowledging that the magic of teams lies in their ability to generate output greater than the sum of individual parts, particularly in diverse teams. The range of knowledge, skills, and experiences within a diverse team becomes a powerful resource that drives the group toward significant achievements. As we move forward, we might face challenges like labor union issues and time constraints, but these are just part of the journey towards creating a team that truly represents diversity, equity, and inclusion. The main goal is to ensure that all members of the squad are committed to an overarching Vision 4 Justice and ensuring access to STEM for all.

#4Real Reflection Prompts

Intentionally Cultivating Your Squad

How can the intentional cultivation of a diverse and supportive squad, as emphasized by Will Franzel and Elena Aguilar, contribute to the successful implementation of a culture of STEM, especially considering the intersections of personal and professional identities in the journey toward inclusivity and equity in STEM education?

Career Stability versus Systemic Equity

In the context of dismantling systemic inequities and fostering a culture of belonging in STEM education, how can individuals balance the understandable concerns about personal stability and career repercussions with the imperative to actively challenge and reshape existing power dynamics? Additionally, how might the qualities outlined for crafting an effective squad contribute to navigating these challenges and creating meaningful change within educational systems?

Representation and Diversity Matters

How can individuals be intentional about promoting diversity, representation, and ensuring that multiple voices and perspectives are honored within their squad? How can you establish a shared understanding of terms like anti-racism, social justice, equity, and anti-bias to strengthen the collective commitment toward justice in STEM education, aligned with Vision 4 Justice and the creation of access to STEM for all?

CHAPTER 3

Who Are My Students? The Case-Study Student Analysis

Why are all the Black kids sitting together in the cafeteria?

—Beverly Daniel Tatum

Beverly Daniel Tatum's work *Why Are All the Black Kids Sitting Together in the Cafeteria?* explores the complexities of racial identity development and the ways individuals navigate their sense of self within a racialized society. The concepts presented in Tatum's work are highly relevant to the lack of belonging students of color experience in STEM. Tatum's model of racial identity development emphasizes the stages individuals go through in understanding their racial identity. This begs the question: Where are the students of color in STEM? In the context of STEM education, students of color may grapple with stereotypes, biases, and a lack of representation, impacting their sense of belonging.

The isolation observed in the cafeteria metaphor can extend to STEM classrooms, where students might feel more comfortable with peers who share similar racial backgrounds due to shared experiences and understanding. This is why building a culture of STEM begins with the importance of creating inclusive environments where individuals feel seen, heard, and valued. In a culture of STEM, efforts should be made to address systemic inequities, provide diverse role models, and create spaces where students of color can fully engage in learning without the burden of racial isolation.

In June 2023, a teacher performing the retirement walkout from her school was captured giving loving hugs to the young white students who leaned in for a moment of embrace from the beloved teacher. When a young Black girl leaned in with the same glee to get a loving hug from this same teacher, the teacher responded with a dismissive pat on the back and then proceeded to embrace full hugs from even more white children thereafter.

The video clearly depicted the ignoring and dismissing of a young Black girl seeking the same love that her white counterparts received from this teacher. There were comments that defended this teacher, stating that it was not possible for her to give a full hug to all of the students. Regardless of the intent, the impact was real, and the environment created in that retirement walkout was not inclusive to all children, especially the young Black girl. Experiences like this run rampant among communities of color, teaching and codifying racism in the narratives formed among children.

Similarly, students of color in STEM may face microaggressions, implicit biases, and stereotyping, creating a hostile environment. These experiences don't just erode a sense of belonging, but they also hinder academic success. Stereotypes about the abilities and interests of certain racial or ethnic groups can influence educators' expectations. Cultural biases may lead to the perception that students of color are less capable or interested in STEM fields (Steele, 1997). The best way to truly understand the all-encompassing cultures of our students is to understand our students and their families through qualitative relationships and interviews.

Exploring the Case-Study Student Analysis Protocol

The case-study student analysis protocol is part of a comprehensive protocol designed to illuminate the intricate layers of students' lives and experiences, enabling educators to forge deeper connections and provide tailored STEM instruction. Dr. Sheldon Eakins, educator, author, and equity advocate refers to this as "avenues of authenticity." "Each of us has a story. As our classrooms are becoming more and more diverse, it is crucial for students to share their stories and their cultures to make learning relevant and authentic." The following questions delve into different categories that make up the whole child. From mental health to data and assessment, gathering this information allows educators to leverage the students' cultural capital. As Professors Takeshia Pierre and Chonika Coleman-King from the University of Florida state, "Positioning students as contributors to the learning process and believing they are fully capable of applying themselves can further motivate Black students to excel in STEM education." This case-study protocol aligns to any school or district's MTSS plan that looks at academic, behavioral, and social-emotional instruction. Conversations around these three buckets allow teachers, coaches, and administrators to collect qualitative data that can support student programming.

Mental Health

- How is their overall mental health? How have they been feeling lately?
- How are they adapting to their current learning style (distance, hybrid, independent study, traditional classroom, community school)?
- How do students overcome and persist through challenges?

Lived Story

- What are the students' lived stories? What are their likes? Dislikes? Life-changing events?
- What are the students' identities, families, ethnicities, and cultures?
- What stories or passions drive them?
- What are some fun and random facts about them that may not come up in school?
- What are the students' likes or hobbies and what do they do in their free time?
- What do the students dislike? What activities would they avoid?
- What are the known stories of trauma?

Home Language

- What are the students' home languages? Are translation services necessary and available?
- What is their primary language and are they receiving the language support they need?
- What are the different ways students perceive, comprehend, and understand language in your classroom?

Strengths

- What are their academic strengths?
- What are they really good at doing?
- How do we tap into the students' strengths?
- How are you building relationships to create community and create connections with students?
- What supports have you tried with each student? (What has worked well? What did not work as well?)
- What is an emotional intelligence strength?

Data

- What qualitative data do we have access to that can inform us more?
    - Healthy Kids Surveys
    - District/State test scores
    - Language test scores
    - Grades and grade point average (GPA)
- What specific grades and test scores are noteworthy to capture?

Challenges

- What opportunities/ challenges do you think each student would have with the learning sequences?
- Where have students struggled in the past?
- What supports have not worked well in the past?
- What learning barriers can you anticipate for each student?

- What disabilities do your students have? How are these connected to IEPs and 504s (SPED Toolkit)?

Multi-Tiered System of Supports (MTSS) and Universal Design for Learning (UDL)

- Academic: How does this student access the STEM academic content?
- Behavior: How does this student behave in class and school?
- Social-Emotional Instruction: What social-emotional supports are available?
- What social-emotional learning opportunities exist for the student? (This connects to providing options for self-regulation.)
- In what ways can you (the teacher) create moments of belonging for students?

Creating a Home-School Partnership Plan

- Where does each student live?
- Who are the key adults in your students' lives?
- Do they have siblings? In the same school?
- Do your students have adult mentors? Who are they?
- Who looks after the students before and after school?

Communication

- When is the best time to call parents/guardians?
- Do parents/guardians prefer e-mail, calling, or home visits?
- Do the parents attend any school or district meetings (e.g., IEP, ELL, ELAC, PTA, etc.)?

Expectations and Shared Vision

- What are the expectations of each student from their parents?
- How can you best help the students achieve this?
- How are we recovering from the pandemic and what additional support is needed?
- How can we reach our goals?

Case-Study Student Analysis through a Universal Design for Learning (UDL) Lens

As schools and districts are adopting the UDL model, the goal of this section is to **align the analyses of the case studies** through the lens of Universal Design for Learning (UDL), emphasizing the importance of understanding students' diverse backgrounds, abilities, and learning styles. Each of the following questions serve as guiding prompts for educators to explore various aspects of their students' experiences, including their lived stories, disabilities, emotional intelligence, and language preferences. By examining case studies, educators can uncover unique factors influencing students' learning journeys and tailor their instructional approaches accordingly, embracing equity, engagement, and success in STEM education. As districts are adopting MTSS models that assess the academic, behavioral, and social-emotional learning of students, this process supports all three dimensions with qualitative data collection. Through this personalized and inclusive approach, educators can address systemic barriers and cultivate a supportive ecosystem that empowers all students to thrive in STEM fields.

What is their lived story? UDL calls upon educators to create multiple means of representation. CAST is a nonprofit education research and development organization that created the UDL framework. According to the principle of representation, learning differs in the ways that different students perceive and comprehend information that is presented to them. Learning and the transfer of learning occurs when multiple representations are used because they allow students to make connections within and between concepts. I joke that I know organic chemistry really well because I had to take it twice. I took my familiar walk to Dr. Pedersen's lecture and sat in the sea of students. In the front of the lecture hall, I see Dr. Pedersen wearing a headband and carrying a target with two Velcro balls attached to the target. The two balls represented the two electrons that formed a chemical bond. Dr. Pederson then asked if there was a student in the hall that wanted to throw the third ball at him. He asked the class, "Who wants to throw a ball at me? Come on!" I remembered my failing grade and could not have raised my hand faster. Dr. Pedersen chose another student and instructed him to use all his energy to throw the third ball at the target. Dr. Pedersen squinted while we all watched the student wind up his pitch and throw the hardest ball. I wondered if the student throwing the ball had also failed the class previously because he sure threw the ball like he was dealing with some negative feelings. The third ball hit the target, knocking down the other two electrons, thus breaking their bond. Dr. Pedersen then said, "Now I want you to remember how much energy it took you to break that bond. Let's never forget that it takes energy to *break*." In that moment, Dr. Pedersen was able to connect with hundreds of students in the lecture hall by creating a learning moment that involved a common childhood toy that we all could relate to. He connected the concept to something that was memorable and humorous as well. In coaching the STEM4Real teachers we work with, we ask, "What ways have you tried to personalize instruction in the past?" Case studies can reveal unique factors that influence a student's learning, enabling educators to personalize their approach. By knowing your students' cultural context, you can incorporate relevant examples, materials, and teaching strategies, making the learning experience more meaningful and engaging for all students. Integrating cultural responsiveness aligns with UDL by offering diverse and culturally relevant materials and activities. This ensures that the learning environment is engaging and meaningful for students with varied cultural backgrounds.

What disabilities does the student have? What are their strengths? Is there a 504 or Individual Education Plan (IEP)? For each IEP and 504 plan, there are supports listed for mathematics and literacy; there is no mention of science. This is why science and STEM teachers are not exempt from culturally responsive teaching. We are in a system that ignores the needs for a comprehensive STEM education. When we do not include our students with disabilities in STEM, we are essentially saying that we are comfortable with excluding certain student groups. We encourage teachers to ask what barriers they can anticipate for their case study students. Case studies can uncover any barriers to learning that students may be facing, whether they are related to socio-economic factors, language proficiency, or other cultural considerations. Knowing these barriers allows educators to provide appropriate support and interventions. According to the CAST guidelines for interaction, "It is important to provide materials with which all learners can interact. Properly designed curricular materials provide a seamless interface with common assistive technologies through which individuals with movement impairments can navigate and express what they know—to allow navigation or interaction with a single switch, through voice activated switches, expanded keyboards and others." Identifying and addressing barriers to learning is at the core of UDL. Understanding the unique challenges students face allows educators to provide multiple options for action and expression, accommodating diverse needs. Dr. Jennifer Muñoz, Senior Program Director at STEM4Real, states that UDL encourages creating an inclusive learning environment. By valuing and incorporating diverse perspectives, educators contribute to a classroom culture that respects and appreciates the uniqueness of each learner. Understanding the cultural backgrounds of students contributes to a richer classroom dynamic. It promotes a sense of community, where students feel valued for who they are, and it encourages positive interactions among classmates with diverse backgrounds.

What is an area of emotional intelligence strength/area of growth? Are there known stories of trauma? Exploring students' stories and passions not only uncovers hidden facets that may go unnoticed in the traditional classroom setting but also offers insights into the motivations that drive their academic pursuits. This knowledge becomes a powerful tool for educators, allowing them to design STEM instruction that aligns with students' interests and aspirations. The emphasis on building relationships and creating a sense of community further enhances the learning experience, contributing to increased engagement and a more positive attitude toward STEM subjects. For example, this teacher shared this anecdote: *This student is outgoing, friendly, and talkative during class discussion. She would openly contribute by offering her opinions about the topics she connected to, like sharing that her mother would wear a donut on her head to carry water when she was a girl. She would come to the front of the classroom to locate the country where her mother was raised.*

The student felt an increased connection to the lesson plan because of the personal experience she was able to share. The protocol's focus on respecting diverse cultural backgrounds and acknowledging multiple means of expression acknowledges the cultural capital and diverse identities within the classroom. This intentional approach creates an inclusive atmosphere, where students feel seen and valued for who they are. Addressing disabilities, learning barriers, and emotional intelligence strengths enables educators to implement targeted interventions, ensuring that STEM instruction is accessible and tailored to the diverse needs of each student. We specifically seek out support for 504 and IEPs and can further dictate the documentation that is specific for science and STEM instruction. Understanding students' experiences of trauma, their social-emotional learning opportunities, and their overall mental health creates a foundation for holistic support. Educators equipped with this knowledge can provide nuanced strategies for self-regulation, persistence through challenges, and the development of academic strengths. Cultural responsiveness recognizes the interconnectedness of cognitive and emotional development. Knowing your students allows you to create a learning environment that supports both their academic growth and emotional well-being. Educators can ask what social emotional learning opportunities exist for students. UDL recognizes the importance of addressing both cognitive and emotional aspects of learning. Understanding students' backgrounds allows educators to provide options that support emotional well-being and self-regulation. When students see themselves reflected in the curriculum and teaching methods, they are more likely to be engaged and motivated. Culturally responsive teaching helps bridge the gap between students' lived experiences and the content being taught, making learning more relevant and interesting.

What is the primary language? What is the home language? Are there auditory, visual, or other ways of presenting information to be considered? A culturally responsive approach contributes to the promotion of equity and inclusion in education. It helps to address systemic inequalities and ensures that all students, regardless of their cultural background, have equal opportunities to succeed. Both UDL and cultural responsiveness share a commitment to equity and inclusion. Designing learning experiences that consider the diverse needs and backgrounds of students contributes to creating an equitable and accessible educational environment. This is why we at STEM4Real have incorporated this question: "What are the different ways students perceive, comprehend, and understand language in your classroom?" This is especially important when addressing the concept of *translanguaging*. Translanguaging refers to the practice of using multiple languages flexibly and simultaneously in communication and learning contexts. It involves drawing upon the linguistic resources available to multilingual individuals to support understanding, expression, and learning. Authors of *The Translanguaging Classroom*, Ofelia García Otheguy, Susana Johnson, and Kate Seltzer state that "Translanguaging allows students to make connections between their home language and the language of instruction, leading to deeper comprehension of STEM concepts." According to professors Peter Licona and Gregory Kelly, translanguaging supports the logic of everyday sense-making by using out-of-school linguistic practices as resources for learning inside the classroom. Translanguaging can be used to draw from students' full linguistic repertoires, which have developed outside the classroom, in order to leverage them as sense-making tools in science teaching and learning. Using language translation resources and artificial intelligence (AI) tools can support the incorporation of multiple languages within the context of STEM learning.

Ideally, you want to engage in the practice of case-study student analysis with every student; however, teachers do not realistically have the time. This is especially true for secondary and science specialist teachers who might see hundreds of students per year. This is why we suggest identifying one or two students to use as case studies. When you universally design for one student, your work can apply universally well to others. Just as we designed curb cuts to accommodate people in wheelchairs, it turns out that runners and families using strollers also benefit from having a ramp instead of a step. By probing students' lived stories, preferences, and life-changing events, educators gain a nuanced understanding of their unique identities and the factors that shape their engagement with STEM content. This personalized layer of understanding is crucial for cultivating a learning environment that resonates with individual students, fostering a sense of belonging and unlocking their full potential.

The inclusion of academic supports, such as multi-tiered systems of support (MTSS), ensures that STEM content is accessible and scaffolded according to individual learning trajectories. The protocol extends beyond the classroom, delving into the dynamics of home–school partnerships. By examining family structures, communication preferences, and engagement levels, educators can establish meaningful connections with families, creating a collaborative support system for the student. This personalized approach not only contributes to increased student engagement, but also has broader societal implications. It lays the groundwork for dismantling systemic barriers in the school-to-STEM pathway ensuring that all students, regardless of their background, have equitable access to and representation in STEM fields. When we get to know our students and their families, we are essentially creating a client profile where the educators are the business that is serving their clientele. Once we see what the patches are, we can ultimately fix the gaps in the school-to-STEM pathways.

Why Are Students of Color Pushed Away from STEM?

When I walked into a third-grade classroom, I was introduced as Dr. Leena Bakshi by the teacher that I was supporting. She told her class that I was a scientist that helped her become a better science teacher. I was flattered by the marvelous introduction that I received and immediately started questioning whether I was a real scientist or not since I had not been in a lab since graduate school. Nonetheless, as I was internally fighting imposter syndrome, I politely smiled, greeted her class of curious third graders, and exited the classroom to support my next teacher. The teacher later called me and said, "Leena, one of my students asked me if you were really a scientist and I told her, 'Yes!' She responded, 'But she has Brown skin like me.'" Many students have moments where they feel like they can be a scientist and they can do STEM. Unfortunately, many students also have experiences where they do not feel like they belong. There are many reasons that students, especially students of color, are pushed away from STEM. Students of color often face a lack of representation in STEM fields. When individuals cannot see people who look like them succeeding in STEM careers, it may create a perception that STEM is not a space where they belong or can excel. The absence of diverse role models can contribute to feelings of isolation. For this young third grader, seeing another woman of color called a scientist was a new experience for her. It showed her a new reality that she did not know was even possible for her. This is why there is a trend to portray scientists of color and display posters of diverse scientists.

Many teachers begin their school year with the activity "Draw What a Scientist Looks Like." In this activity, students portray their version of what a scientist looks like and most of the images portray a young, white, male figure with a white lab coat. As the years have progressed, the images have evolved to include many other diverse individuals, dismantling the strongly held image of what a scientist has historically looked like. STEM curricula that lack cultural relevance may fail to connect with the experiences and backgrounds of students of color. A disconnect between the curriculum and students' lived realities can lead to disinterest and disengagement. Many curriculum and publishing companies are staffed with teams where the diversity is not representative of the student populations. For example, in one textbook, the first chapter included an example based on planning an island vacation to Hawaii. While this story may work great in terms of tourism, it does not address the sociocultural history of Hawai'i, the fact that the sunscreens they want to pack may actually deteriorate the coral reef, or the connection to the local people and history of Hawai'i. The Eurocentric nature of STEM education can alienate students from diverse cultural backgrounds. A more inclusive approach that recognizes diverse knowledge systems is crucial for fostering a sense of belonging. A curriculum that reflects diverse perspectives and incorporates real-world examples can enhance interest and participation (National Academies, 2011).

Lack of diversity in curricular materials coupled with a lack of representation of diverse individuals in STEM fields can contribute to implicit biases and microaggressions in the classroom. Implicit biases and microaggressions can manifest in educational settings, affecting the experiences of students of color. Some systems have tracking practices that are based on teacher recommendation and student behavior. The practice of tracking students into different academic pathways in science can perpetuate disparities. Many of the tracking practices use standardized test scores to make placement decisions. Students of color may be disproportionately placed in lower-level classes, hindering their access to advanced STEM coursework (Oakes, 2005). Systemic disparities in access to quality education and resources can impact students of color disproportionately. Disparities in access to high-quality education disproportionately affect students of color. Schools in low-income neighborhoods may lack resources and advanced STEM courses, limiting opportunities for underrepresented students (Ladson-Billings, 2006). Students may not have had the opportunity to express interest because their exposure to STEM was significantly reduced or eliminated, especially in the early formative years. Prevailing social and cultural stereotypes may perpetuate the idea that certain racial or ethnic groups are not naturally inclined toward STEM fields. Such stereotypes can influence students' self-perceptions and discourage them from pursuing STEM careers. Though these stereotypes are not intended to manifest in curriculum and instruction, the impact exists and we see trends of students veering away from STEM as we repair our school-to-STEM pathways. Students of color may also face challenges in accessing support systems that can guide and mentor them through STEM education and career pathways. The absence of mentors and advocates can contribute to a sense of isolation and hinder their ability to negotiate the complexities and persistence necessary when navigating STEM fields.

In the process of choosing case-study students, I encourage you to choose students who are in special education, emergent multilingual learners, or come from an underrepresented minority background in STEM. This process allows the teachers to explore the qualitative characteristics of students that go beyond the labels that are placed in their cumulative files.

Why Do This Part? What Does the Research Say about Case-Study Student Analysis?

In creating our framework at STEM4Real, we realized that CONNECT had to be the first phase that spearheads our work. If we do not know our students or the profile of our audience, then how can we create instruction that truly reaches them? Research indicates that students bring diverse cultural backgrounds, perspectives, and prior knowledge to the classroom (Gay, 2002; Ladson-Billings, 1995). In order to understand the specific cultural capital that students have, we have to take the time to gather an ethnographic account of our students. Case studies allow educators to explore the cultural nuances and lived experiences of individual students, leading to a deeper understanding of their identities and backgrounds. It also allows educators to learn from their students versus making assumptions on their behalf.

During a teacher's case-study student analysis, she gathered this: *This student has shared with me her story about how she and her siblings were adopted, as well as her biological parents' struggle with substance abuse. Family does play an important role in her life, and she is resilient and has a great attitude and disposition toward life, which is a great benefit for her. She prefers to work by herself and on paper rather than on the computer.*

The teacher now has an actual student's story in mind when they build out their instructional sequence. This story serves as a baseline data point for teachers to longitudinally monitor the student throughout the year.

Longitudinal case-study student analysis in STEM offers several researched-backed benefits, providing educators with a comprehensive understanding of students' educational journeys. Tracking students longitudinally helps identify patterns and trends in their academic performance, behavior, and engagement. According to a study by Rumberger and Larson (1998), findings demonstrate that longitudinal analyses enable the identification of academic trajectories, helping educators intervene early to support struggling students.

In the STEM4Real case-study student analysis, we encourage teachers to ask their students how they learn something new and what learning supports have proven successful in the past. Gathering this qualitative data informs personalized instruction by uncovering individual learning styles, strengths, and areas for improvement. A student can self-report their own strengths and describe hobbies such as video games, sports, and technology interests that could potentially be woven into future STEM content.

The CASEL (Collaborative for Academic, Social, and Emotional Learning) framework emphasizes the importance of social and emotional learning (SEL) to promote students' overall well-being and academic success. Case-study student analysis aligns with the CASEL framework by providing a comprehensive understanding of students' social and emotional needs, contributing to the development of emotionally intelligent and resilient individuals. However, taking the time to learn deeply about our case-study students is considered an extracurricular task that means going above and beyond the workload. This mentality inhibits the process of case-study student analysis because teachers do not have the time or capacity to invest in the deep learning of our students. Administrators and district leaders can rethink the job descriptions of teachers to allocate the necessary resources and time to support case-study student analysis as a tool to facilitate personalized instruction.

Educators need time to conduct these studies because longitudinal case studies inform personalized instruction by uncovering individual learning styles, strengths, and areas for improvement. This also allows for early interventions and supports throughout each lesson study cycle. Educators can identify challenges early in a student's educational journey, allowing for timely interventions and support. A study by Jones et al. (2018) argues that understanding students' social and emotional experiences contributes to creating supportive learning environments, fostering positive outcomes. Many of the interstitial connections that we learn from our students come from their family and home environments.

A Window into the Student Is Their Family

Family and community engagement has oftentimes been relegated to the office staff, counselors, and family engagement liaisons. When students have a home language other than English, the language barriers often create a wall between teacher and student communication with families. In order to understand who our students are, we have to get to know their families and their home situation. This also provides a window into any trauma-informed practices that are necessary. In *The Body Keeps the Score*, Bessel A. van der Kolk states: "Since emotional regulation is the critical issue in managing the effects of trauma and neglect, it would make an enormous difference if teachers, army sergeants, foster parents, and mental health professionals were thoroughly schooled in emotional regulation techniques."

In order for us as educators to understand the entire emotional package that comes with each of our students, we must do our due diligence in getting to know the families and communities of our students. For example, doctors and the medical community spend time understanding each patient's family history, and their interaction with minors involves conversations and surveys filled out by family members. During one workshop, when we brought up the concept of calling parents, one teacher asked, "So, when we call the parents, what do we say?" The parent phone call is not just a call to inform the parents that their student is not behaving well. It is an opportunity to get to know the student and their family. As teachers, we are caring for the academic, behavioral, and social-emotional well-being of their child. That is why having the perspective of their family can inform us about how we teach and design instruction.

As our STEM4Real team engages with teachers, some of the biggest pushback we get is the lack of time or desire to interact with the parents and families of our students. With the very full plates that teachers have, it is a difficult expectation to ask teachers to interact with all of their students' families. Some of the teachers are preparation period teachers who see hundreds of students throughout the week. In such cases, it could be very taxing for teachers to get to know the families of each of their students.

As a remedy, we recommend getting to know one to two case -study students on a deeper level, along with understanding their families. Understanding the unique needs, strengths, and learning styles of individual students allows teachers to personalize their instruction. When teachers know their students on a deeper level, they can tailor lesson plans, activities, and assessments to better meet the needs of each student. This personalization fosters a more inclusive and effective learning environment. For example, when working with a team of district instructional coaches, we encouraged them to choose case-study students alongside the teachers that they coach. During that process, one coach shared a finding, "John loves math and has great strength in math. ELA is challenging, he is an EL learner, he sees [the EL specialist]. [He] struggles with reading but speaks/communicates well. He loves to support peers during math and gains confidence through it." The role of instructional coaches can be further and further removed from the classroom. Case-study student analysis offers coaches the opportunity to ensure that they are student centered and gather the qualitative data necessary to inform instruction. Now that the coach and teacher have gathered this information on John, they can design instructional situations whereby he is practicing more of his speaking and listening skills to help his peers with mathematics instruction.

The next step would be to get to know John's family and understand the home language, environment, and stories that make up John's lived reality. Deepening the understanding of case-study students and their families provides insight into their cultural backgrounds and experiences. This knowledge is invaluable in making STEM curriculum and content more culturally relevant. Teachers can incorporate examples, case studies, and real-world applications that resonate with the diverse experiences of their students, enhancing engagement and connection to the subject matter. Learning about students' backgrounds, home environments, and potential challenges allows teachers to identify and address barriers to learning. For example, understanding a student's home language, family dynamics, or socioeconomic factors can inform differentiated instruction and support systems. This knowledge helps teachers provide equitable opportunities for success.

Case studies also provide a window into the social-emotional aspects of students' lives. This knowledge is crucial for implementing SEL strategies effectively. Teachers can create a supportive environment that acknowledges and addresses the emotional well-being of students. SEL skills contribute not only to academic success but also to the overall development of students. Educators can then take case studies to the next level and use this data to establish a home-to-school partnership plan. This allows the educator to look at the family structure, modes of communication, and the creation of expectations and a shared vision. Educators can learn information such as where the student lives, the key adults in the student's life, family structure and siblings, and whether they are in the same school, district, or charter. We can also seek out information on expanded learning programs and what the student does before and after school. This is especially beneficial if the student is involved in a STEM-related expanded learning program such as Black Girls Code. Educators can also learn when is the best time to call and what is the parent's preferred way of communicating. As a parent myself, I love using apps such as Remind as a tool to build relationships. Some teachers use it as a tool to congratulate their students, shore up where they have struggled, and offer opportunities for growth through tutoring or peer-to-peer mentoring. With services such as Google Translate, teachers can also communicate with families in their home language. We can also explore whether families attend events and meetings geared toward emergent multilingual learners. This dismantles the false idea that "parents who speak another language do not care." Extending opportunities to create safe and inviting spaces for families strengthens the home-to-school partnership. Together, educators and families can create a series of shared expectations in order to learn how to best help their students. Creating this partnership plan delineates a series of teacher actions, student actions, and family actions. Though we rely on the counselors and school administrative teams to handle family engagement, as STEM educators, increasing family engagement provides us with this crucial window into the student's whole self. This is valuable cultural capital that will strengthen our instructional design. That is why I emphasize doing this with 1 or 2 students and their families.

The CASEL Framework: Social-Emotional Learning Is STEM Learning

There are five components of the CASEL framework to address: self-awareness, self-management, social awareness, relationship skills, and responsible decision-making. In a quest to address the social-emotional learning components of a student, educational leaders are rushing to the next SEL-marketed curriculum and boxed solution. While these solutions may be helpful, it is important to note that there should not be a disconnect between SEL and academic STEM learning. As leaders frame their MTSS plans, there is a planning space for academic, behavioral, and social-emotional learning. This is because teaching the whole child means we cannot compartmentalize the child and address each part in a piecemeal.

One of our teachers responded with these attributes about their case-study student:

> Recent drastic change in how she expresses herself (especially with her clothes). How she learns: She grasps things quickly; in mathematics, understanding abstractly but will show it conceptually when asked by teacher; sometimes takes a few times to practice and apply; earlier this year, asked about pronouns for herself (went by he/they for awhile); sometimes gets caught up in social problems with peers; had some home issues prior to winter break. Strengths: Growth mindset, wants to learn and experiences success; friendly. She likes: socializing at recess (teacher is unsure of other interests, as she has not expressed them in class).

This student is struggling with identity issues along with social issues as she navigates her school environment. Classroom teachers tend to focus solely on the academics of the student and in doing so, are not teaching the whole child. Incorporating the CASEL framework into STEM instruction for this student involves creating a learning environment that values both academic and socio-emotional development. By addressing the student's unique characteristics, strengths, and challenges within the framework, educators can tailor STEM instruction to foster a positive, inclusive, and responsive learning experience. For example, with respect to **self-awareness,** the teacher can understand and acknowledge the recent changes in self-expression, especially with clothing. Recognize and validate the exploration of pronouns as an aspect of self-awareness. This is something that even if their feelings of self-expression are not aligned with the teacher, the student still feels affirmed in their exploration of gender identity. As they are learning the STEM concepts, they can open up their focus knowing that they do not have to invest a lot of time in covering or hiding their identity. The teacher can create this space of safety and belonging with the simple gesture of providing permission to the student to be who they are.

As a **self-management** strategy in the STEM classroom, we can continue to encourage SEL by supporting the growth mindset and cultivating an environment that values effort and persistence. Provide opportunities for the student to set personal learning goals in STEM and celebrate these successes. This way, SEL is not seen as a separate class or separate curriculum. Rather, these supports are added within the fabric of their core academic classes.

As the teacher in our earlier example described about the student, the student gets caught up in social issues at the school site. The logical approach is to separate social issues at school from the academic learning; however that separation is unrealistic to the average adolescent. In terms of **social awareness**, educators have to be attuned to the student's social interactions and challenges with peers. This allows educators to create a classroom atmosphere that encourages positive social engagement and addresses any social problems through open communication. As this student continues to build their **relationship skills,** it will solidify social-emotional interactions when implementing teamwork, team building, and group projects. The teacher can build strong teacher-student relationships by showing understanding and empathy for what the student has shared during the empathy interviews. This provides guidance and support for navigating social challenges and fostering positive connections with peers. Now the teacher can create lesson designs that build in assignment and assessment choices and allow for the student to track their progress. This can support **responsible decision-making** by involving the student in goal-setting for STEM learning. The teacher can provide opportunities for autonomy and choices in how they approach and express their understanding.

Incorporating Cultural Relevance as a Tool for Engagement

Research supports the use of case-study student analysis as a valuable tool for culturally responsive teaching in STEM. By delving into the unique experiences, backgrounds, and learning styles of individual students, educators can better understand and address the diverse needs within their classrooms. Carlone et.al. (2014) referred to this as being "Becoming (less) scientific: A longitudinal study of students' identity work from elementary to middle school science. Counterintuitively, I would argue that it is more scientific to incorporate students' social identity to increase deeper engagement with robust science learning." This study emphasizes the importance of culturally responsive teaching, aligning with the goals of longitudinal case studies to create inclusive and equitable learning environments. As an example of how this can work, one of our STEM4Real teachers created a lesson plan in partnership with Sayap Africa and about creating a water well in Eseka. We will explore more details of this lesson in the following chapters on instructional design, but there were pieces of the lesson that were specifically designed and tailored to her case study students.

Netty Spotlight: Jacqueline Lafitte's Case-Study Student Analysis

This student attends a speech class in a weekly pull-out session. His speech is very low and difficult to hear even when you give him a microphone. He was not really shy about sharing his opinion in front of the class. Fortunately, when you actually hear what he has to say, you get the depth of his empathy and comprehension of the abundant need for Eseka High School to get a clean water well, soon. He partnered with another student with a low speaking voice, who seemed to hear each other just fine. His fine motor skills are as challenging as his speech. He continued to persevere with each writing assignment draft. I could see the satisfaction in his eyes when his handwriting looked clearer and readable on the accordion book pages. He wanted me to take a picture of his pages to send in as examples of his work. In the challenge to carry a gallon of water, he and his partner chose a container without a top, like Jackson in On the Way to School. *Although he didn't travel up and down a hill or run from elephants, he expressed how sorry he was for spilling a few inches from the top of the precious water. He knew how Jackson felt when he dropped a gallon of sandy water and only had one left to share with his sister. They got soaked. His book has so many statements of empathy that I would love to share. I will share this quote, "I promise one day we will give Eseka High School a clean water well that is close to their school so the students don't have to walk miles every day to get a cup of water." His accordion book is complete. Both he and his partner chose to add an author's page in their book which includes their picture. I am proud to share their creative work.*

This anecdote illustrates the impact of case-study student analysis and culturally responsive teaching on the educational journey of a student with unique challenges. Through careful observation and understanding of this student's needs, the teacher not only identified specific areas requiring support, such as speech and fine motor skills, but also recognized the depth of the student's empathy and comprehension. By leveraging the student's strengths and acknowledging the challenges, the teacher created a learning environment that allowed the student to persevere and experience the joy of achievement. Culturally responsive teaching is evident in connection between the student's experiences and the broader issue of access to clean water for Eseka High School and demonstrates the power of weaving cultural relevance into the learning process. This not only engages the student personally but also fosters a sense of social responsibility and empathy. The emphasis on perseverance, satisfaction in improvement, and expression of empathy through the creation of the accordion book reflects the teacher's commitment to a comprehensive understanding of the student's strengths and areas for growth. The student's desire to share his work and express a promise to contribute to Eseka High School's well-being exemplifies the potential for students to become advocates and contributors to broader societal issues when their education is rooted in culturally responsive and inclusive practices.

Say My Name: Do Systems Stifle Relationship Building in STEM?

One of the participants from our STEM4Real Case -Study Student Analysis training happens to be a science specialist and expressed the following concern: "A huge barrier includes the amount of time we spend with each class. Many of us don't even have kids' names committed to memory because we see so many during the week. Also, the amount of time that passes from one week to the next doesn't help either." If specialty and preparation teachers have a limited time with students, how can we ensure that their names are prioritized so that each student has an identity and sense of belonging in the class? Here is how another science specialist teacher addressed this concern: "I had this problem last year. My first year at a new school and 570 students a week. It was really hard. The kids didn't feel respected and I felt bad every time I had to say '*Hey,* you!' This year I made simple name plates out of index cards (older kids made theirs) and put each class in a sandwich bag and a bin for each day. I hand out the names as students come in and take their seats each day. This takes an extra few minutes but has made a huge difference in behaviors, participation, and overall happiness! It is so important to use a person's name—no matter their age."

This teacher saw that by investing the extra time for each class period, she was actually able to gain additional time by dealing with fewer behavioral issues and increasing classroom engagement and joy. Whether you have a science specialist model or a classroom teaching model, which model puts student learning first? Either way, we have to say their names. Names are the first window into a student's identity. If they don't have an identity in their science class, then it is difficult to create a culture and sense of belonging.

When we encourage science specialist teachers to choose a case-study student, we get the most pushback because of the time constraints involved in getting to know their students on this deeper level, coupled with getting to know their families as well. Some administrators have argued to dismantle the content specialist program in elementary years and have the classroom teacher take on the core subjects. However, one content specialist stated:

> *Content specialists help deepen the understanding of what is to be learned. In my school, we rotate 5th and 6th graders with a Math Teacher, Science Teacher, Reading Teacher, and Writing/Social Studies. We each have our homeroom class that we develop a stronger connection with but we work to support all of our students. It provides a great balance and focus on both the content and the relationships.*

In this model, the school was able to maintain the academic rigor and expertise of content specialists and still maintain a homeroom period to foster mentorship and relationship building. Case-study student analysis contributes to the development of strong teacher-student relationships, enhancing communication and trust. Pianta and Stuhlman (2004) highlight the positive impact of teacher-student relationships on students' academic and social development, emphasizing the importance of sustained connections. The benefits of these case-study student analyses are grounded in their ability to provide nuanced insights into students' multifaceted experiences, supporting educators in creating tailored, inclusive, and effective STEM learning environments.

Implications for Increasing the School-to-STEM Pathways

The current reality is that we are losing students of color in the so-called school-to-STEM career pipeline, and this chapter seeks to find out the transformative impact of case-study student analysis and culturally responsive teaching, showcasing the potential for all students, regardless of challenges, to actively engage in meaningful learning experiences that align with their unique identities and perspectives. Case-study student analysis serves as a testament to the importance of recognizing and celebrating the diverse strengths and contributions of every student in building an inclusive and empowering educational environment. If we are able to increase the number of educators who implement this practice, we will be able to create content through an anti-racist lens because of the deeper emotional connections that are unraveled through this process.

Every single student needs one adult to see their whole self and all of the academic, behavior, and emotional interactions. In order for an MTSS plan to be fully implemented, one adult on campus must be able to speak about the academic, behavioral, and social-emotional interactions of each child on campus. This can be an unrealistic request because the teacher-to-student ratios are getting larger and larger as the teaching profession sees a decline. Educational leader Dr. Stephen G. Peters states that the main difference between successful teachers and unsuccessful ones is an understanding of their students—not just as students who need to be taught, but also as people who want to learn. This makes it imperative that we share who our children are with their teachers. Therefore, we have to create systems that normalize getting to know your students and their families as part of the job description for teachers. Whether it is one to two case-study students or a homeroom class period, every school system must ensure that each student has one adult that they can lean on who will support the SEL connections that contribute to academic success. Reverend Harry Louis Williams II is a prominent community leader and author in the Bay Area. He served as my supervisor for case management at Glide Memorial Church where I worked as an intern and currently serves on the board of directors for Homies Empowerment a community school in East Oakland. In his book, Street Cred, A Hood Minister's Guide to Urban Ministry, he speaks with the founder of Homies Empowerment, Dr. Cesar Cruz who said this: "I can't let someone who just cussed me out move me. I can see past the alcohol and the weed. He might be wearing the armor of society and not the armor of honor. What you look at as thug gear, he might wear as the new body armor for survival. If I were to talk to this young person, I'd be trying to give off as much positive energy as I can. It's not my place to judge his clothes or the fact that he's smoking weed. The young man you're talking about may have had a father who was killed. His mother might have post-traumatic stress disorder but been diagnosed as 'crazy'. No one will hire this kid, so he may have turned to the underground economy."

Case-study student analysis emerges as a powerful tool not only for enhancing individual student support but also for dismantling stereotypes, uncovering implicit biases, and catalyzing a transformative shift in the school-to-STEM-pathways. By delving into the unique stories, passions, and cultural nuances of each student, educators can proactively confront and dispel stereotypes that often hinder students of color from pursuing STEM paths. This personalized approach enables teachers to challenge preconceived notions and biases, fostering an environment where every student is recognized for their diverse strengths. Moreover, case study student analysis serves as a pivotal means to address the societal impact of systemic inequities in STEM education. As educators gain deeper insights into the multifaceted identities of their students, they are better equipped to tailor instruction that resonates with diverse perspectives. This, in turn, contributes to a more inclusive and culturally responsive learning environment. Breaking down stereotypes and biases at the individual level has a cumulative effect on the broader educational landscape, progressively dismantling barriers that hinder students of color from thriving in STEM fields. The personalized understanding gained through case -study analysis not only challenges educators to reassess their assumptions but also prompts them to intentionally design instruction that reflects the varied experiences of their students. This shift has far-reaching implications, potentially increasing the representation of students of color in STEM careers. By normalizing this practice within educational systems, we pave the way for a more equitable and accessible school-to-STEM pathways, ensuring that all students feel valued, seen, and empowered to pursue their passions. Knowing who students are transcends the confines of individual classrooms, echoing throughout society by nurturing a generation of STEM learners who defy stereotypes, challenge biases, and actively contribute to a more inclusive and equitable STEM landscape. As educators commit to this transformative approach, the ripple effect has the potential to reshape not only individual student experiences but also the broader narrative of diversity and representation in STEM fields.

#4Real Reflection Prompts

Culturally Responsive Teaching and UDL

Considering the challenges and barriers faced by students of color in STEM education, how can educators leverage culturally responsive teaching strategies and the principles of UDL to create inclusive and equitable learning environments? How might integrating students' lived stories, cultural backgrounds, and diverse learning preferences enhance their engagement and success in STEM subjects?

Integrating Social-Emotional Learning into STEM Education

How can applying the principles of the CASEL framework enhance the effectiveness of STEM instruction, fostering not only academic achievement but also the holistic development of students' social and emotional skills?

Creating a Sense of Belonging

What additional strategies can educators implement to further enhance this sense of belonging for all students, especially those from underrepresented backgrounds? How might incorporating culturally relevant curriculum, establishing inclusive classroom norms, and promoting diverse role models contribute to creating an environment where every student feels valued, respected, and empowered to succeed in STEM?

CHAPTER 4

It Takes a Village: The Families and Communities of My Context

Alone we can do so little; together we can do so much.

—Helen Keller

San Leandro, a small suburban town south of Oakland, California, currently has a diverse population comprising 9.71 percent Black or African American residents. Blogger Richard Mellor recalls that the city bears a racist history and was previously referred to as "Klan Leandro." In fact, there are anecdotes of people recollecting an image of a cross burning on a Black family's lawn as late as 1984. In 1971, a group called the National Committee Against Discrimination in Housing labeled San Leandro "a kind of racist bastion of white supremacy." The documentary *The Suburban Wall* depicted the difficulty that Black people faced when finding a home due to blatantly racist practices of redlining, discrimination, and zoning. Why is this story significant? Many historically racist practices can still manifest in the current foundations of a city and school system. Knowledge of and understanding a town's racist history can have significant implications for the educational systems within it that hail from that same history This awareness can foster cultural sensitivity among educators and students and lead to a more nuanced understanding of the experiences and perspectives of different racial and ethnic groups, promoting empathy and tolerance in the school community. As we analyze the history of our community, we have to ask how these events and policies have shaped the current educational landscape.

Who Are Our Students? Leveraging Demographic Data

Every student makes up the entire cultural capital that is contributed to the classroom and school community. Many of these labels are stamped and measured on standardized tests such as "Black or African American," "Hispanic or Latino," and so on. As educators, we want to dig deeper than these labels. More often than not, stereotypes dictate the treatment and perception of each of these demographic groups. We must seek out the cultural capital ourselves in order to combat the negative stereotypes that hang over the shoulders of our students.

In the previous chapter, we learned about seeking out the deeper story of our students. Now we want to explore the demographic trends that can ultimately build our overall classroom and school culture. Examining demographic data allows educators and policymakers to identify disparities in access to STEM education among different demographic groups. This insight is essential for addressing inequities and ensuring that all students, regardless of their background, have equal opportunities to engage with STEM subjects. You can also use this information to analyze enrollment patterns, master scheduling, and the number of students obtaining access to rigorous STEM courses. Another demographic trend to explore is the number of students who are enrolled in free or reduced lunch. This statistic is an indicator of socioeconomic status and income levels. Knowing this information leads to whether or not the school or district falls under state and federal funding formulas such as Title I funding versus basic-aid funding. Some districts offer universal free lunch and have done away with this metric; however, there may be other ways that schools measure the number of socioeconomically disadvantaged (SED) students. Examining achievement data across demographic groups can reveal efforts to close gaps in performance.

The next layer is to explore the number of students that are emergent multilingual learners or English earners and what students are classified as special education, 504, and any other learning differences. Demographic data can shed light on any gender, racial, or socioeconomic biases that may exist within STEM education. In navigating the landscape of family engagement, language barriers should not serve as a deterrent but rather as an opportunity to foster meaningful connections. When families do not speak English, it is imperative not to let this be a reason for communication gaps about their students. In fact, families might harbor feelings of shame regarding their non-English proficiency, prompting them to conceal their native languages. To address this, educators should actively seek to understand and appreciate the diverse cultures within their school community. Instead of relying solely on students for translation, educators should proactively research and utilize resources, ensuring that student translation becomes the last resort. By recognizing and addressing these biases, educators can work toward creating a more inclusive and welcoming learning environment that challenges stereotypes and promotes a sense of belonging for all students and their families. Examining demographic data over time allows educators to track the retention and success rates of different student groups in STEM courses. This information is crucial for identifying barriers that may hinder the progress of certain demographics and implementing interventions to improve retention and success rates.

Spotlight, Galvez Unified School District

Galvez Unified School District (GUSD) serves approximately 2,254 students with 87.4 percent socioeconomically disadvantaged (SED), 13 percent students with disabilities (SPED), and 97 percent Hispanic or Latino. Almost all of the students are from families working in the agriculture industry, the heart of the Salinas Valley's economy. GUSD stands as the only school district in the community, thus underscoring the need to serve students and educators from rural populations. According to the Galvez Youth Council Survey, 88 percent of student responses indicated that they are struggling with learning/understanding their lessons. As evidenced in our recent student performance levels over the past 24 months, GUSD has seen very low/red performance levels district wide for mathematics with declining patterns in the last several years. When looking at suspension rates when compared to all students, ELL, SED, and SPED student groups were placed one performance color below. For chronic absenteeism, two performance colors were below for SPED. With ELL and SPED students being the most adversely affected by disengagement in the classroom, it is clear that we must address the implicit and explicit biases in many of these systemic policies. Based on this evidence of disengagement for our most vulnerable populations, GUSD seeks to target district-wide anti-bias professional learning with a focus on lesson study. We also build in case-study student analysis, family engagement plans, and understanding the school context into the lesson study process to increase a sense of belonging and community for both students and teachers. In looking deeper into our student achievement data, all student subgroups are not achieving, and based on feedback from stakeholder groups, there is an urgent need for increased focus on student achievement and improving ELD instructional practices, plus the needs to increase staff efficacy in rendering quality instruction, to calibrate PLC practices across sites, and to address the high rate of staff turnover.

Rural educators must especially seek out additional resources to support equitable science and STEM education. Rosanna Ayers, science educator, administrator, and lead STEM4Real instructional coordinator, presented this for her doctoral research study:

"The context of rural life coupled with the small populations of Black students in these areas creates a need to understand how science instruction must be realized for these students. It appears as though a rural environment does not equalize access to science learning and that Black students are not achieving the same levels of proficiency as white students. Issues of scalability, culturally responsive pedagogy, language demands of science, and educator self -awareness have created a vacuum for science educators to imagine their approaches to be sufficient even in the face of consistently poor outcomes for BIPOC (Black, Indigenous, People of Color)." Armed with demographic data, educators can design targeted interventions and support programs to address the specific needs of underrepresented groups, especially in STEM. This may include mentorship programs, additional resources, community partnerships, and initiatives aimed at fostering a supportive and inclusive learning environment that supports access to STEM.

Data as a Storyteller

The data and metrics of a student body can tell a collective story. Educators rely heavily on quantitative data such as test scores, graduation, and attendance rates. The art of using data as our storyteller is to collect both quantitative and qualitative data on a larger scale. This involves taking a historical and ethnographic approach to data collection while understanding the root causes of how our communities were built. One can start with the basics such as figuring out the learning management system used to house all of the data. We can then explore overall test scores for mathematics, language arts, and science. Some states only post mathematics and language arts while other states are still debating whether to collect data on science and social studies. Students are also monitored with their English language acquisition and each state has a language proficiency assessment.

Demographic Data Collection Sheet

- Survey of learning management system
- ELA and mathematics scores
- Science, social studies, and other subject-matter assessments
- Language proficiency
- Special education status
- Attendance rates
- Graduation rates
- Free and reduced lunch

After collecting this data, we have to ask ourselves, "What does the data say about our school or classroom?" Analyzing data can tell a compelling story about building a community that fosters STEM education for all by revealing key insights, trends, and successes. Regularly researching and analyzing demographic data supports a culture of continuous improvement. Educators can use data to assess the effectiveness of their teaching methods, identify areas for growth, and make informed adjustments to enhance the overall quality of STEM education. One of our schools was able to monitor the rates of underrepresented minority students in the Advanced Placement (AP) chemistry and physics courses. This data may show an increase in the enrollment of students from diverse backgrounds in STEM programming. Highlighting the growing diversity within STEM classes can underscore the community's commitment to providing equal opportunities for all students. As example of why data collection is so important, consider this: When a principal asked his peers for the pros and cons of implementing a STEM elective at the elementary school, he was met with a series of data points that included the increase in student engagement levels, connections to career-technical education pathways, and partnerships with local labs and universities to support training and professional development. Data on student participation in STEM-related extracurricular activities and events can illustrate the community's enthusiasm for STEM. This can show increased participation rates over time, which suggests a growing interest and engagement in STEM subjects.

Shifting the narrative surrounding at-promise students is fundamental in cultivating an asset-based model as opposed to a deficit model. Rather than focusing on perceived deficiencies, educators should embrace and celebrate the strengths of families. Collaborating with parents to impart skills and behaviors conducive to home learning creates a collaborative and supportive educational environment. Delving into discussions about family cultures and routines while forging partnerships with community organizations further strengthens the bonds between schools and families. Dispelling misconceptions about time constraints is pivotal in revitalizing family engagement efforts. Statements like "We don't have time to call the parents" should be countered with the resounding affirmation that taking time for parental communication is an investment with significant returns. By recognizing the interconnectedness of student success, classroom management, community, and overall school climate, educators can appreciate the multifaceted benefits of robust family engagement.

What's Not in the Data? Conducting an Ethnographic Tour

After researching the demographics, enrollment data, graduation, and attendance rates, educators need to explore the qualitative aspects of a community that are not necessarily found in these standardized statistics. If we are teaching and learning in a particular community, it is important to explore the school's culture, atmosphere, and overall learning environment that may not be fully captured in statistical data. An ethnographic tour of a school can provide educators with valuable insights that go beyond the standardized demographic data of a school or city. Educators can immerse themselves in the physical environment of the school, gaining a deeper understanding of the context in which students learn. As Mr. Evans, an educator from North Carolina, said:

> I try to always live and shop in the community in which I teach and only missed doing so for one semester. It is advantageous because not only do I get to know more about my student body, I also get to know about the community: the good, the bad, the ugly. Instead of simply living there I attend all school events and many of the events around town. I usually don't drive, so they see me walking through the community every day and always stop and talk to me. Trust me, it is indeed a blessing.

Even if you aren't able to live in the community you teach, here is how you can conduct an ethnographic tour:

1. **Make Community Observations:** Observe people in their natural environment rather than in a formal research setting. Reach out to a community expert and learn more about their stories and experiences. Educators can witness firsthand the interactions among students, teachers, and other staff members during an ethnographic tour. This observational data can reveal nuances in social dynamics, relationships, and communication styles that may influence the learning experience.

2. **Take an Ethnographic Experience Tour:** Visit key city landmarks, museums, festivals, food spots, local farms, or shopping malls. Take photos and make it a day of exploration. Educators can engage with the broader community surrounding the school, gaining insights into the cultural and socioeconomic context that may influence students' lives. Understanding the community's values, challenges, and aspirations provides a more holistic view beyond demographic statistics. Educators can also use the tour to gauge the school's relationships with local businesses, organizations, and community leaders. The tour allows educators to assess the school's efforts in promoting cultural sensitivity and inclusivity.
3. **Get a "Home-Eyed" View:** Talk to counselors to get a picture of the students' life at home and schedule a time to speak with the families in person or virtually. When I was a first year teacher, my colleague Ms. Gutierrez and I conducted home visits for every single student that did not show up for parent/family teacher conferences. I do want to acknowledge that at the time, Ms. Gutierrez and I did not have any children of our own and we had additional funding through the Nell-Soto Grant Program that funded the Parent/Teacher Involvement Program in California. Of course, this was the ideal situation to conduct these home visits and it served a very rich purpose. If you are able to make time for this experience, I highly recommend it; however, I am also acknowledging the demands that educators have on their time already. Getting a "home-eyed" tour can involve joining a family at a school or community event. This part of the ethnographic tour allows educators to observe aspects of student well-being, such as their behavior, engagement, and overall sense of belonging. Non-verbal cues and the general atmosphere can provide a more nuanced understanding of students' emotional and social experiences. Informal conversations with students during the tour can also offer valuable insights into their perspectives, interests, and concerns. Hearing directly from students and families provides a qualitative dimension to complement quantitative data on student demographics.

Incorporating the findings from an ethnographic tour alongside standardized demographic data enriches educators' understanding of the school community. It provides a more nuanced and contextually rich view, supporting informed decision-making, tailored instructional approaches, and targeted interventions that address the unique needs of the school's population. As an example, this is what Mr. Davis from New York City public schools did: He researched Black-owned businesses in the Lower East Side of New York City. He personally reached out to the owners and discussed how he would like to take his students on a tour and requested them to share their origin story, a bit about their business, and the importance of STEM within their business. He also applied for a grant to compensate the business owners for their time. The business owners responded with enthusiasm and even committed to his work regardless of whether he received the grant.

Community Knowledge and Environmental Science

The power of an ethnographic tour can lay the foundation for STEM instructional design, especially when discussing environmental science and climate education. One common factor that unites us all is our ability to breathe in air as aerobic respirators. For example, if you were to take a moment to go outside and inhale a whopping breath of fresh air, would you take in fresh air or would you take in fresh pollution? The impact humans have on the environment extends beyond personal habits or obvious sources of pollution. It also encompasses government regulations, urban planning, and legislative actions that shape our daily lives. Unfortunately, systemic racism often permeates these measures. As STEM educators, we have a duty to address the environmental principles and concepts that directly affect our community. Families and communities play a vital role in shaping students' perspectives, values, and understanding of environmental issues. By engaging families and communities in environmental education, teachers can encourage a sense of shared responsibility and collective action toward addressing environmental challenges. Community organizations such as Comite Civico del Valle can play a significant role in supporting environmental education initiatives. These organizations often have deep roots in their communities and possess valuable expertise and resources that can enhance classroom learning. By partnering with community organizations, teachers can access guest speakers, field trip opportunities, and hands-on learning experiences that enrich the curriculum and provide students with a holistic understanding of environmental issues. To increase community involvement in environmental education, teachers can take several steps:

1. **Establish partnerships:** Reach out to local community organizations, environmental groups, and grassroots initiatives to explore collaboration opportunities. Building strong partnerships can facilitate the exchange of knowledge, resources, and support for environmental education initiatives. The State of California has the State Seal of Civic Engagement to encourage service learning as a critical component of a student's high school education.
2. **Host community events:** Organize workshops, seminars, or community forums focused on environmental issues that invite families, community members, and stakeholders to participate. These events can serve as platforms for dialogue, knowledge-sharing, and collective problem-solving that pertain to specific community issues. As you delve into the communities of your students to gather evidence, encourage them to examine the phenomena within their own community context.

3. **Incorporate community-based projects:** Design curriculum projects that involve students in addressing local environmental challenges or conducting research relevant to their communities. Engaging students in meaningful, hands-on projects creates a sense of ownership and empowers them to make positive contributions to their communities. It is our responsibility as educators to present these situations to students so that they can weigh the evidence themselves. This step grounds students in crafting their arguments when discussing issues of environmental racism. When we tap into the local communities of our students, we can elicit examples that provide students with first-hand experiences. This allows them to understand the multiple perspectives involved when discussing complex community issues and develops their argumentative skills.

Survey of STEM Resources

Conducting a survey of resources to support STEM instruction involves systematically assessing the available tools, materials, and facilities that can enhance the teaching and learning experience. The first step is to inventory existing resources and to take stock of the current STEM resources available in the classroom or school. This includes textbooks, lab equipment, software, and any other materials related to STEM subjects. Some specific items to add to your list could include the following: microscopes, beakers, test tubes, additional laboratory equipment, and consumable supplies for experiments and hands-on activities. One school created a "STEM Materials Storage Room" where they collected common items such as cotton balls, paper clips, magnets, hydrogen peroxide, empty water bottles, Styrofoam, and other materials they can readily use for inquiry-based activities. You can also evaluate the availability and functionality of technology resources, such as computers, tablets, and other devices, and ensure that these resources are up-to-date and suitable for STEM applications.

Many labs and workshops may not be well-equipped or in working condition. Some teachers use this as a reason not to teach STEM. However, STEM can be taught anywhere as long as the tools and materials have been inspected beforehand. The resource is the school or district curriculum adoption for STEM. Evaluate the current STEM curriculum materials in use. Identify any gaps or areas where additional resources may be needed to enhance instruction.

Spotlight on Golden Springs Community Schools:

The teachers use multiple phenomena from the adopted curriculum to drive student learning. For example, Mr. Rogers began his lesson starting with an archaeological dig and connecting the work on dinosaur fossils and the Indiana Jones movie series. He had the class take on the role of doctoral archaeologists as they started the dig in order to bring the lesson to life and connect career exploration into the lesson design. The teacher created a science learning wall to add their own perspectives and embrace the diversity within their own classroom.

In this example, the current curriculum provided the base set of activities that were aligned to the Next Generation Science Standard: "Construct an explanation based on evidence for how geoscience processes have changed Earth's surface at varying time and spatial scales. MS-ESS2-2". He created additional connections to the curriculum by tying in potential careers in archaeology and science academia. To create something similar, teachers can look into online platforms and educational websites that offer STEM resources, lesson plans, and interactive activities and consider how these digital resources can supplement traditional teaching materials. In the next chapter, we will be discussing how to align these resources to be culturally responsive to each of your students.

As you are exploring the resources you have, create a low-cost engineering and tinkering center that can serve as a classroom or school makerspace. Makerspaces can foster creativity, collaboration, and hands-on learning. Start by identifying a dedicated space within the classroom or school, ensuring it's conducive to exploration and project work. Next, gather a diverse range of materials, from basic craft supplies like cardboard, glue, and markers to more specialized tools such as 3D printers, robotics kits, and electronics components. Consider leveraging cost-effective resources, repurposing materials, and seeking donations from families, local businesses, or community members to build your inventory. You can develop a culture of curiosity by encouraging students to contribute ideas and take ownership of the makerspace. Provide flexible workstations that accommodate various projects and learning styles. Offer guidance and support, facilitating a dynamic environment where students can tinker, innovate, and bring their ideas to life. Once you survey all of your school and community resources, you can offer these as training and community building opportunities for families and community members interested in supporting STEM and environmental education efforts. Empowering individuals with knowledge and skills enables them to become effective advocates for justice-centered STEM within their communities.

STEM and Social Media

Over the past decade, social media has evolved into a global platform that significantly impacts education, particularly for STEM educators. Handles such as **@TeachForTheCulture** and **@SurvivingMSScience** have emerged as influential voices, attracting thousands of followers by sharing ideas on educational equity and innovative instructional programming. These platforms offer STEM educators a unique opportunity to stay informed, connected, and inspired. By following these creators or even becoming content creators themselves, teachers can access a wealth of resources, strategies, and insights aimed at fostering equitable STEM education.

Social media also serves as a dynamic space where educators can showcase their own work, highlight student achievements, and engage in collaborative idea-sharing. This interconnected digital community not only empowers STEM educators with diverse perspectives but also plays a crucial role in advancing the collective goal of creating inclusive and equitable content that prepares students for success in STEM fields. In this way, social media can be a powerful catalyst for community building among STEM educators.

Platforms like Instagram, X (formerly known as Twitter), LinkedIn, and Facebook foster virtual communities where educators can connect, share experiences, and draw inspiration from one another. The comment sections on posts from handles like **@TeachForTheCulture** and **@SurvivingMSScience** become virtual forums for discussions on best practices, challenges, and strategies for promoting equity in STEM education. These platforms create spaces for educators to engage in meaningful dialogues, offer support, and exchange valuable insights that transcend geographical boundaries. Social media can facilitate collaboration beyond the confines of school walls by giving teachers from different regions and even different countries a chance to collaborate on projects, share lesson plans, and co-create resources. This collaborative approach not only enriches the diversity of educational perspectives but also provides STEM educators with a global network of like-minded professionals. Through collaborative efforts initiated on social media, educators can pool their expertise, contributing to the development of innovative, inclusive, and culturally responsive STEM content.

Who Is Responsible for STEM?

The allocation of responsibility for STEM education often resembles a game of hot potato, passing the STEM baton from person to person or classroom to classroom. One prevalent model is the science specialist approach, where elementary schools hire a dedicated professional to cover all science standards outside the regular classroom. This model, while allowing classroom teachers a preparation period, results in the specialist teaching one subject across multiple grade levels. Unfortunately, this setup raises issues of access, particularly since the science specialist cannot engage students in science and STEM on a daily basis. It is only in middle school that students begin receiving daily science instruction, typically from a specialized science teacher. However, the delayed exposure to STEM during the foundational years of learning and development can create significant gaps in the school-to-STEM pathways, potentially contributing to disparities in STEM opportunities. Bridging these gaps early on is crucial for ensuring equitable access and fostering interest in STEM fields from an early age.

Moreover, in the elementary schools, there is a hyperfocus on mathematics and ELA instruction because those subjects are heavily tested. Focusing primarily on mathematics and English language arts (ELA) while neglecting science during the foundational elementary years can have several factors that negatively impact students' holistic development and future success. Science education fosters curiosity, critical thinking, and problem-solving skills, which are crucial for a well-rounded education. Neglecting science may hinder the development of these essential skills, limiting students' ability to approach real-world challenges with a scientific mindset. Without exposure to science in the early years, students may miss out on opportunities to develop a genuine interest in STEM fields, potentially leading to a disinterest or disconnection from these subjects later in their academic journey. This is where, under the science specialist model, specialist and classroom teachers can collaborate to ensure that science is taught daily and there is an intentional structure that includes interdisciplinary instruction so that students can receive this well-rounded education.

Expanded Learning Programs

Expanded learning refers to educational programs and opportunities that extend beyond traditional school hours and settings, providing students with enriching experiences such as after-school programs, summer camps, and community-based learning initiatives. Many schools and districts, recognizing the importance of STEM education, often turn to expanded learning programs like MESA (Math, Engineering and Science Achievement) and Girls Who Code to provide additional opportunities for students beyond the regular school day. These programs play a crucial role in leveling the playing field and creating access points for a diverse range of students who may not have exposure to STEM activities otherwise. However, the limitation of these programs lies in their after-school nature, as participation is contingent on students being available during those hours. While these initiatives are phenomenal in their impact, the after-school setting can restrict access for some students due to various reasons, including transportation issues, conflicting responsibilities, or other extracurricular commitments. In contrast, embedding STEM programming and content into the fabric of the regular school day offers a comprehensive solution. By integrating a STEM curriculum within the school schedule, educators can reach the entire school community, ensuring that all students have access to these enriching experiences. This approach helps align STEM education with academic standards and curriculum goals, making it an integral part of the learning journey for every student.

Additionally, integrating STEM into the school day reduces barriers to participation, allowing a more inclusive representation of the student body. While expanded learning programs like MESA and Girls Who Code provide invaluable opportunities, they are inherently limited by factors such as time constraints and enrollment capacity. We had the opportunity to work with the MESA program at the University of Washington and discuss culturally responsive teaching within their expanded learning and after-school context. One of the graduates from our Leadership 4 Justice Program, David, said this, "L4J will shape my teaching methods in the future by adding a level of awareness regarding social justice and equity to my lesson planning and delivery." Many local businesses and community organizations provide expanded learning opportunities that schools and districts can take advantage of, and they can consider building in components that are woven into the school day. Some of the educators we work with in the expanded learning world also work within the school day as well and that is why we have to build in consistent professional learning models that center anti-racism and culturally sustaining pedagogies.

Curriculum and Community: Consequences of Omitting the Community

Omitting the community from STEM education curriculum can have significant consequences, particularly when relying on generic curriculum developed without consideration for local contexts. Many curriculum companies, often originating from states like California and Texas, may create materials that lack alignment with the diverse and ever-changing student rosters in different regions. The consequence of this generic approach is the difficulty in achieving true cultural responsiveness in STEM education. As a middle school teacher from Hawai'i Tina Chan aptly puts it, "I worry greatly that the state of Hawai'i is about to adopt one mainland-based curriculum for the state. Teachers can submit a teacher-written one; however, to submit all the components of a formally written curriculum while simultaneously teaching is a daunting task."

The impact of using a one-size-fits-all curriculum becomes apparent when it fails to address the unique needs, backgrounds, and perspectives of students in a specific community. STEM education should be a dynamic, evolving process that reflects the local context and engages students in culturally relevant ways. A curriculum that does not adapt to the local community may struggle to capture the interest and experiences of students, potentially leading to disengagement and a missed opportunity to connect STEM concepts with real-life applications. Involving the community in curriculum writing is a crucial step toward creating an educational framework that is not only reflective of local contexts but is also responsive to the ever-evolving dynamics of the real world. By incorporating the insights and contributions of community members, educators can design a curriculum that is culturally relevant, meaningful, and resonant with the lived experiences of the students. For example, the Na Hopena A'o (HA) framework is a culturally responsive teaching framework developed in Hawai'i. It recognizes the importance of integrating Hawaiian cultural values and practices into education to foster holistic student development. The HA framework consists of five components: belonging (Nānau), responsibility (Kuleana), excellence (Noho me ka hoi), aloha, and total well-being (Lōkahi). Each component plays a vital role in shaping a culturally responsive educational experience. Culturally responsive teaching, as exemplified by the HA framework, involves a deep understanding and incorporation of these components into the educational experience. It goes beyond acknowledging diversity to actively embracing and integrating cultural values and practices that empower students, foster a sense of identity and belonging, and promote their overall well-being.

One of our STEM4Real teachers, Pua Pali, leverages her ancestral knowledge and Hawaiian culture when teaching earth and space science: *During the STEM4Real Institute the facilitators shared the importance of social justice and incorporating culture into lessons and I agree 100%. I have always incorporated the Hawaiian culture into my lessons. As a native Hawaiian educator who teaches in Hawai'i, it has always been important for me to share mo'olelo and both modern and ancient cultural practices with my students. For example, when covering NGSS standard for understanding the Big Bang Theory, I share with them the Kumulipo, an ancient Hawaiian genealogical chant that begins in darkness then eventually describes the evolutionary process from the first coral polyp to the birth of the first human. By incorporating culture into lessons, many students find personal connections and develop a sense of pride in what they are learning. They are also highly encouraged to go home and talk with family members to learn more about their own family history and cultural background, and some come back to class excited to share their families stories with their peers.*

Flexibility in curriculum is equally important, especially in the context of real-world phenomena happening in real time. The world is dynamic, and events unfold that directly impact communities. A curriculum that allows for adaptability enables educators to integrate current, real-world examples into their teaching, making lessons more engaging and applicable. Whether it's scientific discoveries, technological advancements, or social issues, a flexible curriculum permits educators to seize teachable moments and connect classroom learning to the world outside.

Creating Access to STEM for All through Project-Based Learning

Creating access to STEM for all students within schools, districts, and the surrounding community is essential for fostering a holistic and integrated approach to education. When a district dismisses STEM as a focal point, it not only hampers the professional growth of educators but also limits students' exposure to critical 21st-century skills. Leadership plays a pivotal role in shaping the educational landscape, and when leaders actively encourage and support STEM initiatives, it sends a powerful message to teachers, students, and the community about the importance of these subjects. Leadership encouragement for STEM education involves providing professional development opportunities, allocating resources, and integrating STEM principles into the overall educational philosophy. When leaders endorse STEM, it trickles down to classrooms, inspiring teachers to infuse STEM concepts into their curriculum and teaching practices. Moreover, community engagement becomes more meaningful when schools and districts actively involve local businesses, professionals, and organizations to showcase the real-world applications of STEM skills and career pathways.

Project-based learning (PBL) is a powerful instructional strategy that aligns well with creating a STEM culture. PBL engages students in authentic, hands-on projects that address real-world problems and challenges. Importantly, leveraging the community in PBL enhances the authenticity of projects and reinforces connections between classroom learning and the local environment. For example, in Kentucky, teachers researched the community and recognized the environmental injustices and disparities present in the state. They framed their project around designing buildings that mitigate heat and pollution, particularly in marginalized neighborhoods. This not only addresses a relevant local issue but also empowers students to become problem-solvers and change-makers within their community. It also aligns with the principles of culturally responsive teaching, acknowledging the historical context and designing projects that address real concerns in the community. By involving the community in PBL, students see the direct impact of their work, creating a sense of purpose and relevance in their education. Additionally, community members become active participants in the learning process, providing valuable insights, mentorship, and potential resources for the projects.

STEM through the Eyes of Community Events

Another way to open doors and generate buzz around STEM is to host events that center STEM learning experiences for all. Curating a STEM community event with diversity and inclusion in mind requires intentionality. Dr. Jaguanana Lathan, Antioch Unified School

Board Member and CEO of New Generation Equity, orchestrated a groundbreaking event named InLiving Color: A Hands-On STEM Community Event, which highlighted representation in STEM fields. Here, our youth glimpsed themselves as scientists, tech enthusiasts, engineers, and mathematicians, poised to tackle current and future global challenges through equity and STEM. STEM4Real proudly sponsored this event, aligning with our mission of fostering access and opportunity in STEM for all. A City Council candidate, reflecting on the event, remarked, "New Generation Equity and STEM4Real coordinated a STEM event called STEM In-Living Color. My eldest daughter proudly represented the East County Youth NAACP at a booth. Heartfelt gratitude to Dr. Jag Lathan for bringing this event to Antioch. Our youth deserve creative platforms that unify the community and empower them to shine." We actively engaged teachers in the event's planning, recognizing their pivotal role in shaping educational experiences. Such community gatherings render STEM tangible, particularly in cities where exposure is limited. Phelicia Lang, an educator within the Antioch Unified School District and founder of Me on the Page Publishing, shared her insight:

> My key takeaway was that this event could thrive here [in Antioch]. As a Bay Area native, I've experienced innovative and excellent programs for children both as a student and a mother. Having resided in Antioch for 37 years, I've seen many ideas, programs, and initiatives come and go. Not very many had a true interest/investment in changing the trajectory of Black and Brown students. This event helped me to believe again that it is possible. Our children are full of promise and deserve these experiences. Thank you for mixing and changing the narrative, here.

These inclusive community initiatives extend a welcoming invitation to all. By designing with intentionality and inclusion, we can further widen the gates to STEM opportunities.

Systemic gaps contribute to the perception that involving parents and families is solely the responsibility of teachers or the counselor, or the school administration. It is not one person's sole responsibility; it is the collective responsibility of all of us. Educators must actively work to redefine and fortify these collaborative partnerships so that family and community engagement is not seen as a daunting task. Building trust between parents, families, schools, and the community requires breaking the cycle of negative interactions and dispelling preconceived notions on all sides. It is a collective responsibility to bridge the gap between schools and families, moving beyond automated calls and technological platforms to restore the authentic human connection that underpins meaningful family engagement. While technology and artificial intelligence is great at mass communication, human connections are also necessary in creating inviting communities of learning. Reflecting on and addressing the existing holes in school or district-wide family engagement plans is the first step toward fostering an environment where collaboration and trust can flourish anew.

#4Real Reflection Prompts

Understanding Student Diversity

How does the chapter's emphasis on leveraging demographic data challenge your perceptions of student diversity, especially considering the limitations of standardized labels?

Reflect on ways you can go beyond stereotypes and actively seek out the cultural capital of your students to create a more inclusive learning environment.

Data as a Storyteller

Consider the role of data in telling the story of your student body. How can both quantitative and qualitative data contribute to a more comprehensive understanding of your students and the community?

Reflect on the potential challenges and benefits of using a historical and ethnographic approach to data collection in your educational context.

Ethnographic Tour and Community Engagement

Reflect on the importance of conducting an ethnographic tour to understand the qualitative aspects of a community. How might immersing yourself in the physical environment of the school enhance your understanding of the context in which students learn?

Based on Mr. Evans' experience, consider the impact of actively engaging with the community beyond the classroom. How might this practice benefit both educators and students in building a supportive and trusting educational environment?

PART 2

Create

CHAPTER 5

Culturally Responsive Phenomena: Standard-Hook–Society (SHS)

Why are you showing us only Black scientists?

—A high school student from California

One of my preservice teachers was very excited to introduce a series of Black chemists to her high school chemistry class. Her high school was located in an affluent beach town in southern California. Without saying anything about the race of the chemists that she was sharing, one white student noticed that all of the scientists shown were Black. He raised his hand and asked, "Why are you showing us only Black scientists?" The teacher was taken aback and did not know how to respond. For example, she included Alice Augusta Ball, a pioneering Black chemist who revolutionized the treatment of leprosy by discovering the ester ethyl form of chaulmoogra oil, making it injectable and effective. In order to avoid a power struggle, the teacher focused on the chemistry and emphasized that she was highlighting these scientists because of their significant contributions to the field.

There is a lot to unpack here. During my whole schooling, I was exposed to a *lot* of white scientists and mathematicians. However, I was never moved to ask, "Why are you only showing us white scientists?" I wonder what led this student to ask the inverse question? What systems have been in place for decades that allowed the student to question the color of the scientists' skin? The question raised by the white student about the representation of Black scientists reflects the impact of historical underrepresentation and the need for a deliberate shift toward inclusivity in the teaching of science. It underscores the importance of normalizing diverse voices in STEM education.

I had another teacher tell me that they don't have to teach diversity because they have mostly white students. The misconception that teaching about diversity, equity, and inclusion (DEI) is unnecessary when instructing predominantly white students overlooks the broader benefits of normalizing diversity in STEM education. While it is true that DEI education aims to address racial disparities and biases, its impact extends beyond any single racial or ethnic group. Normalizing diversity in STEM creates an inclusive learning environment that fosters a sense of belonging for students from all backgrounds, promoting empathy, understanding, and collaboration.

Think about a Moment in Your Teaching. What Worked? What Didn't Work?

Reflecting on a moment in teaching is a powerful process that allows educators to evaluate both successes and challenges, providing insights into what worked well and areas for improvement. In one memorable lesson, the use of hands-on activities and interactive discussions created conditions for interest, engagement, excitement, and joy among students. The incorporation of real-world examples and connections to students' lives enhanced their understanding and enthusiasm for the subject matter. However, not all aspects of the lesson were equally effective. Some students faced challenges in connecting with certain concepts, pointing to the need for more differentiated strategies to address diverse learning needs. As Gholdy Muhammad, Associate Professor of Literacy, Language, and Culture at the University of Illinois, Chicago, emphasizes, "When students experience identity, joy, and skill development in their learning, they are on the path to unlocking their limitless potential." Reflecting on what worked well in a lesson allows educators to recognize the elements that contributed to students' sense of identity, joy, and skill development.

Understanding the why behind our teaching is a stand for social justice in education. Gholdy Muhammad's work emphasizes the importance of centering identity, joy, and skill development as key components of culturally responsive and relevant teaching. The why behind teaching becomes a commitment to dismantling systemic inequities. To elevate science teaching to culturally responsive science teaching, it is crucial to recognize and address the systemic biases that have perpetuated the dominance of certain voices in STEM. Normalizing diverse perspectives in the curriculum not only broadens the narrative but also enhances the sense of identity and belonging for students from underrepresented backgrounds. Culturally responsive science teaching goes beyond merely acknowledging diversity; it actively incorporates varied cultural experiences, perspectives, and contributions into the curriculum, making science more accessible and relatable to all students. By intentionally showcasing the achievements of scientists from diverse backgrounds, educators can build an inclusive learning environment that not only prepares students for a diverse workforce but also dismantles stereotypes and encourages a more equitable representation in the scientific community.

What Is Phenomenon-Based STEM?

As described in the K-12 Framework for Science Education, the work phenomenon in science means any observable event that occurs in a natural or a designed system.

A ball bouncing is just as much a phenomenon as a volcano erupting. Next Generation Science Standards (NGSS) instruction begins by introducing phenomena, and lessons progress as students apply their learning to understand and explain the phenomena. There are two types of phenomenon: an anchoring phenomenon and an investigative phenomenon. The **anchoring** phenomena is an overarching phenomenon that is introduced to ignite student curiosity and thinking. This phenomenon serves to inspire students to ask questions and allow students to plan and carry out investigations that seek to answer these questions. The anchoring phenomenon serves as an anchor in the instructional learning sequence whereby students reflect on their learning and revisit this phenomenon throughout instruction as they apply their new knowledge and understanding. The **investigative** phenomenon is an observable event on a smaller scale that is simpler and serves to focus the investigations for individual activities.

As an example, let's focus on the topic of ecosystems. For an anchoring phenomenon, consider the observation of a decline in the population of bees in a specific region of the United States. This overarching phenomenon could ignite student curiosity and prompt questions such as, "Why are the bees disappearing?" and "How does it affect the ecosystem?" This anchoring phenomenon serves as a central theme throughout the instructional sequence. As for an investigative phenomenon related to this anchoring phenomenon, students might focus on the observation of a particular plant species not being adequately pollinated in a local ecosystem. This smaller-scale event could serve as an investigative phenomenon, prompting students to delve into activities such as studying the pollination process, understanding the role of bees, beekeeping practices, and conducting experiments to explore factors contributing to the decline in bee populations. The investigative phenomenon allows for a more targeted exploration, contributing to the overall understanding of the broader anchoring phenomenon of ecosystem dynamics and the interconnectedness of living organisms.

Phenomenon versus Topic

Once, when discussing phenomenon-based science, the first response from a teacher was to proclaim that the phenomenon they would teach is cells. This is a place where many teachers often make the mistake of labeling something a phenomenon instead of a topic. In this case, "cells" is actually a topic because there is no observable or head scratching moment that invites students to tap into their curiosity about cells. We can distinguish between a phenomenon and a topic by recognizing the specific characteristics and purposes associated with each. A phenomenon is an observable event or occurrence in the natural or designed world, something that can be directly witnessed and investigated. In contrast, a topic is a broader subject area that encompasses a range of concepts and ideas without necessarily involving a specific observable event.

One hint we use in differentiating whether something is a phenomenon or a topic is whether or not it will inspire curiosity and questioning. As a high school teacher, my students typically did not run into my classroom with a yearning to learn about the endoplasmic reticulum. (Go, ribosomes!) Despite this, if I were to show them diseases such as Friedreich's ataxia that attack a cell's mitochondria, there might be an urge to research the particular organelles of the cell.

When planning STEM lessons aligned with the NGSS, teachers should identify phenomena that captivate students' curiosity and prompt questions, serving as real-world contexts for scientific exploration. These phenomena anchor the learning experiences and connect abstract concepts to tangible situations. Topics, on the other hand, provide the overall framework within which these phenomena can be explored. Teachers can guide students to understand the relationship between a topic and the phenomena within that topic, ensuring that scientific learning is both comprehensive and grounded in observable events. Here is a list of topics versus their associated anchoring phenomena and investigative phenomena.

Topic	Anchoring Phenomenon	Investigative Phenomenon
Ecosystems	The Decline in Bee Populations in a Local Ecosystem	Studying the Impact of Pesticides on Bee Behavior and Colony Health
Forces and Motion	Analyzing the Effects of Gravitational Forces on Planetary Orbits	Simulating Orbital Mechanics to Understand the Factors Influencing Celestial Bodies' Paths
Chemical Reactions	Investigating the Formation of Rust on Different Metal Surfaces	Examining the Impact of Surface Area and Exposure to Moisture on Rust Formation
Human Anatomy	Exploring the Relationship Between Diet and Bone Density	Studying the Effects of Calcium Intake on Bone Health in Different Dietary Conditions
Solar System	Understanding the Correlation Between Solar Flares and Magnetic Storms on Earth	Experimenting with Solar Flare Simulations and Analyzing Their Effects on Magnetic Fields
Electrical Circuits	Investigating the Impact of Wire Resistance on Electric Current	Exploring Factors Affecting Resistance in Conductive Materials
Genetics	Examining the Prevalence of Genetic Disorders in Different Populations	Studying the Inheritance Patterns and Genetic Markers of Specific Disorders
Environmental Science	Analyzing the Consequences of Industrial Pollution on Local Aquatic Ecosystems	Experimenting with Water Quality Testing and Identifying the Sources of Pollution
Robotics	Exploring the Use of Robots in Disaster Response Scenarios	Designing and Testing Robotic Systems for Search and Rescue Operations
Coding and Programming	Investigating the Impact of Algorithmic Efficiency on Processing Speed in Computing	Comparing the Execution Time of Different Algorithms for Common Computational Tasks

From Phenomenon to Culturally Responsive Phenomenon

Now that we have defined phenomenon and differentiated between an anchoring phenomenon and investigative phenomenon, let's look at phenomenon-based instruction through an anti-racist lens. While many of these phenomena are engaging and can potentially ignite interest, they lack the personal connection to our student populations. That is why engaging in STEM instructional design began with Part 1 of understanding your students, their families, and the community. Once we have a vision that is grounded in anti-racism and justice-centered pedagogy, we can intentionally design instruction that prioritizes diversity, representation and belonging. In order to do that, we must leverage the qualitative data gathered in Part I of this book. One way to bring it all together is by using the SHS exercise of Standard-Hook-Society in order to systematically transform each of these anchoring phenomena into culturally responsive phenomena that connect more fully to students' lived experiences.

Standard

The standards help you narrow the basics of your instructional learning sequence. This is where you decide what grade level, content, and set of topics you plan to teach. Because we are teaching STEM, we must leverage the NGSS as the core of our learning. The NGSS are K-12 science education standards developed to provide a consistent and high-quality science education framework across the United States. The NGSS were created through a collaborative effort involving educators, scientists, policymakers, and stakeholders. Balancing the incorporation of critical consciousness, individualized learning, and adherence to state and NGSS is a crucial aspect of effective STEM instruction. This is where the birth of 3-dimensional learning came from, where it is not just about students "learning about" but rather students "figuring out." We will explore these dimensions further in Chapter 6.

Aligning STEM instruction with state and NGSS standards ensures a common set of expectations and benchmarks, providing a structured framework for educators, students, and parents. It helps maintain consistency and facilitates communication within the educational community. Standards can serve as a tool for equity by establishing a baseline of academic rigor for all students. This ensures that regardless of their background or location, students are exposed to a certain level of content and skills necessary for success in STEM pathways. In addition to the NGSS, we must actively weave in the Common Core State Standards (CCSS) for English language arts (ELA) and math into elementary education, which is crucial for promoting interdisciplinary instruction and ensuring a well-rounded educational experience. When there is a lack of alignment with these standards, it can lead to the omission of science from the instructional day, creating significant issues of inequity and limiting access to foundational STEM knowledge.

Common Core State Standards: The interdisciplinary nature of CCSS allows students to apply ELA and math skills in real-world contexts, including scientific inquiry. This holistic approach mirrors the way these skills are used in professional settings and encourages students to see the interconnectedness of different disciplines. Omitting science from the instructional day due to a lack of alignment with CCSS deprives students of exposure to foundational STEM concepts. This omission disproportionately affects students in schools where science is not prioritized, leading to gaps in their STEM knowledge and skills. Since science is often not heavily tested in standardized assessments aligned with CCSS, some schools may allocate less time and fewer resources to science instruction. This creates inequities, as students in schools with fewer resources may miss out on critical STEM learning opportunities, exacerbating existing educational disparities. You can develop curricular strategies that seamlessly integrate science with ELA and math, aligning with CCSS. This ensures that science is not sidelined but rather becomes an integral part of interdisciplinary instruction.

If your state or region has not adopted the NGSS or the CCSS, they may have adopted a set of state or regional standards that are similar in terms of content. For example, the state of Texas refers to their science standards as TEKS (Texas Essential Knowledge and Skills). Either way, tying your phenomena to a set of standards ensures that the rigor of learning is maintained, regardless of topic or choice of phenomenon. When we have created an international community of educators committed to social justice in STEM, having a set of standards also allows for seamless integration and sharing of resources, regardless of location.

Hook

The hook is your direct connection to hypnotize your students and bring them straight into your instructional funnel. In the world of online business, entrepreneurs are looking for "lead magnets" or artifacts that serve as magnets to pull and attract potential leads and customers into their funnel. Similarly, if we look at our students as potential clients, we have to create a level of attraction that pulls them directly into the learning. You will see in the next chapter how this hook is pivotal in creating the "engage" segment of your lesson design. Creating an engaging hook in a STEM lesson is essential as it serves as the foundation for capturing students' attention, sparking curiosity, and igniting their interest in the subject matter. The hook can serve as a tool to pose a problem or unjust situation to your students that inspires questioning, argumentation, and perhaps some controversy. This is the foundational springboard of questioning, observing, and creating a hunger for more information. Many science and STEM curricula base their instructional design on the 5E framework. The 5E Instructional Model, developed by the Biological Sciences Curriculum Study (BSCS), is a pedagogical framework designed to guide inquiry-based science teaching. It consists of five phases: engage, explore, explain, elaborate, and evaluate. The engage phase captures students' attention and activates their prior knowledge, setting the stage for learning. In this phase, teachers present phenomena or questions that provoke curiosity and stimulate interest, fostering an engaging and interactive learning environment.

This initial engagement is particularly crucial during the engage phase and also aligns with the principles of the Universal Design for Learning (UDL) framework. The UDL Framework is an educational approach discussed in Chapter 3. It aims to address the diverse learning needs of all students by providing multiple means of representation, expression, and engagement. Engagement is crucial in both the 5E Instructional Model and the UDL Framework as it serves as the foundation for effective learning experiences that ignite students' curiosity and motivation, creating a positive learning environment where they are actively involved in the exploration of STEM concepts. Similarly, in the UDL framework, engagement is essential for capturing students' interest and maintaining their focus throughout the learning process. If the standards are the WHAT of your instruction, the hook serves as your WHY. The Engage phase of the 5E model aims to stimulate students' curiosity and highlight the relevance of the upcoming lesson. An engaging hook serves as the catalyst for piquing interest, making students eager to explore the topic further. This also allows students to activate their own prior knowledge or real-world experiences, creating a bridge between what they already know and the new concepts being introduced. The hook will set the tone for the entire lesson by establishing a positive and motivated learning environment. An engaging hook creates a sense of excitement and hunger, making students more receptive to the upcoming content.

Universal Design is the Tier 1 instruction that is accessible to all students in a general education classroom. It incorporates principles of UDL to cater to diverse learning styles and abilities. Therefore, your hook is the window into a classroom's Tier 1 instruction and ensures that students are cognitively engaged for their upcoming instructional learning sequence. As Katie Novak, renowned UDL and MTSS education consultant states, "Student engagement is equal parts attention and commitment. For students to pay attention, they need learning opportunities that are relevant, authentic, and meaningful" (Novak & Rodriguez, 2023). An effective hook establishes a clear connection between the students' prior knowledge and the learning objectives from the selected standards. We spent an extensive amount of time in Part 1 to gather information on the interests and cultural capital that students bring into the classroom. STEM4Real Teacher Tricia Dennis stated this: "When I teach through a culturally relevant lens, my elementary students are usually looking for visual, linguistic, or geographical representation of themselves." When she began her unit on water conservation, she opened with a picture book called A *Cool Drink of Water* by Barbara Kerley. It shows pictures of people all over the world as they collect, contain, and store water. Students were able to share what they noticed, what they wondered about, and what personal connections they had to what they were seeing. Students spoke about where they were from, how they had experienced collecting water, their personal long walks, and pride in the culture, their home, and their strength. Tricia further went on to say, "Yes, my academic goal was to talk about the importance of water conservation and promoting peace, but students' prior knowledge and experiences blew my mind, far beyond what a standard would ever ask for." By tapping into students' interests and culture, an engaging hook helps build intrinsic motivation. Students are more likely to be invested in the learning process when they find the content personally relevant and interesting. UDL promotes offering multiple means of engagement to address diverse interests and motivations. An engaging hook aligns with this principle by capturing students' attention through varied and interesting stimuli, motivating them to actively participate in the learning process. This personalized learning cannot be found in a boxed curriculum set that is meant to educate the masses.

Netty Spotlight

One teacher from the continuation school expressed frustration because he felt that the girls in his class were only interested in makeup. He was having a hard time figuring out a phenomenon, especially after learning that his case-study student was only interested in makeup. One of our coaches took this as an opportunity to showcase the chemistry of makeup. She discussed melanin, chemistry, and makeup brands for different skin tones. They co-created the following activity: Cosmetic Chemistry: Investigating pH in Makeup Products, where they explored the acidity or alkalinity (pH) of different makeup products. Students chose a variety of makeup products representing different types and brands. Using disposable applicators or cotton swabs, students collected small samples of each makeup product. They placed a small amount of each sample in separate containers and dipped pH test strips into the samples. Alternatively, students could also have added a few drops of pH indicator solution. Students observed color changes on the pH test strips or in the indicator solution and matched the color to the pH scale provided with the strips or solution. They then had the following discussion: Are makeup products generally acidic or basic? How might pH impact skin health? Students went on to research and discuss the role of pH in skincare and how certain pH levels may affect different skin types. This teacher took it upon himself to embrace makeup as his hook.

Guidelines for your hook

- *What will ignite curiosity and questions from your students?*
- *Is it interesting?*
- *Will students ask questions?*
- *Pose the (unjust) situation to the students.*
- *Have them generate questions and observations.*

Society

Society serves as the crucial third element in the equation of Standard + Hook + Society when creating a culturally responsive phenomenon in STEM. It ensures that educators adopt a justice-centered lens and actively address societal issues within their lessons. Dr. Daniel Morales-Doyle emphasizes the importance of justice-centered science pedagogy, stating, "Justice-centered science education requires that educators embrace an equity stance, one that actively confronts and seeks to dismantle systems of oppression." By considering societal implications, educators can take on an anti-racist stance in planning and lesson design. When selecting a phenomenon, teachers should ask questions such as, "What societal issue would need science to understand?" This prompts educators to choose phenomena that not only ignite curiosity but also have real-world relevance and implications for society. Reading the news and staying informed about current events, particularly those affecting communities of color and lower socioeconomic communities, provides valuable insights into issues that can be woven into the science curriculum. To actively incorporate society into lesson planning, teachers can follow a protocol that leverages resources such as Google News and NewsELA. This protocol requires teachers to:

1. Stay Informed: Regularly check news sources to stay current on trends, real-time phenomena, and local community issues. Focus on stories that intersect with scientific and STEM concepts and have societal relevance.
2. Analyze and Connect: Analyze news articles critically, considering the STEM principles involved and their societal implications. Connect these issues directly to the chosen standard and hook, ensuring alignment with curriculum and instructional goals.
3. Evaluate Local Impact: Consider the local impact of societal issues. Explore how these issues resonate with the communities where students live, creating a more meaningful and culturally responsive learning experience.
4. Collaborate with Community: Engage with local community organizations, experts, or guest speakers related to the identified societal issue. This collaboration enhances the authenticity of the learning experience and connects classroom learning to real-world contexts.

This is exactly why we spent time in Part 1 learning about the community and establishing local and global partnerships so we can ensure that societal implications are at the forefront of our instructional planning. Now let us put the formula into practice:

Here is an example:

Phenomenon: The Decline in Bee Populations in a Local Ecosystem:

Standard:

- Elementary (5th grade): 5-ESS3-1 - Obtain and combine information about ways individual communities use science ideas to protect the Earth's resources and environment.
- Middle School: MS-LS2-4 - Construct an argument supported by empirical evidence that changes to physical or biological components of an ecosystem affect populations.
- High School: HS-LS2-7 - Design, evaluate, and refine a solution for reducing the impacts of human activities on the environment and biodiversity.

Hook: Showcase an actual beehive or a video clip of honeybees and discuss the essential role of bees in pollination, encouraging students to ponder the reasons behind the decline.

Society: The decline in bee populations can lead to reduced crop yields and negatively impact ecosystems, affecting food production and biodiversity.

Culturally Responsive Phenomenon: Examining Bee Population Decline and Its Disproportionate Impact on Food Insecurity in Marginalized Communities

What Is the *Why* behind Your Instruction?

Now that we have established a formula for creating a culturally responsive phenomenon, we as educators, have to ask ourselves how we know our instruction is relevant and reaching our students. What is the *why* factor that inspires intrinsic learning? If classroom attendance were optional, would students still flock to learn STEM in our classrooms?

This process goes beyond STEM for STEM's sake and creates an intentionality of prioritizing justice-centered pedagogy through an anti-racist lens. When we create STEM learning opportunities that are relevant to the lived realities of our students, then students are more likely to engage with and retain information that directly connects to their lived experiences. Educators can address real-world issues, including systemic injustices. These discussions can be related directly to key practices such as arguing from evidence and constructing explanations. Elevating science phenomena to scenarios with societal and community implications ensures that learning is meaningful and relevant to students' everyday lives. This process also allows for cultural inclusivity. Recognizing and integrating diverse cultural perspectives into science education fosters a sense of belonging for students from various backgrounds. It validates their identities and promotes an inclusive learning environment. By intentionally incorporating anti-racist principles, educators can dismantle stereotypes and biases embedded in traditional science narratives. This promotes an understanding of the value of diverse perspectives and contributions in the scientific community. Phenomena-based instruction can serve as a powerful tool for community engagement and service learning. Elevating science phenomena to scenarios with societal implications encourages students to become active participants in addressing local and global challenges. By selecting phenomena that align with students' cultural contexts and community experiences, teachers bridge the gap between abstract scientific concepts and the lived realities of their students, making learning even more accessible and relatable.

Spotlight on Ramada Unified School District:

For this school district located in the Inland Empire of Southern California, we used our process, which involves having teachers use case study student analysis to address academic, behavioral, and social-emotional needs in tandem with the theory of service-learning to advance access and ensure that students are creating service-learning projects dedicated to societal justice within their community context. Culturally relevant pedagogy, identity, and belonging had to be incorporated into the service-learning and civic engagement framework because of the student populations that this district served. Leading up to 12th grade, there were various classroom labs that addressed working in the gardens and groves, watershed health, air quality, heat islands, atmospheric carbon sequestration, habitat destruction mitigation, and tree planting. Particularly, looking at the student population subgroups, the district monitored potentially identified middle or high school students that have discontinued high school to provide services that will motivate them to remain in school. We particularly sought to recruit these students as part of the service learning program to decrease chronic absenteeism.

Empowering students with the skills to critically assess societal issues prepares them for active civic engagement. Connecting science phenomena to issues of environmental justice, health disparities, or other social justice topics allows students to explore and confront systemic racism. It empowers them to advocate for positive change within their communities. Elevating science phenomena to justice-centered narratives also promotes critical consciousness. Students learn to question, analyze, and understand the broader societal impacts of scientific principles, developing a deeper understanding of science as a social endeavor. Additionally, educators can encourage students to critically examine the historical context of scientific knowledge. This approach helps dismantle the idea of science as neutral and highlights the role of bias in shaping scientific narratives.

Additional Standards to Consider

In addition to the NGSS and CCSS for ELA and math, educators should consider these other standards to provide a comprehensive and well-rounded education. Incorporating standards related to environmental principles, social justice, and computer science further enriches the comprehensive STEM learning experience. For example, in California they adopted the Environmental Principles and Concepts (EP&Cs). The EP&Cs, often associated with the Next Generation Science Standards (NGSS), emphasize the importance of environmental literacy. Integrating EP&Cs into the curriculum allows educators to address environmental issues and sustainability within the context of science education. This interdisciplinary approach helps students appreciate the impact of human actions on the environment and encourages environmentally conscious decision-making.

California has also taken on the field of computer science. Computer science is a rapidly growing field with increasing relevance in various industries. The California Standards for Computer Science provide a framework for developing computational thinking skills, digital literacy, and coding proficiency. Integrating computer science standards into the curriculum equips students with essential skills for the digital age. This includes problem-solving, algorithmic thinking, and understanding the societal implications of technology. Such integration ensures that students are well-prepared for the demands of an increasingly technology-driven world.

Some states have also instituted English language development (ELD) standards on a scale of emerging, expanding and bridging language development. ELD standards emphasize vocabulary development. Teachers can embed STEM-specific vocabulary in lessons and provide explicit instruction on key terms. Lessons can use visual aids, graphic organizers, and hands-on activities to reinforce vocabulary in meaningful contexts. Educators can create interactive vocabulary walls or use concept maps that connect STEM terms with visuals and real-world examples. In order to draw connections, teachers can have students engage in activities that require them to use and discuss STEM vocabulary, promoting language acquisition in a context-rich environment. Because there are so many standards to keep track of, the intention is to design interdisciplinary projects that incorporate elements from multiple standards, creating connections between different subject areas. For example, a project on environmental conservation could integrate science, ELA, ELD, and social justice standards.

The Phenomenon Find!

Engaging in a phenomenon find for 10–15 minutes is an immersive experience that encourages educators to explore the natural world around them, leading to a direct connection with potential phenomena for their STEM lessons. This exercise, inspired by the San Diego County Office of Education, is a dynamic way to ground STEM instructional design in real-world observations. During the phenomenon find, educators immerse themselves in the local environment, keenly observing natural occurrences. This firsthand experience helps educators understand the context in which their students live, providing insights into the local ecosystem, environmental challenges, and community dynamics. By choosing phenomena that are locally relevant, educators can create a bridge between scientific concepts and the cultural context of their students, encouraging a deeper connection to the learning material. The exercise also encourages educators to explore diverse aspects of their community, considering different ecosystems, landmarks, and environmental factors. Actively exploring the natural world sparks curiosity and inquiry, creating a foundation for the Hook component of the SHS method. Educators can leverage the observations made during the phenomenon find to design intriguing entry points that capture students' interest and curiosity, setting the stage for meaningful STEM exploration. In the previous chapter, we discussed going on an ethnographic tour of your school community. Conducting a phenomenon exploration elevates this ethnographic tour to think about the local phenomena surrounding their students. Educators can establish connections between STEM and the communities in which students live. This allows students to recognize the relevance of science in addressing local issues, building a sense of responsibility and empowering them to contribute meaningfully to community well-being.

Now you can try this on your own! You can also leverage the support of tools such as MagicSchool AI and ChatGPT. Here are a few AI prompts to consider:

- What is a social justice phenomenon related to this [NGSS Performance Expectation]?
- What accommodations and/or modifications can I make to this learning activity to be more inclusive to emergent multilingual learners and students with disabilities?

Intentional Inquiry versus Activity for Activity's Sake and Whiz-Bang Science

Intentional inquiry in science education is a crucial element for cultivating cultural competence and moving beyond what has been colloquially termed "whiz-bang" science—activities conducted merely for the sake of excitement and engagement without intentional connections to broader societal and community issues. By deliberately infusing inquiry-based practices with cultural relevance, educators can elevate phenomenon-based science to address the diverse backgrounds, experiences, and contexts of their students. Cultivating cultural competence in all students prepares them for a globally interconnected world, where diverse perspectives are integral to innovation and problem-solving. Additionally, dismantling stereotypes and acknowledging the contributions of individuals from underrepresented groups in STEM fields not only enhances the accuracy of historical narratives but also contributes to breaking down systemic barriers. Intentional inquiry ensures that science activities go beyond surface-level engagement. By connecting the inquiry process to real-world phenomena that hold significance for students' lives and communities, educators make science meaningful and relevant, encouraging deeper engagement and interest. The shift from generic science phenomena to justice-centered, culturally responsive scenarios is essential for creating an education system that not only imparts scientific knowledge but also instills a sense of social responsibility and awareness. Professors Emily Adah Miller, Leema Berland and Todd Campbell call upon education leaders to restore teacher professionalization in order to build equity-centered classrooms. They stated that, "Teachers are faced with the demand of making risky decisions around equity in a politically polarized nation, without assurance that administration and parents will back those decisions. If teachers are going to navigate equity learning in their science classrooms, they need to be able to make "equity and social justice judgements" and be invited to safely reflect on those judgments. They go on to discuss the necessary conditions for teacher professionalism with the first one being to, "Trust in, and elevate teacher equity, social justice, and anti-racism advocates' expertise for planning and goal setting, especially with respect to equity-centered and social justice-oriented learning environments." Actively incorporating principles of anti-racism and social justice involves providing teachers with the necessary agency they need to articulate these issues in the classroom. By integrating anti-racism into phenomenon-based instruction, educators contribute to a more equitable and inclusive educational experience, empowering students to become informed, critical thinkers who can actively contribute to positive societal change.

#4Real Reflection Prompts

Student Perceptions and Teacher Responses

In the scenario with the preservice teacher encountering a question from a white student regarding the representation of Black scientists in a chemistry class, reflect on your own teaching experiences: What strategies have you employed to address questions or comments from students regarding the representation of diverse voices in science education? How do you navigate discussions on representation while maintaining a focus on the subject matter?

Standards, Hooks, and Societal Implications in STEM

Consider how you can apply the Standard-Hook-Society framework to systematically transform your anchoring phenomena into culturally responsive phenomena that resonate more deeply with your students' diverse backgrounds and experiences. How do you select phenomena that not only ignite curiosity but also have real-world implications for your students' communities?

Unpacking the Purpose of Your Instruction

Reflecting on your STEM instruction, what is the underlying purpose that drives your teaching choices, and how do you ensure it resonates deeply with your students? Consider the intrinsic motivations that spark engagement and curiosity. If classroom attendance were optional, what elements of your instruction would compel students to participate eagerly, and how do you integrate justice-centered pedagogy through an anti-racist lens into your teaching?

CHAPTER 6

Creating Justice-Centered STEM: The 3D5E Instructional Learning Sequence

Teaching race politics doesn't do anything for students.

—Social Media Commenter

As we have explored in Part 1, culturally responsive teaching involves a careful curation of personal, family, and community artifacts for each of our students. We then braid this cultural capital into our lesson design. In the previous chapter, we used the standard-hook-society (SHS) approach to set the stage for the "Why" behind our instruction. The NGSS calls for thought-provoking phenomenon-based instruction that inspires curiosity and wonder in our students. The SHS approach augments this phenomenon into a culturally responsive phenomenon. In this chapter, we will be creating instructional learning sequences that use these culturally responsive phenomena as the springboards into comprehensive STEM instruction.

Netty Spotlight

Social Justice in the Elementary Science Classroom with Mr. Davis

When I teach a stand-alone science standard, the students are interested in the topic if it's a hands-on activity with moving parts or if they've had prior knowledge at home with the topic. For example, second-grade students learned about plants and grew them because most had experiences with them at home, in school, and in community gardens.

However, when I added a culturally responsive lens to the lesson, students became aware of health inequities in their community. So, they grew their own food and ran a student-led farmers market at school to advocate for healthier food. This opened up curiosity and vulnerability for the students to feel heard.

Through this experience with my students, I was able to see first-hand the impacts of culture in society by connecting with the students and having conversations about their culture. This makes a bridge to the content and specific skills that need to be taught so they can advocate for themselves and question the system using STEM content as their evidence

Learning for Justice has created a set of Social Justice Standards based on a framework for anti-bias education; they can be found at (**https://www.learningforjustice.org/frameworks/social-justice-standards**) The standards are divided into four domains: Identity, Diversity, Justice, and Action. Integrating the Learning for Justice Social Justice Standards with the Next Generation Science Standards (NGSS) presents an opportunity to cultivate well-rounded, socially conscious learners. By connecting the Culturally Responsive Phenomenon from the standard-hook-Society approach with the Social Justice Standards, educators can create phenomenon-based learning experiences that not only promote scientific inquiry but also address societal issues.

In the domain of Identity, science teachers can design lessons that explore the cultural and individual identities of scientists, connecting students with diverse role models in the scientific community. This approach helps break down stereotypes and fosters a sense of belonging for students from various backgrounds. In Diversity, educators can emphasize the global nature of scientific and engineering collaboration, encouraging students to appreciate the multitude of perspectives that contribute to scientific advancements. For Justice, teachers can incorporate discussions on the ethical implications of scientific research, highlighting instances where scientific knowledge intersects with social justice issues. In Action, science and STEM educators can guide students in applying their knowledge to address real-world problems, developing a sense of agency and responsibility.

Incorporating the Social Justice Standards is not confined to humanities teachers; science and STEM teachers play a crucial role in creating a comprehensive anti-bias framework. By infusing social justice principles into STEM education, educators provide students with a holistic understanding of the world, emphasizing the societal implications of their scientific knowledge.

Standards	Justice
NGSS Performance Expectation: Support an argument that animals get the materials they need for growth chiefly from air and water. 5-LS1-1	Students will analyze the harmful impact of bias and injustice on the world, historically and today.
Standards + Justice	
Students will discuss the need for clean water for all for the importance for health and growth. Not everyone has access to clean water historically.	

This interdisciplinary approach encourages collaboration between departments, fostering a schoolwide commitment to social justice. Assessment strategies can be reflective of real-world problem-solving. Students can demonstrate their understanding through project-based learning opportunities that tackle community issues. Assessments can also include reflections on the societal impact of scientific advancements and presentations that communicate findings to a broader audience. This approach not only aligns with the NGSS emphasis on real-world applications but also instills in students the importance of using their scientific knowledge to effect positive change—which we'll explore more in the next chapter. By connecting action to the principles of youth action, educators empower students to become active agents in creating a more just and equitable society.

The DO-KNOW-THINK Framework and 3-Dimensional Learning

The Next Generation Science Standards (NGSS) introduced the concept of 3-D learning, emphasizing three dimensions: Science and Engineering Practices (SEPs), cross-cutting concepts (CCCs), and Disciplinary Core Ideas (DCIs). This framework represents a shift from traditional, content-only learning to a more integrated and inquiry-based approach. In 3D learning, students not only acquire content knowledge but also engage in practices that mirror the work of scientists and engineers, exploring cross-cutting concepts that connect various disciplines and delving into core ideas that form the foundation of scientific and technical understanding. Implementing 3D learning requires a departure from traditional teaching methods.

Rather than focusing solely on delivering content knowledge teaching about photosynthesis, educators need to design lessons that integrate SEPs, CCCs, and DCIs that allow students to figure out photosynthesis. For example, content-only learning might involve memorizing facts about photosynthesis in biology. In contrast, a 3D learning approach would actively engage students in the scientific practices of designing experiments to understand the factors influencing photosynthesis (SEP), exploring the cross-cutting concepts like energy and matter flow (CCC), and grasping the core ideas related to how plants convert energy (DCI). We have expanded this 3D learning to include all of the subjects in STEM using the DO-KNOW-THINK framework. This framework provides a valuable lens for understanding 3-D learning. *Do* corresponds to the Science and Engineering Practices, asking what students are doing. *Know* aligns with DCIs, inquiring about the knowledge students need to acquire. Finally, *think* corresponds to CCCs, focusing on how students are thinking about the content in a holistic and interconnected manner. Teachers can design more meaningful and comprehensive learning experiences that prepare students not just with scientific knowledge but also with the skills and thinking processes essential for scientific inquiry.

Dimension 1: DO (More Than Just the Scientific Method)

The NGSS and the Standards for Mathematical Practice (SMP) collectively emphasize the active engagement of students in meaningful and authentic learning experiences. This "DO" phase of the Do-Know-Think framework addresses the question "What are students doing?" This underscores the importance of students actively participating in the processes of science and mathematics, versus only the content. Both sets of practices highlight the dynamic nature of these disciplines, extending beyond rote memorization to encompass the skills and habits of mind essential for scientific and mathematical reasoning. In the NGSS, the eight Science and Engineering Practices (SEPs) are integral to the "DO" aspect.

- Asking questions (for science) and defining problems (for engineering)
- Developing and using models
- Planning and carrying out investigations
- Analyzing and interpreting data
- Using mathematics and computational thinking
- Constructing explanations (for science) and designing solutions (for engineering)
- Engaging in argument from evidence
- Obtaining, evaluating, and communicating information

These practices encompass the diverse ways in which scientists and engineers investigate the natural world and design solutions to problems. For instance, students engage in asking questions and defining problems, planning and carrying out investigations, and analyzing and interpreting data. These practices reflect the broader aspects of scientific inquiry, including constructing explanations, designing solutions, and engaging in argumentation from evidence.

The progression of the SEPs across grade bands ensures that students develop a deep understanding of the nature of scientific inquiry as they advance through their education. It is more than just the scientific method. The scientific method is no longer the exclusive lens through which the practice of doing science and STEM is viewed. Contemporary science education acknowledges that the scientific method, with its linear and rigid structure of hypothesis formulation, experimentation, and conclusion drawing, offers a simplified representation of the complexities inherent in real scientific work. Modern science, and consequently science education, recognizes the iterative and dynamic nature of scientific, engineering, and mathematical practices. Beyond the traditional steps of the scientific method, doing STEM now encompasses habits of mind, including asking meaningful questions, constructing evidence-based explanations, engaging in argumentation, analyzing data, and communicating findings. This expanded perspective captures the interdisciplinary and collaborative nature of scientific research, encouraging students to think critically and solve societal and community problems.

Similarly, the SMPs outline the same habits of mind that mathematicians employ in their work. These standards go beyond the mere computation of answers and emphasize the importance of mathematical reasoning and critical thinking. The practices include making sense of problems and perseverance in solving them, reasoning abstractly and quantitatively, constructing viable arguments, modeling with mathematics, using appropriate tools strategically, attending to precision, looking for and making use of structure, and expressing regularity in repeated reasoning. The goal of these practices is to emphasize the active engagement of students in the processes of mathematical problem-solving and reasoning.

Let us consider the SMPs of "Model with Mathematics." In a math class, particularly in middle or high school, students can work on a real-world problem that requires the creation and use of mathematical models. For example, students might explore the concept of exponential growth and decay by examining population trends in a local community. They could collect data on the population over several years, analyze the patterns, and then use mathematical modeling to predict future population trends. This involves not only applying mathematical skills but also constructing a meaningful model that reflects the underlying principles of exponential change.

To implement this SMP effectively, students would need to:

1. **Identify the Problem:** Clearly define the problem related to population growth or decay and articulate what mathematical representation is required.
2. **Select and Apply Mathematical Tools:** Choose appropriate mathematical tools and techniques to model the population trends. This might involve using exponential functions, understanding growth rates, and applying relevant formulas.
3. **Construct the Model:** Develop a mathematical model that accurately represents the population changes observed in the data. This requires a deep understanding of the mathematical concepts involved and their application to the real-world scenario.
4. **Interpret Results:** Analyze the results of the model in the context of the original problem. What do the mathematical predictions reveal about future population trends? How reliable is the model, and what factors might influence its accuracy?

5. **Communicate Findings:** Present their findings in a clear and coherent manner, both in writing and verbally. This step involves articulating the mathematical model, explaining the methodology used, and interpreting the implications of the results.

Engaging with the Model with Mathematics SMP in this way not only enhances students' mathematical proficiency but also emphasizes the practical application of math in understanding and solving real-world issues. Many students get upset when there are word problems and writing in mathematics. This is why STEM can reinforce literacy skills through the use of interdisciplinary instruction. In a biology class, students might engage in the practice of asking questions and defining problems by formulating inquiries about the impact of environmental factors on plant growth. Through the planning and carrying out of investigations, they design experiments to test hypotheses, collect data, and analyze results. Applying mathematical practices, students use quantitative reasoning to interpret data and construct mathematical models to represent relationships between variables. In physics, the practice of constructing explanations and designing solutions is evident as students investigate the principles of motion and energy. They may use mathematical practices to develop equations describing the motion of objects or design experiments to test the principles of conservation of energy. Throughout the process, students engage in argumentation, defending their explanations with evidence and reasoning. An example of this is "The Argumentation Toolkit" by The Lawrence Hall of Science at UC Berkeley. It is a collection of resources designed to help teachers understand and teach scientific argument. STEM4Real worked with teachers to design an argumentation activity based on the building of an oil refinery in Dos Bocas, Mexico. Students are urged to think about multiple perspectives such as an oil tycoon president of Mexico, a resident of Dos Bocas, and a real estate developer. Building in this empathy strengthens the practice of argumentation.

Importantly, the progression of the practices in both the NGSS and the SMPs aligns with students' cognitive development and increases in complexity as they advance through grade levels. Early experiences involve asking simple questions and making observations, while more advanced practices include constructing sophisticated arguments and engaging in complex problem-solving. The "DO" part of the Do-Know-Think framework is woven into the NGSS and the SMPs. The SEPs and SMPs are inherently anti-racist in their commitment to equity, inclusivity, and the dismantling of systemic biases within STEM. By emphasizing the importance of asking questions, engaging in argumentation, and constructing evidence-based explanations, these practices promote a classroom environment where diverse perspectives are valued. The SEPs and SMPs underscore the interconnectedness of these disciplines with real-world problem-solving, encouraging students to explore and question scientific and mathematical phenomena within the context of social and cultural relevance. By prioritizing critical thinking and collaborative inquiry, these practices help create a more equitable and antiracist learning experience, preparing students to contribute meaningfully to a diverse and inclusive scientific community.

Dimension 2: KNOW Core Learning Content through a Justice-Centered Lens

The Learning for Justice Social Justice Standards, coupled with Disciplinary Core Ideas and Common Core Math/ELA, can allow for a transformative 3D learning experience. This approach intentionally designs a sense of responsibility, empathy, and critical inquiry in our students. Building a justice-centered lens involves strategic steps to create 3D learning goals that seamlessly integrate the core content with the social justice standards. To build a justice-centered lens, educators should anchor lessons in real-world phenomena that resonate with students' lives.

***Netty Spotlight* Mrs. Kinser's 2nd Grade Classroom**

Mrs. Kinser's second-grade lesson on waste management demonstrates the integration of social justice and content standards. The lesson, centered on the staggering statistics of food waste, not only delves into environmental implications but also addresses issues of racial and socioeconomic disparities in waste management. By introducing students to concepts of recycling and composting, Mrs. Kinser is not only teaching environmental responsibility but also fostering an awareness of racial and economic inequities linked to waste management. The connection to the social justice standard "Identity: 5" is evident as students explore the different ways families and communities handle waste. By recognizing the traits of their own culture and comparing them to others, students gain insights into the interconnectedness of environmental practices and cultural diversity. This approach aligns with social justice goals by acknowledging and respecting diverse cultural perspectives related to waste management.

Combining Learning for Justice standards with content standards in STEM is a powerful way to prioritize equity, inclusivity, and social consciousness.

Step 1: Choose Your Content Standard and Social Justice Standard: Begin by selecting a specific content standard from STEM disciplines (e.g., a Science and Engineering Practice, a Disciplinary Core Idea, or a Math/ELA standard) and a corresponding Learning for Justice (LFJ) standard that aligns with the thematic focus. For instance, if the content standard revolves around environmental sustainability in a chemistry class, consider pairing it with LFJ standards related to environmental justice and action. This intentional selection creates a foundation for the integration of justice-centered principles into STEM education. *Example: Content Standard (Chemistry):*

Analyze environmental factors influencing chemical reactions. Learning for Justice Standard: Students will recognize their own responsibility to stand up to exclusion, prejudice and injustice.

Step 2: Brainstorm and Map Out Possible Connections: Conduct a brainstorming session to identify potential connections between the chosen content and Learning for Justice standards. Consider the broader societal implications, cultural contexts, and the relevance of the content to students' lives. Map out these connections, identifying areas where the content and social justice standards intersect. *Example: Brainstorm Connections: Explore how chemical waste disposal practices disproportionately impact marginalized communities. Investigate the cultural perspectives on sustainable chemistry practices in different communities. Map Out Connections: Environmental factors in chemical reactions → Impact on communities → Environmental justice implications. Sustainable chemistry practices → Cultural perspectives → Bridging cultural responsiveness with STEM concepts.*

Step 3: Craft a 3D Justice-Centered Learning Goal: Build upon the identified connections to craft a 3D learning goal that integrates Science and Engineering Practices (SEPs), Cross-cutting Concepts (CCCs), and Disciplinary Core Ideas (DCIs) with Learning for Justice standards. Ensure that the learning goal reflects a justice-centered lens, emphasizing critical thinking, societal implications, and cultural responsiveness. This goal should guide the instructional design, assessments, and student activities throughout the learning unit. *Example: 3D Learning Goal: Students will critically analyze the environmental factors influencing chemical reactions, considering how these processes impact different communities. In doing so, they will recognize their own responsibility to stand up to environmental injustice. Building on this awareness, students will propose sustainable chemistry practices, actively incorporating cultural perspectives to address environmental justice issues. Through this, students will not only understand the chemical principles but also critically engage with the social dimensions of sustainable chemistry.*

As Dr. Daniel Morales-Doyle, associate professor of science education at the University of Illinois Chicago, states on the Abolition Science Praxis Podcast, "We can't talk about inequity without considering the way those forces manifest in our students' everyday lives and in their communities. To engage in justice-centered pedagogy means that we're constantly asking ourselves, how is our teaching disrupting those forces? A big part of that is to view students as transformative intellectuals, which means believing in their capacity to lead social change."

Dimension 3: Think across the Content with the Cross-Cutting Concepts

The cross-cutting concepts (CCCs) of the NGSS have been referred to as the forgotten dimension. As we have discussed the importance of promoting Dimension 1 with the science and engineering practices to ensure equitable access to Dimension 2 with the core learning content, many are not confident in incorporating CCCs as a tool to promote anti-racism and equitable science classrooms. Despite the CCCs being a critical dimension of NGSS teaching, they are often misunderstood by educators and are not always included as sense-making lenses in the classroom. The reality is the CCCs can promote sense-making for all science students, serve as a lens to better understand real-world phenomena, unify concepts across scientific disciplines, and provide a basis for exploring systemic social injustices. Phenomenon-based instruction serves as the driver of sense-making and is a key opportunity to process these phenomena using the CCCs. In doing so, the CCCs present opportunities for science educators to promote science teaching that emphasizes equitable practice and the CCCs allow students to engage with social injustices that highlight systemic disparities for marginalized communities.

It is vital to choose topics that encourage a culture of discourse that is centered on social injustice. As science teachers, we have a responsibility to practice the nature of science in our classrooms, which includes arguing from evidence on societal issues that directly impact our diverse students. When selecting phenomena to bring awareness to social justice issues, a science educator might ask themselves, "Would examining these phenomena through different CCC lenses impact the takeaways made by students?" or "How might students benefit from using different CCC lenses to explore the same content?" or "How might different lenses promote greater student understanding of the social injustices reflected by these phenomena?" These questions can ultimately help science educators decide how to guide student sense-making through specific CCC lenses in order to bring maximum awareness to a social justice issue. By capitalizing on students' funds of knowledge from their homes and communities, including their everyday experiences with the CCCs, teachers demonstrate value for students' cultural and linguistic resources.

For elementary teachers, this becomes a powerful tool to integrate STEM into their curriculum, transcending traditional silos and enhancing the depth of students' learning experiences. In the early years, where the emphasis is often on math and ELA due to standardized testing, incorporating CCCs becomes a strategic approach to infuse STEM principles seamlessly into foundational education.

The seven CCCs identified in the NGSS are:

- Patterns
- Cause and Effect: Mechanism and Explanation
- Scale, Proportion, and Quantity
- Systems and System Models
- Energy and Matter: Flows, Cycles, and Conservation
- Structure and Function
- Stability and Change

Netty Spotlight, Dr. Nancy Nasr

Dr. Nasr describes an instructional sequence that presents a phenomenon that relates air pollution with marginalized communities. The sequence includes an opportunity for students to analyze data and determine how vehicle age/type ultimately impacts air pollution levels. During the data analysis phase of the lesson sequence, students infer the cause-and-effect relationship between vehicle age/type and air pollution levels to ultimately conclude that older trucks emit higher levels of pollutants than newer cars. The determination of this cause-and-effect relationship sets the stage for students to elaborate their understanding of the social justice issue of air pollution disproportionately plaguing marginalized communities. Examining this social justice issue can be understood through the cross-cutting lens of systems and system models. Students build an understanding of the systems that are in place that perpetuate the issue of marginalized communities and air pollution by recognizing that oftentimes low socioeconomic status is pervasive in marginalized communities. Pervasive low socioeconomic status thereby makes it difficult for those marginalized members of these communities to afford low-emission vehicles. Taking into account marginalized community demographics, income levels, and urban infrastructures, students are better able to examine the phenomenon of the impact of air pollution on marginalized communities through the lens of the cross-cutting concept of systems and system models. Thus students are better able to make connections about the systemic nature of this social justice issue, increasing student awareness of systemic injustices and possibly proposing solutions to these injustices. In fact, the instructional sequence described by Nasr culminates by having students develop an action plan to address the systemic issue of air pollution and its impact on marginalized communities. As students have examined this phenomenon through the lens of systems and system models, they are better equipped to propose solutions as the "key to identifying solutions for a complex system is to apply a systems thinking lens" (Creswell et al., 2022). While Systems and System Models is an appropriate CCC lens through which to examine systemic social injustices, Patterns as a CCC lens can also serve to help students make sense of additional social issues.

To ensure that students develop their understanding of pervasive social injustices, STEM educators can guide student sense-making through specific CCC lenses. As described above, CCCs such as Patterns, Systems and System Models, and Cause and Effect can enable students to explain phenomena that reflect complex interactions in systems wherein social injustices pervade. Additionally, it is important for educators not to lose sight of the importance of the three-dimensionality of the NGSS, with particular emphasis on the CCCs, to promote equity in STEM classrooms. Diverse science students who are offered opportunities to explore the DCIs by using the SEPs through the lens of the CCCs are undoubtedly exposed to science instruction that promotes higher-order thinking and sensemaking, thereby promoting high expectations for all.

The Great Dreamstorm

Once you have decided the three dimensions of your lesson design, you want to now brainstorm or dreamstorm all of the potential activities, readings, discussions, videos, etc. related to your topic, standard, hook, and impact on society. Dreamstorming differs from brainstorming in that it encourages educators to tap into their subconscious thoughts and imaginative ideas, often involving a more open-ended and creative approach. The practice of daydreaming and dreamstorming can benefit educators by establishing a deeper understanding of student needs and interests, leading to the creation of more engaging and personalized instructional learning sequences that resonate with learners on a profound level. During this dreamstorming session, there is no wrong idea. You are using this as an open canvas to throw everything at your lesson design. We will then discuss how to weave all of the activities together into a coherent storyline using your culturally responsive phenomenon and braiding in the 5Es.

The 5E Instructional Design

The 5E Learning Sequence Model is based on the BSCS model and allows educators to map out their culturally responsive pedagogical journey. The model consists of the following stages: engage, explore, explain, elaborate, and evaluate. This model not only promotes active student engagement but also aligns seamlessly with the principles of the CAST Universal Design for Learning (UDL) framework. Through each stage, teachers can create an inclusive and equitable learning environment that connects with students on a cultural level and promotes deeper understanding of STEM concepts. It also provides a platform to actively think about academic discourse and how to strategically build in opportunities for students to talk and process the information. As we are building out learning activities, educators can ask, "Who is doing the talking?" and "What are students talking about?" Students can either talk amongst partners, small groups of three to five students, or engage in a classroom-wide discussion. Dr. Christine Lee Bae, Associate Professor of Education and Director of the Discourse and Learning Lab at Virginia Commonwealth University, conducted a systemic review of science discourse in a K–12 urban science classroom and describes hybrid spaces that are environments that integrate students' everyday, home, and cultural experiences, languages, and identities into the learning process. In the review, she notes, "hybrid discourse spaces that invite students' everyday, home, and cultural experiences, languages, and identities into the substance of disciplinary discourse can support equitable opportunities for participation in science talk." This is where the students' cultural capital gathered from Part One can connect to the culturally responsive phenomenon from the Standard-Hook-Society frame. When brainstorming all of the potential activities throughout your lesson plan, you want to think about the placement of each activity into the appropriate "E." We call this transition from activity to *E-ctivity*. As you build out each E-ctivity, plan out how students will interact with the content through discourse and sense-making.

Engage: Culturally Responsive Phenomenon and the Standard-Hook-Society Connection

Engage, the initial stage of the 5E model, is the hook that captivates students' attention and sparks their curiosity. In a culturally responsive context, this stage serves as an opportunity to connect the learning objectives with the cultural experiences of the students. To establish this connection, educators use the Standard-Hook-Society approach, aligning content standards with a hook that resonates culturally. For example, if the lesson revolves around cellular respiration, a culturally responsive phenomenon might involve exploring how air pollution impacts cellular processes. Connecting this to the CAST UDL framework, the Engage stage directly corresponds to the Engagement domain. This stage allows educators to recruit interest and "optimize relevance, value, and authenticity." The students feel valued, engaged, and connected to the content while we are also enhancing the accessibility of the content. Students can ask questions and generate observations from the captivating phenomenon presented.

Explore: Activity Before Content and Representation in CAST UDL

Explore, the second stage of the model, focuses on engaging students in inquiry-based activities before delving into the content. In a culturally responsive approach, this stage provides an opportunity to embed different types of representation such as presenting content in multiple ways to cater to diverse learning styles and preferences. This is where educators can illustrate the content through multiple media and guide the information processing and visualization for students. Educators can design meaningful inquiry-based activities that embrace STEM practices (DO) and cross-cutting concepts (THINK). For example, students could explore the impact of air pollution on cellular respiration through hands-on experiments, simulations, or multimedia presentations. Representation in UDL ensures that students can access, understand, and engage with the content by decoding text, highlighting patterns and big ideas, and activating background knowledge.

Explain: Fostering Student Discourse and Sense-Making

Explain, the third stage, moves beyond the traditional teacher-centric explanation model. This stage emphasizes the importance of student-to-student discourse and sense-making. It is not just the teacher explaining to the student. This can also be the student explaining back to the teacher or students explaining content to each other. Ensuring content includes moments for student discourse aligns with the principles of cultural responsiveness by valuing diverse perspectives. For instance, in the cellular respiration example, students could discuss the impact of air pollution on cellular processes from different cultural viewpoints, promoting a richer understanding of the topic. This is also an area to overlay the UDL guideline of action and expression where students use multiple media for communication. STEM has a lot of information, and this is a stage where we can facilitate managing the information and resources.

Elaborate: Diversifying Content and Embracing Cultural Capital

Elaborate, the fourth stage, provides an opportunity to diversify content and tell counter-narratives. This is where educators can actively embed the cultural capital of their students, acknowledging and incorporating their unique experiences and perspectives. By incorporating storytelling and actively embracing diverse narratives, educators broaden the context in which STEM concepts are understood. I like to think that in Engage, Explore, Explain, you have taught your students to drive. Now for the Elaborate stage, can you teach your students to drive in Los Angeles rush hour? You have a skill set and now you want to create the opportunity for your students to implement their skills in a new setting or environment. The Elaborate stage challenges students to apply these skills in a new and complex environment. In the context of cellular respiration and air pollution, students might investigate real-world scenarios where environmental justice issues intersect with scientific and STEM principles.

Evaluate: Incorporating Youth Action and Social Justice

Evaluate, the final stage, goes beyond traditional assessments. It is an opportunity for students to demonstrate their learning through scientific communication, diagramming, modeling, and, importantly, youth action. Connecting back to the learning goals established at the beginning of the lesson, students can showcase their understanding by addressing social justice aspects related to the scientific content. In the example of cellular respiration and air pollution, students might create informative campaigns, models, or projects that communicate the impact of air pollution on cellular processes. This not only demonstrates their scientific knowledge but also encourages them to engage with and address real-world issues, fostering a sense of agency and responsibility. It is also an opportunity to explicitly include student goal-setting, self-regulation, self-assessment, and student reflection. In the next chapter, we will discuss designing assessments for all and the art of anticipating student responses as a tool for assessment design.

The 3D5E Instructional Learning Sequence Planner

The full planner can be found at **https://stem4real.org/lesson-planning-tools/**.

Culturally Responsive Phenomenon
Standard (NGSS, CCSS, State Content Standards)
Hook (Local & Global News)
Society (Connect to Social Justice)
Instructional Learning Goal

Additional Standards		
Social Justice Standard (Learning for Justice)	Environmental Principle and Concept (EP&Cs)	ELD Standards

3D: The Three Dimensions		
DO: Science, Math, and Engineering Practices	KNOW: Disciplinary Core Ideas	THINK: Cross-Cutting Concepts

Differentiation for Students (SPED, EML)
Emergent Multilingual Learners
Students with Disabilities
Case Study Students

Engage: SHS: Standard-hook-society. Introduce culturally responsive phenomenon.

Explore: ABC: Activity before content. Plan learning activities before formal explanations.

Explain: Build in opportunities for academic talk. Explanations can occur from teacher to student, student to teacher, or student to student.

Elaborate: Diversify your content and tell the counternarrative.

Evaluate: Formulate claims using claim-evidence-reasoning, youth action, and project-based learning.

5E	Academic Discourse	Learning Activity	Student Work	Accommodations and Modifications
*Engage *Explore *Explain *Elaborate *Evaluate	*Partner Talk *Small Group *Whole Group Who is talkng? What are they talking about? Discussion Prompt(s)	Describe what the teacher is doing, what the students will be doing and how they will be thinking about the concept	This artifact will capture student sense-making. Analyzing this provides a lens into student thinking. Examples include written and oral work.	Place specific accommodations for each learning activity that will meet the needs of each of your diverse learners.

5E	Academic Discourse	Learning Activity	Student Work	Accommodations and Modifications
Engage				
Explore				
Explain				
Elaborate				
Evaluate				

What Culturally Responsive Teaching Is *Not*

Now that we have created this formula for culturally responsive teaching in STEM, it is time that we address what culturally responsive teaching is not so that we can continue to advocate for this work. Unfortunately, culturally responsive teaching has been conflated with Critical Race Theory and reduced to the CRT acronym. In recent years, "anti-CRT" laws have plagued school districts and regions across the United States. Anti-racism and social justice have become political weapons to mobilize voting patterns based on political agendas. Many people race to social media platforms to share their opinions on CRT without taking into consideration the actual meaning of culturally responsive teaching. Let us take some time to discuss what culturally responsive teaching is *not*:

1. **Culturally responsive teaching is not about teaching race politics.** A student's culture is a multifaceted concept that encompasses their background, language, traditions, familial influences, and personal experiences. It's a dynamic force that shapes their worldview and influences their interactions with the world around them. On the other hand, a student's race is a singular aspect of their identity tied to physical characteristics. Embracing a student's culture in education is about recognizing and respecting the diverse elements that contribute to their identity, promoting inclusivity without reducing them to a single dimension. In doing so, educators cultivate an environment that fosters a sense of belonging and acceptance that transcends superficial categorizations based on race.
2. **Culturally responsive teaching is not just for students of color.** Dr. Sheldon Eakins's question "How many students of color do you need in order for the students to matter?" challenges us to reevaluate our educational approach. All students, regardless of their racial or cultural backgrounds, deserve a curriculum and learning environment that values and respects their unique identities. STEM, in particular, does not show diversity in its curriculum. Focusing solely on motivating students of color implies a limited perspective that neglects the diverse experiences within any classroom, especially in STEM. Instead, culturally responsive teaching seeks to create an inclusive atmosphere that recognizes the richness of every student's cultural heritage, creating an environment where everyone feels seen, heard, and valued.

3. **Culturally responsive teaching is not mastering all of the details of every single culture and tradition.** Culturally responsive teaching is not about learning all of the intricacies of every single student's cultures or traditions, as this would be an impractical and overwhelming expectation for educators. Instead, the focus is on recognizing the broader connections between culture and the disciplines rather than memorizing specific cultural details. This approach allows educators to create a foundation for a global perspective in STEM that celebrates the contributions of people from various cultural backgrounds, particularly those historically underrepresented in STEM fields.
4. **Culturally responsive teaching is not about tokenizing people of color.** Culturally responsive teaching goes far beyond surface-level representation and the mere visual inclusion of diverse faces in the classroom. It is not about tokenizing people of color by adorning the walls with posters but rather about intentionally cultivating a culture of belonging. When Christina Taylor, a Black woman, enrolled in the Stanford Physics program, a fellow student questioned whether she was there because of affirmative action policies and not her merit. This illustrates the challenges faced by people of color in academic settings. Tokenism can exacerbate these challenges by reducing individuals to mere symbols of diversity, perpetuating harmful stereotypes and undermining their achievements. True cultural responsiveness involves creating an environment where every student, regardless of their background, feels valued for their unique contributions and recognized for their merits rather than being questioned based on stereotypes or assumptions.

The truth is, culturally responsive teaching, as described by the National Equity Project, is as simple as these three points:

1. a bridge between home and school life
2. affirming of students' history and culture
3. centering student voices and learning styles in all lessons and classroom experiences.

It is almost anticlimactic when you think about all of the political fervor and frenzy that was created by these three simple letters. There have been instances where school, district, and charter boards of education worked tirelessly to eliminate many of the instructional practices that I have discussed. However, if we use this chapter as a guide, educators can see that all of the instruction is tied to standards, while also incorporating justice-centered issues where students can apply their content knowledge. Standards *and* justice: we do not have to choose.

In education, we have something I would like to refer to as *TMF*, which stands for "*too many frameworks*." The STEM4Real 3D5E instructional design plan serves as a guide that weaves together multiple frameworks, including UDL, the TRU (Teaching for Robust Understanding) Framework, Zaretta Hammond's Culturally Responsive Teaching (Ignite, Chunk, Chew, Review), and the 3 Act Model (Hook, Explore, Reveal). Through a deliberate alignment of these frameworks, the instructional plan embraces the common theme of engagement, exploration, play, learning content, review, assessment, and reflection. By intertwining elements from each framework, educators employing the STEM4Real approach can craft a holistic, inclusive, and culturally responsive learning experience. This synthesis ensures that students not only encounter content in a meaningful and accessible manner but are also provided with diverse avenues for understanding and applying knowledge. The 3D5E plan ensures that students are actively involved in the learning process, creating an environment that not only imparts knowledge but also nurtures a deep and lasting connection with the subject matter.

#4Real Discussion Prompts

Implementing the DO-KNOW-THINK Formula

How can educators integrate the three dimensions of 3D learning, emphasizing practices (SEPs/SMPs), cross-cutting concepts (CCCs), and disciplinary core ideas (DCIs), to create a justice-centered STEM instructional learning sequence? Share examples of activities or lessons that effectively engage students in these dimensions while fostering a deeper understanding of social justice issues within STEM.

The 5Es and Too Many Frameworks

Explore the intersections of the 5E Instructional Design and culturally responsive teaching. How can each stage of the 5E model, from engage to evaluate, be approached through a culturally responsive and anti-racist lens? Share insights, examples, or practical tips for educators to align these frameworks, ensuring that STEM education is not only rigorous but also fosters equity and social justice.

Mitigating Misconceptions of Culturally Responsive Teaching

Reflecting on the discussion around what culturally responsive teaching is not, consider how educators can overcome misconceptions and navigate challenges related to cultural responsiveness in STEM education? Discuss specific strategies for creating an inclusive environment that values diverse student identities and ensures equitable access to STEM learning opportunities.

CHAPTER 7

Anticipate and Assess: Bursting the Bubble

Does state testing help or hurt science education?

—California Association of Science Educators

The California Association of Science Educators posed this question in a survey to science stakeholders: Does state testing help or hurt science education?

State testing is federally mandated and in fact, states are heavily fined if they choose to opt out. When we looked at the responses to this question, only 11 percent of the respondents thought tests were helpful. The primary reason mandated testing is seen as beneficial is that it ensures dedicated attention and time are given to science. One administrator admitted that without a science test, science would not be taught at their school. Those who view testing positively believe it helps teachers align their curriculum with standards and focus instruction on key areas. Essentially, testing provides accountability and ensures rigor in education.

However, most respondents felt that state tests negatively impact science education, with 63 percent stating that testing detracts from teaching effective science. The main concern was that testing consumes time and diverts resources toward improving test scores rather than improving quality science education. One person stated, "We are creating a generation of test-takers instead of critical thinkers." As a result, teachers are spending more time on test preparation instead of engaging in sense-making and critical thinking which are key practices of STEM. One educator described state testing as a source of stress and anguish for students, teachers, and families alike. The heightened significance of state testing diminishes the enjoyment of hands-on learning, as highlighted by several teachers who responded to the survey. Additionally, some educators expressed a sense of constraint on their teaching creativity. Many argue that the results of state testing perpetuate unjust and unequal barriers, especially impacting diverse student groups including English language learners, students with special needs, and Black and Latinx students. The administration of state tests via computers exacerbates the pre-existing digital divide, particularly for students and educators who lack essential computer literacy skills needed to navigate these assessments.

When I was a first-year teacher, our school was in a program called Program Improvement (PI), where it was on the verge of getting taken over by the state due to poor test scores. PI serves as a probation period for schools and districts where they are given a certain amount of time to improve and if they do not, they face the consequence of getting taken over by state governments. All of the teachers were given test-preparation packets for the students. I remember having my students memorize that the universe was in the shape of an ellipse so that they would be ready to bubble in the response "ellipse." The good news is that the students performed very well and the school exited program improvement. There were a lot of other practices that the school implemented in an attempt to improve test scores. The principal and administrative team conducted classroom walkthroughs daily, focusing on student instruction. Every department was given collaboration and planning time. The math team hired a coach to support instructional practices. Classroom sizes were reduced to a 1:26 ratio, and teachers implemented an after-school tutoring program. Therefore, I do not believe that the packets for rote memorization contributed to our school's success. Nonetheless, even if we prepared our students to be better test takers, what is the point in creating a generation of "bubble students" instead of "critical thinkers"? According to the California Department of Education, "[It is] imperative to avoid making important educational decisions based on a single test result." However, in practice, numerous school and district administrators rely on high-stakes measures, such as state assessment data, to guide funding allocations outlined in Local Control and Accountability Plans (LCAPs) and Single Plans for Student Achievement (SPSAs). In this chapter, we will discuss assessment strategies that allow teachers to obtain a window into student sense-making and to truly measure understanding instead of memorizing.

Creating a 3D Assessment

The goal of this chapter is to create a student artifact that captures do-know-think learning. In order to do so, we must refer back to the culturally responsive phenomenon and ask: will our assessment help students make sense of the phenomenon? Refer back to the Standard-Hook-Society (SHS) bridge that you created to guide your instruction (Chapter 5). For example, in this bridge, we connect the content standards associated with the water cycle, then show a picture of contaminated water from Flint, Michigan, and then connect to the societal impact of water scarcity. As you showcase the hook to your students, think about the thought-provoking questions that you can use to open instruction. When creating a 3D assessment, there are three dimensions to think about and these dimensions are from the do-know-think frame:

1. Do: What practice are you focusing on? Write this specific language into your assessment prompt. If you are using the science and engineering practices, you can locate them on the National Teaching Association website (**https://ngss.nsta.org/PracticesFull.aspx**). When you click on a practice, it will direct you to the grade-level progression of the

practice. This would be ideal for mathematicians to create these grade-level progressions for the standards for mathematical practice. Choose the specific grade level and then choose the targeted bullet point that you want to focus on for instruction. The Science and Engineering Practices (SEPs) in the Next Generation Science Standards (NGSS) have delineated all of the bullet points for you by grade level. If you are using another practice, such as the Standards for Mathematical Practice (SMPs), you would craft your own specific element. For example:

   a. Practice: Developing and using models
   b. Grade level: Middle school
   c. Specific element: Develop and/or use a model to predict and/or describe phenomena.

2. Know: What content knowledge are you capturing? When you write your assessment prompt, you want the assessment to capture the content that is connected to the standard. For example, if you are assessing students on their knowledge of the effects of resource availability on organisms and populations of organisms in an ecosystem, your prompt to capture whether students understand this would be: "Provide evidence for the effects of resource availability on organisms and populations of organisms in an ecosystem."
3. Think: What cross-cutting concept (CCC) are you focusing on? If you want to explicitly assess how students are thinking about the content, then the language of the CCC should be written in the assessment. For example, for the following performance expectation, "MS-PS1-2: Analyze and interpret data on the properties of substances before and after the substances interact to determine if a chemical reaction has occurred", a teacher can write the following assessment prompt: "*A student conducted an experiment by mixing baking soda (sodium bicarbonate) and vinegar (acetic acid) in a sealed plastic bag. The bag inflated and expanded. Based on your understanding of chemical reactions and the cross-cutting concept of cause and effect, assess the effects of mixing baking soda and vinegar. What evidence supports that a chemical reaction occurred, and what can you infer about the cause of the bag's inflation?*" The prompt explicitly uses the phrase "assess the effects," which directly cues students to focus on the outcomes of the experiment. By asking students to consider "what evidence supports that a chemical reaction occurred," the question guides them to think about the observable results of the interaction (the effects) and link these results to the initial action (the cause). Similar to the practices, you can locate the CCC here: **https://my.nsta.org/ngss/CrosscuttingConceptsFull.aspx**. When you click on the CCC of choice, it will direct you to another grade-level progression. See the example below:

   a. CCC: Cause and Effect
   b. Grade level: Middle school
   c. Specific element: Cause and effect relationships may be used to predict phenomena in natural or designed systems.

The Do-Know-Think Frame

DO	KNOW	THINK
Practice: Developing and Using Models Grade Level: Middle School Specific Element: Develop and/or use a model to predict and/or describe phenomena.	Growth of organisms and population increases are limited by access to resources.	CCC: Patterns Grade Level: Middle School Specific Element: Graphs, charts, and images can be used to identify patterns in data.
Practices [insert practice verb clause]	Core Idea [insert core learning verb clause]	Cross Cutting Concepts [insert CCC clause]
3D Assessment: • Create a model that shows the growth of organisms and populations of organisms when there is access to resources such as food and water. • Use your model to show patterns of where populations would grow based on resource availability.		

Brainstorm All the Ways to Elicit Student Sense-Making

As you refer back to the overarching questions of your unit, use your SHS bridge as your guide when you create your standards-based goal. In designing NGSS-aligned 3D assessments, begin by constructing a SHS bridge to link the content standard, an engaging phenomenon, and its broader societal implications. This bridge serves as the foundation for assessing student learning. To brainstorm ways to elicit student sense-making, collaborate with colleagues to outline various ways students can demonstrate understanding. Consider how students with disabilities, emergent multilingual learners, and case-study students can actively engage. In doing so, teachers need to adopt a mindset that embraces inclusivity, ensuring that activities are accessible and engaging for everyone.

Zaretta Hammond's ignite, chunk, chew, and review principles complement the 5E lesson model seamlessly. The engage phase ignites curiosity through an intriguing phenomenon, the explore and explain phases involve breaking down complex concepts into manageable chunks and facilitating collaborative sense-making (chew), and the elaborate phase extends learning through more complex activities. In organizing these activities into the 5Es, teachers can progress seamlessly from one phase to another, allowing for continuous evaluation and refinement and thus going from activity to E-ctivity. The goal of assessment is to emphasize reflection, feedback loops, and iterative improvement, fostering a dynamic and culturally responsive learning environment.

What Do Students Already Know?

Eliciting prior knowledge is a crucial aspect of effective assessment in STEM. By understanding what students already know or think they know about a topic, educators can tailor instruction to meet their needs and address any misconceptions. Page Keeley's formative assessment probes provide a valuable tool for this purpose, offering a series of questions designed to draw out students' current thinking in various areas of science. These probes allow educators to engage students in evidence-based discussions and monitor their understanding throughout the learning process. When teaching students at Wai'anae Elementary School in Hawai'i, we gauged students' understanding of the phenomenon of waves by asking how big a wave they've surfed. This capitalized on the rich surfing culture of the West Side. We introduced the lesson with the question "Do waves move the boat?" This question serves as a probe to elicit prior student thinking and uncover misconceptions about the phenomenon of waves. Additionally, it sets the stage for the lesson by tapping into the students' existing knowledge and experiences, particularly their understanding of water waves and energy. The probe encourages students to articulate their initial thoughts and ideas, providing valuable insights for the educator to tailor instruction and address any misconceptions. This probe allowed us to understand the students' ideas about water waves and energy. Prompts like this also enable students to change and modify their thinking throughout the unit, creating an inviting environment for mistakes, learning, and reflection. It creates an environment where students feel comfortable making mistakes, learning from them, and engaging in reflective practices. Additionally, the use of prompts such as "What do you know? What do you wonder? What did you learn?" encourages students to reflect on their own learning process and articulate their thoughts and questions. I observed a lesson where the teacher was lecturing on all the different types of DNA enzymes. There were no checks for understanding, which made it difficult for the teacher to figure out whether the students had any misconceptions or difficulty because of information overload. By eliciting prior knowledge, educators can effectively assess students' understanding, identify gaps, and build upon existing proficiency with meaningful learning experiences.

It's Not about the Answer; It's about the Question

Recall that a phenomenon sparks curiosity and ignites questions. The very first practice listed in the science and engineering practices is "Asking Questions and Defining Problems." I used to pat myself on the back for the best questions that I would pose to my students. It turns out, I was doing the critical thinking and heavy lifting for them. I realized that I needed to create the conditions where my students could pose these same questions. When you introduce each phenomenon to your students, the first thing you want to do is light up their curiosity using questioning techniques. The questions generated from these exercises serve as a source for formative assessment.

Question Formulation Technique (QFT): Questioning is such a vital practice that Harvard University created The Right Question Institute, an entire research facility dedicated to the art of questioning. Developed by educators Dan Rothstein and Luz Santana, the QFT involves a structured process for formulating, improving, and prioritizing questions.

1. ***Introduce a Phenomenon***: Start by presenting the phenomenon, or in this case the culturally responsive phenomenon of SHS that captures students' interest and curiosity. This is your hook that could be a text, image, video, or any other material related to the topic of study. The goal is to spark curiosity and create a context for generating questions.
2. ***Ask as Many Questions as Possible***: Encourage students to generate as many questions as they can without evaluating or judging them. The emphasis is on quantity rather than quality at this stage. Students are free to ask open-ended, closed-ended, or any other type of question. Since the QFT encourages generating numerous questions, it provides students with an opportunity to approach the topic from various perspectives. This diversity in questioning allows for multiple entry points into the subject matter.
3. ***Do Not Stop, Judge, or Discuss***: During the question-generation phase, students are instructed not to stop, judge, or discuss the questions. The idea is to create a free-flowing environment where every question is considered valid. This helps in overcoming inhibitions and promoting a nonjudgmental atmosphere.
4. ***Categorize Questions***: After a set period of question generation, students categorize the questions into open-ended and closed-ended. Open-ended questions typically lead to deeper exploration and discussion while closed-ended questions often have straightforward answers.
5. ***Prioritize Questions***: Students then prioritize the questions based on criteria such as relevance, importance, or personal interest. This step involves critical thinking and decision-making, as students evaluate and rank the questions they've generated.
6. ***Develop an Action Plan***: Once questions are prioritized, students can develop an action plan for addressing the questions. This may involve further research, experiments, discussions, or other activities aimed at exploring and answering the questions.

By focusing on inquiry, the QFT helps students make sense of the phenomena under study. The emphasis on questioning as a fundamental aspect of learning encourages a deeper exploration of the subject matter.

Driving Question Board: The Driving Question Board (DQB) is a key component of the OpenSciEd approach to science education. It is designed as an interactive and dynamic tool that serves as a visual guide throughout a unit of study. The DQB supports an iterative questioning process and is considered a living document that evolves as students progress through the unit.

1. ***Introduce Central Driving Questions***: Begin the unit by introducing the central driving questions connected to your SHS that will guide the inquiry. These questions should be open-ended and designed to provoke thought and curiosity.

2. ***Create a Visible Board***: Establish a physical or digital board that is prominently visible in the classroom. This is where the driving questions will be displayed and updated throughout the unit.
3. ***Encourage Ongoing Reflection***: Throughout the unit, encourage students to reflect on their learning and update the DQB based on their investigations and findings. Students will have the chance to check off and answer questions on the DQB. This process not only helps track the evolving understanding of the topic but also provides a sense of accomplishment as students see their questions being addressed.

The DQB is not static; it evolves as the unit progresses. As students engage with the content and conduct investigations, they update the board in real time. This iterative process allows for continuous refinement and deepening of understanding. The DQB is considered a living document because it reflects the ongoing nature of scientific inquiry. New questions may emerge as students uncover more about the topic, and existing questions may be revised or answered based on the evidence gathered during the unit. At the end of the unit, assess the DQB to see which questions have been answered, which remain open, and if any new questions have arisen. This reflective process informs future teaching and learning.

Need-to-Know Questions: Need-to-know questions arise from a genuine need to understand and solve problems related to the project's overarching theme. The need-to-know questions are a protocol that is part of the project-based learning framework that we will discuss later in this chapter. They serve as the driving force for learning, inspiring students to delve deeper into the subject matter and contributing to the definition of the project's problem or challenge by guiding students in understanding its scope and identifying required information and skills.

1. Introduce the Project: Provide context and explain the real-world relevance of the project to pique students' interest.
2. Facilitate Brainstorming: Encourage a brainstorming session where students generate questions related to the project. These questions should focus on what they need to know to address the challenge effectively.
3. Organize Questions: Help students organize their questions into categories, distinguishing between essential, need-to-know questions that are crucial for project success and questions that might be interesting but are not central to the project.
4. Prioritize Questions: Guide students in prioritizing and refining their questions. Emphasize the importance of questions that are directly linked to the project's goals and objectives.
5. Create a Visible Display: Establish a visible display of the need-to-know questions in the classroom.
6. Encourage Continuous Reflection: Throughout the project, encourage students to revisit and update their need-to-know questions based on their evolving understanding and progress.

That was *a lot* on questioning. Why does questioning play such a pivotal role in STEM assessments? It is due to its ability to gauge and foster critical thinking, problem-solving skills, and the application of knowledge. The QFT, DQB, and need-to-know Questions are evident in their shared emphasis on iterative processes, categorization of questions, visual displays for ongoing reflection, and a collective commitment to create meaningful student-driven inquiry. You can choose any of these methods as long as you open each phenomenon with some sort of questioning practice. These questions can guide instructional decisions where we can tailor lessons, activities, and assessments to address the identified needs and ensure that students are acquiring the necessary knowledge and skills. We should celebrate both the journey of seeking answers and the questions gained along the way.

CER and the Evidence-Gathering Organizer

Now that we have created multiple ways of establishing the conditions for students to ask questions using various methods, we can encourage them to make claims using the claim-evidence-reasoning (CER) strategy. CER is a structured framework used in science education as a powerful assessment tool for students to construct and communicate explanations:

Claim: The claim is a statement that directly answers a scientific question or addresses a problem. It is the central idea or conclusion that the student is putting forth.

Evidence: The evidence is the data or information that supports the claim. It involves presenting relevant observations, measurements, or findings substantiating the proposed claim.

Reasoning: The reasoning is the logical connection that explains why the evidence supports the claim. It involves the application of scientific principles, concepts, or theories to interpret the data and make sense of the observed patterns.

Claim	Evidence	Reasoning
The increase in temperature causes the rate of enzyme activity to rise.	In the experiment, as the temperature increased from 25°C to 45°C, the rate of enzyme activity showed a consistent and significant rise.	According to the kinetic theory of enzymes, higher temperatures provide more energy, leading to increased collisions between enzymes and substrates, thus accelerating the reaction rate.

The CER framework encourages students to draw on their own experiences and observations when constructing explanations. This inclusivity allows for a broader range of examples and contexts, acknowledging and honoring diverse cultural backgrounds.

The Evidence Gathering Organizer developed by STEM4Real is a valuable tool that addresses a common challenge in science education—students' tendency to forget details from experiments and activities. This tool not only serves as a memory aid but also guides students through a systematic process of constructing robust CER responses. We have created the Evidence Gathering Organizer as a tool for students to keep track of the pieces of evidence throughout the instructional design. Use the Evidence Gathering Organizer below to gather all of the data collected from experiments and activities in the lesson or unit. Students can use the data to make a claim about a given question and verify whether the data supports their claim.

List of experiments and activities throughout the lesson/unit: The tool prompts students to list and document all the experiments and activities they have completed during a lesson or unit, as well as record data and observations from each experiment. This step ensures that students have a comprehensive overview of their scientific inquiries they can reference when constructing their claims and providing evidence. It addresses the challenge of forgetting important information and ensures that claims are grounded in evidence. The organizer is then able to guide students through a systematic evaluation of each experiment's data to determine if it supports their claim.

Experiment/ Activity	Data & Observations from Experiment	Supports Your Claim? (Yes or No, Why?)
Spinach leaves and hole punch experiment	*After punching holes in spinach leaves and exposing them to light for a period of time, observe any changes in the punched areas compared to the rest of the leaf. Document observations such as color changes, moisture levels, and any visible signs of gas production.*	*Yes. The experiment demonstrates that the punched areas of the spinach leaves show signs of gas production, indicating that oxygen is being released. This supports the claim that oxygen is a byproduct of photosynthesis.*

List of sources of reasoning: Students list out the sources of reasoning, such as readings, lectures, informational texts, and videos. This step helps students recognize and acknowledge the various inputs that contribute to their understanding. Similar to the evaluation of data, students systematically assess whether the reasoning supports the evidence.

Readings, Lectures, and Informational Videos	Does the reasoning support your evidence? (Yes or No, Why?)
Watching an informational video on photosynthesis.	Yes, the video explains the process of photosynthesis, detailing how plants use sunlight, water, and carbon dioxide to produce glucose and oxygen. It provides an explanation of the chemical reactions involved, demonstrating how oxygen is released as a byproduct. This aligns with the claim that oxygen is indeed a byproduct of photosynthesis.

The Evidence Gathering Organizer serves as an organizational tool, helping students build on their learning from previous activities. It supports the idea that scientific understanding is cumulative and interconnected, addressing the challenge of fragmented learning. Through this guided reflective process, students engage in metacognition, thinking about their thinking. This metacognitive approach enhances their awareness of the connections between experiments, evidence, and reasoning.

Project-Based Learning

Project-Based Learning (PBL) is an instructional approach that centers on students engaging in real-world projects to gain practical knowledge and skills. It emphasizes active learning, collaboration, and problem-solving rather than traditional methods of rote memorization. The need-to-know questions strategy stems from PBL philosophy. PBL encourages students to explore complex issues, work collaboratively, and apply their knowledge to solve authentic problems. By selecting projects that highlight societal challenges related to racism, inequality, and injustice, PBL enables students to critically analyze and contribute to solutions, thereby promoting anti-racist values. For example, one of the PBL units used in Louisville, Kentucky, discusses the extreme heat of buildings. The unit poses this question: "How can we collectively design energy-efficient buildings that embrace diversity, challenge power structures, promote equity, and enhance the well-being of occupants in our community?" Kentucky has a history of environmental injustices and disparities in resource and opportunity access. Often, communities of color and low-income groups have disproportionately shouldered the impacts of environmental pollution and resource exploitation. Recognizing this historical backdrop is vital for addressing past injustices and preventing their continuation in energy-related initiatives. The inefficiency of energy use in housing can contribute to increased energy expenses, placing a disproportionate burden on vulnerable populations. Using the principles of PBL, educators can pose this question: How can we create structures that alleviate the effects of substantial heat and pollution, especially in Black and Brown neighborhoods?

Standard	Hook	Society
HS-PS3-2: Develop and use models to illustrate that energy at the macroscopic scale can be accounted for as a combination of energy associated with the motions of particles (objects) and energy associated with the relative positions of particles (objects). HS-PS3-4: Plan and conduct an investigation to provide evidence that the transfer of thermal energy when two components of different temperature are combined within a closed system results in a more uniform energy distribution among the components in the system (second law of thermodynamics https://my.nsta.org/ngss/DisplayStandard.aspx?view=topic&id=43)	Hotter cities, higher heat risks More than half of the global population and about 80% of the U.S. population live in cities. Urban populations tend to experience higher average temperatures and more intense heat extremes than people in less developed areas (**https://www.climatecentral.org/climate-matters/urban-heat-islands-2023**). U.S. Department of Energy awarded Louisville Metro Government with $400,000 from its Buildings Upgrade Prize. According to a news release Monday, the grant will support and scale programs that advance energy efficiency and clean energy in affordable housing. (Copyright 2023 WDRB Media)	Students will collaborate with city planners to develop a comprehensive set of energy efficiency policies and recommendations for Kentucky, promoting sustainable building practices, reducing energy consumption, and enhancing overall quality of life. Using evidence gathered from the project, students will create individual policy reports that cite the need for the Kentucky Institute for Environment and Sustainable Development as well as the Center for Sustainable Urban Neighborhoods and will make their work public to the surrounding city council community meetings and respective departments of planning and building.

PBL involves high-quality performance assessments using the know-do-reflect model. As you can see, this aligns very well with the do-know-think framing. The goal of these assessments is to provide feedback to the teachers and students on progress in understanding the content knowledge and skills or the core learning content standards as discussed in the KNOW section. There is an opportunity for students to demonstrate or apply this knowledge within the assessment using the DO frame as well as reflect on their learning process and growth. This step is pivotal for student metacognition and taking ownership of their learning. The purpose of assessments should always be explicitly communicated to students.

Example Assessment: As a group, design a shoebox building with the given materials that can power your building and reduce the internal temperature of each shoe box when placed under a heat source.

Example Rubric

Criteria	Exceptional (4)	Proficient (3)	Basic (2)	Limited (1)
Design and Creativity	Demonstrates exceptionally creative and innovative design choices that effectively integrate materials and enhance energy efficiency.	Shows creative design elements that contribute to energy efficiency but may lack some innovation.	Design shows basic creativity and some consideration for energy efficiency.	Design lacks creativity and fails to address energy efficiency effectively.
Effective Use of Materials	Skillfully and efficiently utilizes materials to construct a functional shoebox building that effectively harnesses energy and reduces internal temperature.	Effectively uses materials to construct a shoebox building with good functionality in energy harnessing and temperature reduction.	Adequately uses materials to construct a shoebox building, but there are some inefficiencies in energy utilization.	Ineffectively uses materials, resulting in a poorly constructed shoebox building with limited energy efficiency.
Energy Efficiency Strategy	Implements a well-thought-out and innovative strategy to power the building and reduce internal temperature, demonstrating a deep understanding of energy efficiency principles.	Implements an effective strategy to power the building and reduce internal temperature, showing a good understanding of energy efficiency principles.	Implements a basic strategy to power the building and reduce internal temperature, demonstrating some understanding of energy efficiency principles.	Strategy is unclear or poorly implemented, indicating a lack of understanding of energy efficiency principles.
Collaboration and Communication	Demonstrates seamless collaboration, effective communication, and distribution of tasks among group members, leading to a cohesive and well-coordinated effort.	Collaborates well, communicates effectively, and assigns tasks adequately, resulting in a coordinated group effort.	Some collaboration and communication issues are evident, impacting the overall coordination of the group effort.	Poor collaboration and communication significantly hinder the group's ability to work cohesively.
Presentation of Shoebox Building	Presents the shoebox building with exceptional clarity, providing insightful explanations of design choices, materials used, and the overall functionality of the building.	Presents the shoebox building clearly, offering explanations of design choices, materials, and functionality.	Presents the shoebox building with limited clarity, providing only basic information about design choices and materials.	Presentation lacks clarity, and explanations of design choices and materials are unclear or absent.

Criteria	Exceptional (4)	Proficient (3)	Basic (2)	Limited (1)
Terms and Content Aligned to Principles of Energy Heat Transfer	Demonstrates a precise and comprehensive understanding of terms related to energy heat transfer, accurately integrating content aligned with energy efficiency principles.	Displays a solid understanding of terms related to energy heat transfer, incorporating content that is mostly aligned with energy efficiency principles.	Shows a basic understanding of terms related to energy heat transfer, with some inaccuracies or gaps in content alignment with energy efficiency principles.	Lacks a clear understanding of terms related to energy heat transfer, and content is not effectively aligned with energy efficiency principles.

For students to effectively showcase their knowledge and abilities, assessments must be learner-centered, asset-based, and accessible to all. PBL assessments are embedded in meaningful contexts, drawing on students' interests, experiences, and knowledge related to their cultural identities and communities, as seen in this location-specific example. To ensure engagement for all students, these assessments utilize and allow for multiple modalities, are developmentally appropriate, and offer varying degrees of scaffolding based on individual needs, with particular attention to the requirements of multilingual learners and special education students. The following are the guidelines provided for designing a PBL experience:

- **A Challenging Problem or Question:** Frame the project around a meaningful problem to solve or a question to answer, ensuring it is suitably challenging for the students.
- **Sustained Inquiry:** Engage students in a thorough, ongoing process of posing questions, seeking resources, and applying information.
- **Authenticity:** Incorporate real-world contexts, tasks, tools, and quality standards into the project, or ensure it addresses personal concerns, interests, and issues relevant to the students' lives.
- **Student Voice & Choice:** Allow students to make key decisions about the project, including their approach and what they create, enabling them to express their ideas in their unique voices.
- **Reflection:** Encourage students and teachers to reflect on the learning experience, the effectiveness of their inquiry and project activities, the quality of the work produced, and any obstacles encountered, along with strategies to overcome them.
- **Critique & Revision:** Facilitate an environment where students give, receive, and apply feedback to improve their processes and products, with opportunities for iteration and reflection built into the project.
- **Public Product:** Have students share their project work publicly by presenting it to audiences beyond the classroom, such as city officials, local businesses, and community members.
- **Connections to Social Justice and Anti-Racism:** in this section, your project should connect back to the social justice standards chosen and how students can think critically about the goals of the project with respect to the impact on society and the local community.

Student Voice and Student Choice

Incorporating student voice and student choice into science and STEM assessments not only enhances engagement but also aligns with the principles of Universal Design for Learning (UDL).

1. **Project-Based Assessments with Student Choice:** Just as we discussed in creating project-based learning, project-based assessments can provide student choice. Allowing students to choose topics or themes for projects gives them the opportunity to explore areas of personal interest, connect learning to their lives, and express their unique perspectives. For example, students might choose a real-world problem to investigate such as renewable energy sources. Allow students to choose a specific aspect of renewable energy that interests them the most, such as solar power, wind energy, or hydropower. Provide multiple means of engagement by offering a variety of resources. Students can explore readings, watch videos, or listen to podcasts about their chosen renewable energy source, ensuring accessibility for diverse learning preferences. Allow students to use multiple media for communication and construction. They can create presentations, infographics, or even build physical models to demonstrate their understanding of the chosen renewable energy source.
2. **Flexible Assessment Formats:** Let students choose how they want to demonstrate their understanding. This could include traditional written reports, oral presentations, multimedia projects, or even hands-on demonstrations. For example, if you are teaching forces and motion, some options could include writing a traditional report, creating a stop-motion animation, or designing an interactive simulation. Students might use software for animation, create physical models, or design interactive simulations, showcasing their understanding in diverse ways.
3. **Collaborative Inquiry and Problem-Solving:** Collaborative inquiry projects promote multiple means of engagement by encouraging social interactions and shared learning experiences. Students can collaborate on research, share ideas, and collectively work toward solutions. If students are exploring environmental conservation, they can work together to address an environmental conservation issue. Allow them to choose a specific problem, such as pollution, deforestation, or habitat loss. Draft a list of possible topics that provides students with focused autonomy that still connects to the standard-hook-society bridge.

Modeling Iteration: Assess, Revise, Assess Again

The practice of modeling allows students to construct conceptual models as a tool to represent ideas and explanations. Model representations can include diagrams, drawings, physical 3D replicas, mathematical models and representations, analogies, and computer simulations. In the following diagram, the student is drawing out the demonstration where there is a light source, current, motor, and battery.

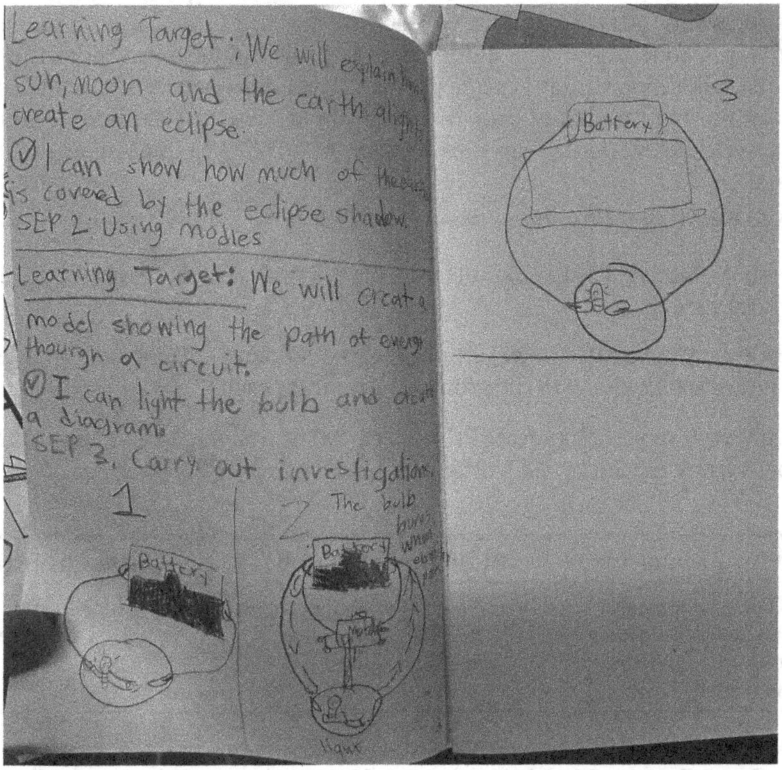

Use the following prompts:

1. Ask students to draft a diagram or image of what they think is happening. This is where some students may push back and say that they are not good at drawing. The more you normalize modeling as a practice, the more the students will get used to demonstrating their thinking using pictures from the mental models they envision.
2. Have students tap into their prior knowledge by recording what they initially think: "First I thought, now I think . . ." This part is an important step because it normalizes not having the "correct" answer from the beginning. It also lets the students know that they can always revise their thinking.
3. When you begin direct instruction, you can ask students, "What do you think about common terms we see and hear?" This also broadcasts student thinking so that as you progress through the lesson, you can rectify any misconceptions. The key is to highlight all wonderings without shutting down wrong answers. This builds a perpetual culture of curiosity.

The process of modeling is iterative with the focus on modeling as a verb versus a noun. Gone are the days of the static dioramas and Jell-O cell models. Modeling is an ever-changing flow of ideas, iterations, and information gathering to assess, revise, and assess again. As an assessment, you do not want your grade to be based on first-draft thinking. Modeling allows students to approach STEM concepts from various entry points. Whether a student excels in visual representation, hands-on construction, or abstract thinking, modeling provides multiple avenues for expressing understanding. The practice of modeling can also be used in building a consensus model among group members:

Steps to Building a Consensus Model

1. Individual Model (5–10 minutes): Allow students to construct their own individual model.
2. Small Group Consensus Model (15 minutes, 3–5 students): Allow each student to share their individual model with the group (1–2 minutes each).
3. Peer Review Using a Sticky-Note Protocol (2–3 minutes per round): Have students give feedback using the Sticky -Note Protocol. Do this for about 3–4 rounds.

Clarification of Ideas	Build on Ideas	Agree about Ideas
• What do you mean? • Can you elaborate on how _____ supports the model?	• I want to add to your idea on _____ because _____.	• I agree with your thinking on _____ because _____.

4. Small Group Revision Model (10 minutes): Have students review peer feedback and use the feedback to revise their group consensus model.
5. Revise Individual Model (5 minutes): Have students use a different colored pen to revise their initial individual model.

The process of creating models encourages students to connect abstract ideas to tangible representations, fostering a deeper understanding. Students can choose from various media and tools to construct their models, providing flexibility in how they express their ideas. The iteration of models and the continuous updating of versions of thinking play a pivotal role in sense making. This iterative process reflects the journey of hypothesis testing, evidence gathering, and refining conceptual mental models. The subsequent iterations, influenced by feedback, new evidence, and evolving insights, prompt students to confront and address misconceptions, enhancing their critical thinking skills. It allows students to mirror the authentic practices of scientists who refine their models in response to emerging data. As students encounter discrepancies between their models and real-world observations, they are prompted to reconsider and adjust their thinking.

The Worksheet Is Not Working: STEM Notebooking

Instead of passively filling out worksheets, students are involved in documenting their observations, posing questions, designing experiments, and reflecting on their learning. Standardized worksheets tend to focus on rote memorization and recall which can stifle creativity. Worksheets often prioritize correct answers and final products, emphasizing the destination rather than the journey of learning. In contrast, STEM notebooking aligns with anti-racist teaching practices by valuing and validating diverse ways of thinking, learning, and expressing understanding.

Notebooking is more than taping and gluing worksheets into your notebook. Jennifer Weibert is a science coordinator and founder of Weibert Science. She focuses on supporting teachers in creating phenomenal science notebooks. She discusses tips on how to scaffold the notebooking process so that you aren't left with a series of blank pages. Two important takeaways are 1) have students set up the page with a template so that students know how to use their space and 2) tell students what to put in the space. Being explicit with these two steps of scaffolding can help you avoid blank pages and incomplete work. Template out your notebooks and allow students to take ownership of their pages and learning. This is how students can become highly engaged in the content. STEM notebooks serve as a personalized space for students to document their observations, questions, investigations, and reflections. Here are some fundamental strategies to implement STEM notebooking:

Use Notebook Templates: Design and provide notebook templates to structure students' entries. Templates can include sections for observations, arguments, claim-evidence-reasoning, and scientific communication. This organizational framework helps students structure their thoughts coherently. Templates can incorporate prompts or guiding questions to support students in articulating key aspects of their investigations. While providing structure, templates should also allow flexibility for students to adapt the format based on the nature of their inquiries. For students with disabilities, consider offering alternatives such as audio recordings or dictation for entries.

Provide Scaffolds for Creativity and Visual Representations: Offer scaffolds that guide students on what to write in designated spaces while leaving room for creativity and visual representations. For example, you can include prompts like "Illustrate your observations" or "Draw a model to explain the process." These prompts guide students in incorporating visual elements into their notebooks, promoting creativity and enhancing their ability to communicate scientific concepts visually. Encourage collaborative notebooking where students work in pairs or small groups. Scaffold language support by providing sentence frames, vocabulary lists, or graphic organizers.

Add Space for Reflection: Dedicate specific sections or pages in the STEM notebooks explicitly for reflection. This could include prompts such as "What did you learn from this activity?" or "How does this connect to your everyday life?" Reflection spaces encourage metacognition, helping students think critically about their learning experiences.

***Go Outside—Nature Journaling*:** The three prompts of nature journaling—"I notice," "I wonder," and "It reminds me of" —provide students with a structured framework to observe, question, and connect their experiences, enhancing learning and retention. This process not only models STEM inquiry but also establishes a deeper connection with the natural world. Nature journaling also allows students from various backgrounds to share their unique observations and cultural connections with nature.

Encourage students to use their notebooks for inquiry-based entries, posing questions, and designing investigations. Using color, pictures, and text allows the brain to remember and retain content. STEM notebooking provides a space for creativity and individual expression and allows students to fully embrace the practices such as modeling. The process of documenting and revisiting information in STEM notebooks also supports memory consolidation and reinforces learning over time. Students can go back and revisit their learning through a different lens such as crosscutting concepts. In addition, STEM notebooking enables students to connect their learning to real-world experiences. Angela Calabrese Barton, professor of educational studies at the University of Michigan, emphasizes the importance of incorporating students' cultural and community knowledge into science classrooms. Through documenting observations, reflections, and investigations, students bridge the gap between abstract concepts and their lived experiences.

Youth Action: Incorporating a youth action or social justice component into assessments is a powerful way to engage students and promote societal impact. By crafting assessments that allow students to address real-world issues through these mediums, they are not only demonstrating their understanding of academic content but are also actively contributing to societal change. Examples of Youth Action assessments are as follows:

- Letter-writing campaign
- Informational poster
- Marketing campaign
- Social media design
- Website or video
- Podcast or radio
- Virtual or live presentation

This approach connects to students by tapping into their interests, empowering them to use their skills for meaningful purposes. This form of assessment serves as culturally responsive teaching by acknowledging and incorporating students' diverse backgrounds, perspectives, and ways of expressing themselves through action and advocacy. It promotes equity and social justice by providing students with the opportunity to make a positive impact on their communities, creating a sense of agency and responsibility.

Anticipate Student Responses

The magic of designing assessments is found in anticipating student responses. If we anticipate all possible student responses, even the off-the-wall responses to our most advanced assessments, we can stay ready so that we don't have to get ready. That means we don't have to revise the assessment because we've already thought of all of the possible responses. Some questions to ask include "What can students say?" Think through the spectrum of student responses that you can predict. Additionally, what would your case-study students say? Imagine all of the possible student responses. This ensures that you're not caught off guard but are prepared to guide and support students at every turn. Anticipating student responses in STEM assessments is also a proactive step towards dismantling biases, fostering equity, and promoting an anti-racist teaching approach. Biases may exist within assessment practices, and by anticipating student responses, we are actively working to mitigate these biases.

Netty Spotlight

Ms. Bravo introduced the culturally responsive phenomenon SHS of food insecurity. She described the *why* behind the learning as follows: "We need to care about how we get our food. In case of a food shortage, we need to know how to grow our own food. Refer back to how we experienced and saw empty shelves as we had to endure the pandemic. How can we be more prepared so that we can continue to survive as a population? Understanding growth and survival can help feed your family, school, and community and helps save money as we embrace a new hobby." She then showed her students two pictures: one of a dilapidated and dying school garden and the other of a local grocery store with empty food shelves.

She then asked her students to brainstorm all of the questions they had. While planning the lesson, she anticipated the following student questions:

1. Why is it all dead?
2. Why is the garden dead, why is there no food?
3. Where did the food go?
4. What happened?
5. Who was responsible?

(continued)

(*continued*)

6. Who bought *all* that food?
7. When did this start?
8. Why are there empty shelves?
9. Can that come back to life?
10. What are we going to eat?
11. Did that happen in all stores?
12. Is every state like this?
13. Can the food we grow be sold in the store?
14. What did people who didn't get food do?
15. How can we grow food to survive?
16. Is that fair?
17. What was growing there?
18. What can we do about the garden?
19. Did the garden get polluted?
20. Who was responsible for watering?

Strategies for Anticipating Student Responses in STEM

1. Prior Knowledge Surveys: Conducting surveys at the beginning of a STEM unit to gauge students' prior knowledge provides insights into the diversity of their backgrounds. This information helps you anticipate a range of responses so you can tailor instruction accordingly.
2. Peer Collaboration: Promoting peer collaboration provides students with opportunities to share their diverse approaches to problem-solving. This strategy also broadens the spectrum of anticipated responses.
3. Varied Assessment Formats: Using diverse assessment formats accommodates different learning styles and preferences. Anticipating responses in written, visual, or interactive formats ensures that students can express their understanding in ways that align with their strengths.

You can then differentiate your assessment based on the needs of your students. Think about how to create voice and choice in the assessment. Leverage education technology and embed simulations and other technological tools. Utilize flexible grouping for language support and revisit any reading and writing scaffolds. The art of anticipating responses allows the teacher to be ready for multiple situations.

What will you look for in the observation? Aligning observations with anticipated responses creates a holistic understanding of student learning. If an assessment task involves a hands-on project where students are designing a solution to an engineering problem, observing students in the classroom provides real-time data on how they collaborate, apply critical thinking skills, and creatively solve problems. The alignment between anticipated responses and observed behaviors creates a feedback loop that informs instructional decisions, ensuring that teaching strategies are responsive to the evolving needs of the students. Recall in the Netty Spotlight with Ms. Bravo and the brainstorming of questions during the engage phase of the lesson, she can now generate pieces of evidence to look for during the classroom observation.

- Looking for students asking the questions and driving the questioning.
- (Have different pictures ready to ignite questions and conversations.)
- Students are writing down all of the questions that they are coming up with and the list of the questions can be used as a formative assessment.
- Have other students connect with other tables and share their questions with other tables.
- Listen for students sharing their questions out loud. Assign roles where a student is a recorder, taskmaster, or a presenter and listen for each student in their respective roles.
- Show pictures of a local grocery store as a HOOK and listen for students relating to the content.
- Show empty shelves and prices. Listen for students asking where the food comes from?

This evidence allows Ms. Bravo and the observers to ask the question: "How will you know that your students are engaging in do-know-think learning?" Let us look at another example of observing 3D instruction:

Netty Spotlight

The teacher designs an assessment where students are asked to draw and explain the water cycle in their own words. Anticipating various student responses to this assessment prepares the teacher for what to look for during a classroom observation of the same lesson. She takes a particular look at her case -study students and the possible responses to the prompt. Here are the anticipated student responses:

- Anticipated Response 1: Student draws a classic representation of the water cycle with arrows depicting the stages of evaporation, condensation, precipitation, and runoff. They may use scientific terms and demonstrate a conventional understanding of the process.
- Anticipated Response 2: Student uses visual metaphors to represent the water cycle. They compare the water cycle to a giant recycling system, emphasizing the cyclical nature of water movement on Earth.
- Anticipated Response 3: Student from a coastal region emphasizes the role of the ocean, and also integrates cultural symbols related to water.

(continued)

(continued)

- Anticipated Response 4: Student expresses their understanding predominantly through drawings or diagrams.

During the observation, teachers can look for the following:

- The teacher looks for individualized approaches to the water cycle. This includes noting the variety of visual representations and the extent to which students incorporate their unique perspectives, experiences, and cultural elements into their drawings and explanations.
- The teacher observes collaboration such as peer interactions, noting instances where students share their perspectives, and considers how collaborative discussions enhance the overall understanding of the water cycle.
- The teacher pays attention to cultural elements incorporated into the drawings and explanations. This includes recognizing and valuing diverse cultural representations.

This is why we must burst the bubble because standardized tests cannot possibly give us the information gathered by all of the assessments listed in this chapter. By anticipating these varied student responses beforehand, the teacher is better equipped to focus the classroom observation on specific aspects that align with the learning objectives. This proactive approach ensures that the teacher can tailor instructional strategies to meet the diverse needs and perspectives of the students, creating a more inclusive and effective learning experience. This is where the teacher can create differentiated assessments based on the particular needs of students and specifically, the case-study students. The careful examination and research of our case-study students come into play here in our powers of anticipating their responses to the assessment we craft.

We are now ready to observe STEM instruction. Whether you are observing classrooms or small group instruction, the goal is to enter the observation with a set of responses that we can expect from the assessment and witness how the instruction, assessment, and observation are all interconnected. Assessment extends beyond a mere measurement of what students know; it is a process aimed at unraveling how students make sense of information. We are bursting the bubble of conventional assessments because the true focus lies in understanding the students' comprehension, their unique ways of processing information, and a window into their thinking. The goal is not just to quantify knowledge but to appreciate the diverse pathways through which students construct meaning. A measure of success in assessment lies in our ability to nurture the web of thoughts, ideas, interpretations, and sense-making processes that students bring to their learning journey in STEM.

#4Real Discussion Prompts

Reflecting on High-Stakes Testing in Science Education

Considering the discourse around state testing in science education, reflect on the impact of high-stakes testing on both teaching and learning. So your own experiences or observations regarding the influence of high-stakes testing on STEM education, drawing parallels to the practices discussed in the chapter. In what ways do high-stakes assessments shape classroom instruction, student engagement, and educational equity? Consider the broader implications of relying on standardized testing as a measure of academic success and its alignment with the goals of fostering critical thinking and sense-making skills in STEM education.

Empowering Inquiry-Based Assessment Strategies

How can we leverage questioning techniques such as the Question Formulation Technique (QFT), Driving Question Board (DQB), and need-to-know questions to encourage student-driven inquiry and deeper understanding in STEM assessments? Reflect on ways to integrate these strategies into your instructional design to promote critical thinking, metacognition, and inclusivity in assessment practices.

Student-Centered Assessment Approaches in STEM

Consider the various assessment strategies discussed in this chapter, including project-based learning, student voice and choice, modeling iteration, STEM notebooking, youth action assessments, and strategies for anticipating student responses. How might you integrate these student-centered approaches into your own teaching practice to promote deeper understanding, engagement, and equity in STEM education? Reflect on the potential benefits and challenges of adopting these strategies and identify specific steps you can take to enhance your assessment practices moving forward.

CHAPTER 8

Observe and Debrief: Opening Our Classrooms for Student Learning

If we create a culture where every teacher believes they need to improve, not because they are not good enough, but because they can be even better, there is no limit to what we can achieve.—"

—Dylan William

If you have experienced lesson study before, you know that the observation is where the magic happens. This is the moment when we get to see all of our ideas, research, and methods come together in unison. Even if the observation is seen as a disaster, it is our moment where we innovated, took risks, and most importantly, watched student instruction. Before we get into the details of observation, let us talk about what it is not.

Dog and Pony Show *versus* Authentic Observation

When I was teaching my lesson on sugar content and common snack foods, I set up the common inquiry lab where students burned a cheese puff to measure the calories. I remember while I was explaining the directions, one of my students was talking to his seatmate about something completely unrelated. I did the usual teacher look coupled with the "I'll wait until you're done" comment. He immediately looked at my face and paused his conversation. I continued my directions, and we engaged in an awesome day of inquiry and discussion.

I finished the day feeling like I had knocked my lesson out of the park. I was even quite pleased that it happened to be my evaluation lesson. I met with my assistant principal to discuss the highlights of my lesson. During that evaluation, she wrote that I "exhibited sarcasm with my students and should work on developing more positive relationships with my students." In my head, I immediately got defensive. Does she not know that I had a lengthy conversation with that student's grandmother and know his family? Does she not know that I talk to my students every day, and we have our own banter and know when to get down to business? I got more upset remembering that the assistant principal came from an elementary background and had no idea how an HS classroom functioned. Of course, I said all of this in my head, and in person, I nodded and thanked her for the feedback.

We then had our spring observation and I completed yet another amazing lesson. I did the same thing as my fall observation. When I had my post-observation meeting with my assistant principal, she looked at me in awe of my teaching practice and said, "Wow, Leena, your students really love you." She realized that coming into my classroom for a 40-minute snapshot was not an accurate reflection of my teaching as a whole. She decided to remove the sarcasm comment from my observation, realizing that it was the relationship of banter and fun that I had established with my students. While this observation had a happy ending, and my evaluator was able to witness my teaching as a whole (from two observations), not every teacher has this experience. Moreover, the process can bring up feelings of defensiveness and anger. I personally started researching the background of my evaluator just to attempt to discredit her. This is because observations as evaluative seek out punitive measures that are not conducive to growth and reflection. Most importantly, the observation is centered around the teacher and not on student instruction.

Observations are not the time to look at classroom walls and whiteboard organization. I remember getting docked during an observation once because I didn't have student work updated on my wall. I was also docked once for not having the full standard written on the whiteboard. When administrators come in and look at the walls and whiteboard, they aren't looking at the students and what practices they are engaging in. Classroom observations are not intended to be isolated snapshots for the purpose of assigning blame or judgment. They are not punitive measures designed solely for evaluating a teacher's performance based on superficial criteria. And yet some observers use observations as a way of catching teachers off guard or seeking out flaws. When observations are weaponized like this, it becomes impossible to use them for collaborative reflection and professional growth.

Netty Spotlight: *How did the educators implement the Standard-Hook-Society (SHS) bridge in their lessons?*

The teachers used multiple phenomena to drive student learning. For example,

- *Mr. Russ Robb began his lesson with an archaeological dig and connected*
- *the work to dinosaurs and Indiana Jones. He had the class take on the role of*
- *doctoral archaeologists as they started the dig.*
- *In Ms. Georgina Alcantara's class, STEM4Real modeled a lesson based on the*
- *phenomenon of alcohol evaporating much faster than water. Students made*
- *observations that led to the discussion of the chemical structures of water and*

(continued)

(continued)

- *alcohol.*
- *Ms. Yolanda Jones enhanced her lesson by having her students discuss how*
- *damage to the biosphere and hydrosphere is correlated to our health and desire to enjoy the outdoors.*

Ms. Terra Uppstad hooked her students to human impacts on water sources through stories of people and ecosystems around the world affected by overpopulation. Students then related the topic to the impact of overpopulation in the Bay Area..

Creating a Mindset for Open Doors

Observations have to be a way of life versus a task to complete. The focus should always be on student learning and student interactions. When we ask teachers to open their doors, it is an invitation that should not be taken lightly. We are opening our classrooms to learn, not to judge. Author and marketing strategist Seth Godin posed these questions: "What's it for, and who's it for?" The questions underscore the importance of intentionality in educational practices, particularly in the context of observations and feedback. Intentionality in observations is crucial because it shifts the focus from mere assessment to reflective learning and growth. When educators approach observations with intentionality, they prioritize understanding, reflection, and collaboration over evaluation. This deliberate approach allows for deeper insights into teaching practices, student interactions, and learning outcomes. Observations should not be conducted merely for assessment or evaluation purposes but should primarily serve the needs of student learning and teacher professional growth. Observations and feedback should be tools to serve as meaningful dialogue about professional growth and reflection. With the onset of ChatGPT and machine learning, some administrators had the audacity to provide rote feedback from AI instead of authentic feedback from each observation. Most educators would rather receive one to two sentences of quick feedback from their administrator rather than a lengthy AI-generated essay. This is not to say AI has no place in education. It can be valuable in replacing mundane tasks; however, observation is a practice that is personal, vulnerable, and requires personalization, especially as we dissect the power dynamics between administrators and teachers.

Once we set the stage that observations and walkthroughs are part of the non-evaluative school culture, we can then plan for intentional observations that actually look at student instruction and outcomes. Emphasizing nonevaluative observations encourages educators to view observations as opportunities for professional development rather than assessments of performance. By removing the pressure of evaluation, teachers can engage more authentically in reflective practices, explore new teaching strategies, and take risks in their instruction without fear of judgment. If students know that classroom observations are happening twice a year, then the culture of observation has not been fully built out as part of the normalized classroom day. Students can potentially behave differently with the presence of another person in the classroom. The teacher is also made to feel that the administrator is strictly there to observe and evaluate, but not to use those findings as a tool to build school culture and student relationships. Observation facilitates meaningful relationships between teachers and students. By actively engaging with students in the classroom, educators can build trust, rapport, and empathy, which are essential components of culturally responsive teaching. Through observation, teachers can better understand the lived experiences of their students and create instructional experiences that resonate with their cultural identities and backgrounds. Observation also helps educators identify any biases or assumptions they may hold and work to mitigate them. By critically reflecting on their observations and interactions with students, teachers can continuously refine their practice to ensure it is culturally responsive and equitable.

Classroom observations are an integral part of the STEM4Real Lesson Study Process because it is where we get to collectively see the instructional learning sequence come to life. However, when teachers hear the word observation there is often a visceral and adverse reaction. This is because there can be trauma associated with this process. Many teachers have experienced negative evaluations that have led to a cascade of punitive measures such as changes in assignment, dock in pay, or even getting fired. There may be situations where some of these events are valid and warranted; however, judging a teacher based on two 56-minute observations a year does not seem like a fair evaluation of the teacher as a whole. For example, I had a colleague who awarded his students with a donut party if they behaved well during the two observations. It was a win all around: The teacher received a stellar observation, the students received a donut party, and the world never got to find out that this teacher had actually come to school drunk other days that year. The point is, sporadic observations alone cannot evaluate a teacher. Because of the adversarial nature of past observations and the connection to punitive measures, we must create a new mindset for teacher observations. We must think of observations as a nonevaluative tool for reflection. This is the time for peers, colleagues, and administrators to see student instruction. That's it. If students are used to a revolving door of adults entering and exiting the building, they will be used to showcasing their learning, regardless if it is an "observation day" or not.

Creating Indicators for Observation

Recall in the last chapter, we discussed anticipating student responses. In this section, we will discuss observing evidence of student learning for each section of the instructional sequence. In preparing for the observation, educators can list the anticipated student responses for each section of the 5E instructional learning sequence. In the adjacent column, educators list the pieces of evidence that demonstrate what observers should look for during this stage of the lesson. We can see the evidence is aligned to the anticipated student responses. Observers can clearly see that "looking for students asking the questions and driving the questioning" is evidence of students engaging in the practice of questioning. They can also look for potential responses that may have been anticipated by the teacher.

5E Engage Explore Explain Elaborate Evaluate	Anticipating Student Responses: *What are the students potentially going to say when they engage with each of these activities? What will your case-study students say?*	Observations Evidence: *How will you know that your students are engaging in DO-KNOW-THINK learning?*
Engage	Questions: **1.** Why is it all dead? **2.** Why is the garden dead, why is there no food? **3.** Where did the food go? **4.** What happened? **5.** Who was responsible? **6.** Who bought *all* that food? **7.** When did this start? **8.** Why are there empty shelves? **9.** Can that come back to life? **10.** What are we going to eat? **11.** Did that happen in all stores? **12.** Is every state like this? **13.** Can the food we grow be sold in the store? **14.** What did people who didn't get food do? **15.** How can we grow food to survive? **16.** Is that fair? **17.** What was growing there? **18.** What can we do about the garden? **19.** Did the garden get polluted? **20.** Who was responsible for watering?	• Looking for students asking the questions and driving the questioning. • (Have different pictures ready to ignite questions and conversations.) • Students are writing down all of the questions that they are coming up with and the list of the questions can be used as a formative assessment. • Have other students connect with other tables and share their questions with other tables. • Listen for students sharing their questions out loud. Assign roles where a student is a recorder, taskmaster, or a presenter and listen for each student in their respective roles. • Show pictures of a local grocery store as a HOOK and listen for students relating to the content. • Show empty shelves and prices. Listen for students asking where the food comes from.

We must always begin by looking at the overarching driving phenomenon. What are we getting students curious about? As we begin each section, we constantly go back to this phenomenon because we want to create a storyline that consistently returns to this phenomenon that is driving learning. We can then create indicators of learning for each of the three dimensions: do, know, and think.

DO What actions and activities related to the practices will we see in the lesson? As we have discussed all of the science and engineering practices and the standards for mathematical practice, it is important to zoom in on the particular practice that you witness for the observation period. Once you decide the specific practice you will be teaching, think about the verbs that make up each practice. Decide what actions and activities the students will be engaging in during this segment of the lesson. For example, if the practice is modeling, your observation indicators will involve looking for students creating and labeling diagrams. Below are the key practices for science engineering and mathematics. As you can see, there are many similarities and overlap between the two domains. This is why when we discuss three-dimensional learning as described in the Next Generation Science Standards (NGSS), we can easily expand it to include mathematics and computer science instruction.

Science and Engineering Practices (SEPs)	Standards for Mathematical Practice (SMPs)
• Asking Questions and Defining Problems • Developing and Using Models • Planning and Carrying Out Investigations • Analyzing and Interpreting Data • Using Mathematics and Computational Thinking • Constructing Explanations and Designing Solutions • Engaging in Argument from Evidence • Obtaining, Evaluating, and Communicating Information	• Make sense of problems and persevere in solving them • Reason abstractly and quantitatively • Construct viable arguments and critique the reasoning of others • Model with mathematics • Use appropriate tools strategically • Attend to precision • Look for and make use of structure • Look for and express regularity in repeated reasoning

KNOW For this dimension, we ask what words, terms, and vocabulary are related to the content. This is where you want to dictate the concepts that you will be listening for as students work. You can consider the operations and equations that you will be looking out for as well. For example, if you are observing population dynamics, you may add in your observation indicators the Hardy-Weinberg equation. This is where the technical information of vocabulary, terminology, definitions, and processes go. If you are using the Evidence Gathering Organizer from the previous chapter, use this tool to pick out pieces of evidence to listen for during the observation. Select the topic and standard that you will be focusing on and then decide what terms and vocabulary the student will be interacting with. Create a list of indicators to let you know that the student is learning the material. For example, if the standard is on photosynthesis, you will look for water, carbon dioxide, oxygen and sugar.

THINK This is the most difficult dimension to observe because you are essentially attempting to observe how a student thinks and a lot of thinking patterns are invisible.

Our goal in this section is to make student thinking and sense-making as visible as possible. This is where we build in thinking routines, discourse, and problem-solving techniques that are explicitly related to the crosscutting concepts. We ask this question: How are students making connections, solving problems, and discussing solutions? First, select the cross-cutting concept that you will be focusing on and then decide what sense-making and discourse the student will be engaging in. Create a list of indicators to let you know that the student is engaging in this type of thinking. For example, if the cross-cutting concept is patterns, how will you observe students making sense of patterns in the lesson?

Netty Spotlight: Jessica Bravo

When Jessica was teaching her lesson on infant developmental stages, she explicitly included the cross-cutting concepts during her lesson. She connected cause and effect to when the baby was crying and what the causes of infant crying were. She then had her students look at their actions to see if any of them would cause the crying to stop. She also explicitly taught the patterns of the life stages and developmental milestones with each stage. The students were able to conceptualize the different stages from infant to toddler. In the STEM4Real Observational Tool, there is a table that lists each of the cross -cutting concepts (CCC) and poses the question about how students are thinking and processing information. Observers can mark which CCC they observe and how they are observing this in the instruction. Perhaps students are discussing patterns or engaging in an argument about cause and effect. In Ms. Bravo's classroom, observers saw students discussing that humans experience predictable life stages that contain developmental milestones. Her team also noticed that students were discussing that when a baby has its needs taken care of, the baby thrives.

THINK: How are students thinking and processing the information?						
Patterns	*Cause & Effect*	*Scale & Proportion*	*Systems*	*Energy & Matter*	*Structure & Function*	*Stability & Change*
X	X					
The human experiences predictable life stages with developmental milestones within each stage.	When a baby has its needs taken care of, the baby thrives.					

Forms of Data Collection

Understanding and evaluating student learning experiences is foundational to effective teaching; however, we cannot all have a different compass. This is why professional learning squads can co-create observation indicators such that there is a common target to look for. The do-know-think framework provides a structured approach for educators to assess the three dimensions of learning as delineated in the NGSS. In this table, we explore different forms of data collection aligned with each dimension of the framework: do, which focuses on students' implementation of the practices; know, which is centered on disciplinary core ideas; and think, which addresses cross-cutting concepts. These observation indicators offer educators insights into student behavior and understanding across different learning contexts. By leveraging these indicators, educators can gather comprehensive data to inform their instructional practices, encouraging deeper student learning and acquisition.

DO-KNOW-THINK Dimension	Observation Indicators
DO: The Practices	Observing students designing their own experiments, constructing their explanations, analyzing data, tables, and graphs
KNOW: Disciplinary Core Ideas	Observing students reading and summarizing informational text, discussing key vocabulary terms, arguing about concepts and ideas
THINK: Cross-Cutting Concepts	Observing students diagramming different patterns, modeling energy and matter cycling, discussing the cause and effect of something

The #4Real Observation Tool: Observation in Collaboration versus Evaluation

Let's set the stage. You are a teacher, and you just designed your 5E lesson with all of the anticipated student responses and potential indicators for observation. Yet you are horrified to let anyone observe your lesson plan because you are having a hard time with the behavior issues in one particular class period. If someone were to walk into your classroom and witness students throwing paper airplanes at each other, there would be no place on the tool to write down that notation. The worst evaluation that a teacher can receive is a blank document. This is because the tool itself allows observers to document what the students do, what the students know, and how the students think. Ensuring transparency and collaboration, we share the observation tool with all stakeholders involved, including the teacher, administrator, and professional learning team. This proactive sharing ensures that the teacher is well-informed about expectations and what the observers are specifically looking for, while administrators have a designated observation partner for calibration and feedback discussions. Through this collaborative process, timely instructional feedback is facilitated, directly impacting student learning outcomes.

Step 1: The foundation of science instruction centers around utilizing phenomena to spark curiosity and ground learning. Phenomena-based instruction provides the *why* behind the learning and is applicable across content areas. Observers focus on engaging phenomena that offer the rationale for the instruction, such as starting a U.S. history lesson with a real-world phenomenon like the controversial swearing-in of Supreme Court Justice Brett Kavanaugh.

Step 2: Both science and engineering practices and standards for mathematical practice emphasize the actions students are undertaking—essentially, the *do* of the do-know-think framework. This prompts teachers to create instructional sequences with specific, action-oriented verbs in mind. Observers take note of the actions students are performing during the observation session, checking relevant boxes and providing detailed comments.

Step 3: The *know* frame grounds instruction in state standards to ensure alignment with grade-level measures. Observers assess how the instructional sequence aligns with the relevant standards, acknowledging that not all lessons will cover every standard. The framework accommodates interdisciplinary lessons, allowing observers to evaluate how standards are woven together across disciplines.

Step 4: The *think* frame explores how students are thinking about information through cross-cutting concepts. Observers note cross-cutting concepts explicitly integrated into instructional sequences, making students aware of the lens through which they should view the learning. Observers check relevant boxes and elaborate on their observations.

Step 5: The academic discourse component breathes life into the do-know-think framework by allowing for intentional student-to-student academic discourse. Observers assess evidence of partner talk, small group talk, or whole group talk, providing insights into opportunities for student discourse throughout the lesson.

Step 6: This section addresses other school or district-wide initiatives linked to a multi-tiered system of support (MTSS). It explores components beyond the main instructional sequence, such as social-emotional curricula or metacognitive strategies for student reflection.

We recommend applying this tool for at least 15 minutes of instruction or more, allowing for a comprehensive assessment aligned with the do-know-think Framework. This is a win-win-win situation because:

1. teachers feel empowered and know what the observation tool looks like so they plan instruction accordingly based on the instructional strategies learned in the professional learning series;
2. administrators are able to observe for shifts in instructional practices and look at evidence directly related to quality student-centered learning directly found in the observational tool; and

3. instructional coaches and professional learning providers are able to see the evidence of their work and the direct impact on student learning.

This creates a concrete accountability system where professional learning providers are held accountable with real-time classroom data to verify impact and reach. By shifting the focus from teacher to student, the evaluation veil is lifted, emphasizing student learning under the do-know-think framework and promoting student-centered professional learning.

Universal Design for Learning and Teaching for Robust Understanding

The Teaching for Robust Understanding (TRU) framework is an instructional framework developed by Alan Schoenfeld, Distinguished Professor of Education and Mathematics at UC Berkeley. It focuses on enhancing teaching practices to foster deep and meaningful understanding among students. The TRU framework emphasizes the importance of helping students develop robust understanding rather than merely memorizing information. The following is an observation guide aligned to the elements of the TRU Framework:

Content: What is the big idea in this lesson? How does it connect to what students already know? During classroom observations, observers can look for evidence of topics that stimulate curiosity and critical thinking in STEM subjects. Are teachers selecting topics that allow for in-depth exploration and inquiry? Content refers to the extent to which classroom activity structures provide opportunities for students to become knowledgeable, flexible, and resourceful disciplinary thinkers. Discussions are focused on coherence, providing opportunities to learn disciplinary ideas, techniques, and perspectives, make connections, and develop productive disciplinary habits of mind.

Cognitive Demand: How long are students given to think and make sense of things? What happens when students get stuck? Are students invited to explain things or just give answers? Observers can assess whether understanding goals are clearly defined and if instructional strategies align with promoting deep comprehension of STEM concepts. Are students challenged to connect ideas and transfer knowledge? Cognitive demand refers to the opportunities students have to engage with and understand important disciplinary concepts. Students learn most effectively when they face challenges that offer both room and support for growth, with tasks ranging from moderately difficult to demanding. The level of challenge should facilitate what is known as "productive struggle."

Equitable Access to Content: Do students get to participate in meaningful learning? Can students hide or be ignored? In what ways are students kept engaged? Classroom observations can assess whether teachers promote knowledge integration across STEM disciplines. Are students encouraged to make connections between different concepts and apply their understanding in interdisciplinary ways? Equitable access is the extent to which classroom activity structures invite and support the active engagement of all of the students in the classroom with the core disciplinary content being addressed by the class. Classrooms in which a small number of students get most of the "air time" are not equitable, no matter how rich the content. All students need to be involved in meaningful ways.

Agency, Ownership, and Identity: What opportunities do students have to explain their ideas? In what ways are they built on? How are students recognized as being capable and able to contribute? Observers can gauge the level of collaboration and discussion within the STEM classroom by asking these questions. Is there evidence of a learning community where students actively participate in meaningful discourse and learn from each other? Agency is the extent to which students are provided opportunities to "walk the walk and talk the talk"—to contribute to conversations about disciplinary ideas, to build on others' ideas and have others build on theirs. This contributes to their development of agency (the willingness to engage), their ownership over the content, and the development of positive identities as thinkers and learners.

Formative Assessment: How is student thinking included in classroom discussions? Does instruction respond to students' ideas and help them think more deeply? Observations can focus on the types of assessments and activities used in STEM classrooms. Are students engaging in performances of understanding that go beyond memorization, such as applying concepts to real-world problems? Formative assessment, as discussed in the last chapter can be summed up as the extent to which classroom activities elicit student thinking and subsequent interactions respond to those ideas, building on productive beginnings and addressing emerging misunderstandings. Powerful instruction "meets students where they are" and gives them opportunities to deepen their understanding.

We have gone over a lot of frameworks. Let us now talk about how these frameworks can work in tandem. Between 3D, 5E, UDL, and TRU, our heads are spinning. We have created a summary table below to compare these frameworks and how we pulled them together.

Framework	Organization	Main Idea	Implications for STEM Educators
3-Dimensional Learning	Next Generation Science Standards (NGSS)	Integrates three dimensions: Science and Engineering Practices (DO), Disciplinary Core Ideas (KNOW), and Crosscutting Concepts (THINK).	Encourages educators to focus on the interconnectedness of science concepts and practices, fostering a deeper understanding of STEM content through inquiry-based learning. It emphasizes active student engagement in scientific practices and the application of knowledge to real-world problems.

Framework	Organization	Main Idea	Implications for STEM Educators
5E Lesson Design	Biological Sciences Curriculum Study (BSCS)	Structured around five stages: Engage, Explore, Explain, Elaborate, and Evaluate.	Promotes student-centered inquiry and exploration, facilitating a gradual transition from exploration to explanation. It encourages educators to design lessons that actively engage students in hands-on activities, collaborative learning, and reflective thinking.
Universal Design for Learning	Center for Applied Special Technology (CAST)	Emphasizes flexibility and inclusivity in lesson design, catering to diverse learner needs through multiple means of representation, engagement, and expression.	Encourages educators to create accessible and engaging learning experiences for all students, including those with disabilities or diverse learning styles. It promotes the use of varied instructional strategies, technologies, and materials to support individualized learning and remove barriers to achievement.
TRU (Teaching for Robust Understanding)	Teaching for Robust Understanding Project (Alan H. Schoenfeld)	Focuses on developing deep conceptual understanding through rich, authentic learning experiences that promote critical thinking, problem-solving, and metacognition.	Challenges educators to move beyond surface-level learning and rote memorization, encouraging them to design instruction that fosters students' ability to transfer and apply knowledge in novel contexts. It emphasizes the importance of active engagement, reflection, and feedback in promoting robust understanding.

We can avoid overwhelm by thinking about the framework as a lens and not a checklist. These guides are meant to be used as reflection tools for lesson planning and design. Though the frameworks give us a great guide for instruction, the instruction should be standards based, not standardized. We have seen the drawbacks of standardized anything in education, and the goal of these frameworks is to serve as a guide for good teaching. Each of these frameworks centers student self-regulation and student agency. By putting these frameworks together, we can create a common definition of student-centered learning and well-rounded teaching. STEM4Real's Connect-Create-Cultivate design brings together these different ideas. Through the creation of 3D5E justice-centered content, STEM4Real ensures that learning experiences are engaging, relevant, and aligned with both academic standards and social justice principles. By making sure that the content is joyful and relevant to everyone, using the Connect-Create-Cultivate frame prioritizes student-centered learning, authentic experiences, and the development of critical thinking skills within a supportive and inclusive classroom environment.

Case-Study Student Analysis: Observation Stage

In the process of conducting classroom observations, closely observing the case-study students becomes a valuable lens through which to glean rich, context-specific data for instructional design. Integrating the ethnographic knowledge gathered from interviews and assessments of the whole child allows the teacher to implement culturally responsive teaching practices, especially when teachers gain additional insights about students' families and communities. With specific observations of case-study students during classroom activities, educators can gain nuanced specifics into their individual needs, learning styles, considerations for any IEP, 504, or language plans, and responses to instructional methods. The case-study student serves as a not-so-secret recipe, providing a longitudinal study that spans from initial interviews to classroom observations and analysis of student work. This comprehensive approach allows teachers to identify patterns, strengths, and areas for growth specific to each case-study student.

While applying this approach to all students may be constrained by time and capacity, strategically choosing case-study students as a statistical sample enables educators to extrapolate insights and lessons learned to inform broader educational planning. The depth and specificity offered allow for a more tailored and effective instructional design that considers the diverse needs of students within the larger classroom context. Observe instances where the teacher demonstrates empathy towards students, including case study students, in understanding their individual challenges and strengths. The case-study student analysis process is intended as an empathy-building exercise that encourages educators to get to know their students on a deeper level that otherwise would not have happened. We can also use observations as an opportunity to evaluate the overall classroom culture, considering whether it promotes inclusivity, respect, and a sense of belonging for all students, including case-study students. What makes up the entire classroom ecosystem and does every student feel valued and represented? Classroom observations in a STEM classroom can significantly contribute to anti-racist instruction when coupled with a deep understanding of case study students. Let's discuss what to observe when looking for particular evidence of anti-racist instruction.

Observation and Anti-Racism

The goal of the observational process is to allow educators to gather specific observational data connected to the classroom environment, instructional practices, and student interactions. It is not a reflection on the teacher. Nor is it a proverbial witch hunt to accuse teachers of racism. Here's how this process can inform next steps, promote empathy, and foster anti-racist instruction in a way that encourages reflection and learning.

1. **Culturally Responsive Teaching:** Pay attention to how the students learn about diverse examples as they interact with culturally relevant materials. Assess whether the curriculum includes content that challenges stereotypes, addresses systemic biases, and promotes a critical understanding of STEM concepts within a broader social context. For example, in a science class, the teacher incorporates examples of diverse scientists and engineers from various cultural backgrounds in their lessons. When discussing the history of scientific achievements, the teacher includes stories of scientists of color, female scientists, and individuals from underrepresented communities. This approach not only challenges stereotypes but also provides students, including case-study students, with role models they can relate to. One student saw a teacher's wall and actually changed his career path because he saw a computer engineer who looked like him and realized he too could become one.
2. **Equitable Participation:** Observe how students, including case-study students, are encouraged to participate in class discussions, group activities, and hands-on experiments. Look for any disparities in participation rates, especially for girls and students of color. Examine how the case-study students are participating and if they feel supported or included within the classroom environment. Look to see if any students are receiving any individualized support. For example, during a group project on renewable energy, the teacher ensures equitable participation by assigning roles that leverage each student's strengths. The teacher implements the think-pair-share strategy to give all students, including those who may be less inclined to speak up, an opportunity to contribute.
3. **Student-Teacher Relationships:** Observe the quality of relationships between the teacher and students, including the rapport with case-study students. Pay attention to communication styles, feedback, and support provided. Do all of the students feel like they belong in that classroom? Observe instances where the teacher demonstrates empathy towards students, including case-study students, in understanding their individual challenges and strengths. For example, a case-study student faces challenges

outside the classroom that affect their participation in the student's STEM notebook. The teacher actively listens to the student's concerns, offering support, and providing looseleaf paper while he gets his STEM notebook together. This can also look like providing additional resources, adjusting deadlines, or connecting the student with counseling services.

Debriefing the Observation: From Evaluative to Collaborative

The purpose of this debriefing protocol is to engage in a collaborative, student-centered discussion that promotes a deeper understanding of anti-racist practices in STEM education and the integration of NGSS standards. The observation debriefing protocol outlined here is designed to prioritize a collaborative and supportive approach, ensuring that there is no blame or shame associated with teacher observations.

Do-Know-Think Observations

Do (What was observed): Begin the debriefing by sharing concrete observations made during the classroom observation. Focus on observable behaviors, teaching strategies, and interactions that relate to anti-racist practices, STEM instruction, and NGSS alignment.

Example: "I observed the teacher using hands-on activities to explain photosynthesis, incorporating diverse examples of agricultural farming methods to highlight the contributions from various backgrounds. Encourage descriptions of student interactions, engagement, and teacher-student dynamics."

Know (What content was learned): Discuss the specific standards learned, vocabulary terms, and general concepts about the learning objectives. Discuss specific instances where student understanding, engagement, or misconceptions were evident. Reflect on how the observed teaching practices contributed to or impacted student learning experiences. Explore the alignment of the observed teaching methods with NGSS or content standards. Discuss how the lesson supported NGSS disciplinary core ideas or content learning overall. Example: "How did the hands-on activities in the lesson align with NGSS content and contribute to students' understanding of scientific concepts?"

Think (How students thought): Discuss how critical thinking was observed about the observed cross cutting concepts. How did the observed teaching practices encourage students to make connections between STEM concepts and other disciplines by looking at patterns, systems, or cause and effect? In what ways did students demonstrate an understanding of how scientific principles relate to real-world scenarios or other areas of study? How did the lesson encourage students to think about systems and the interrelationships within them?

Anti-Racist Lens: Discuss the observed practices specifically through an anti-racist lens. Analyze how the teacher's approach addresses equity, representation, and cultural responsiveness. Example: "How did the teacher ensure that all students, including those from diverse backgrounds, felt seen and represented in the lesson content?"

NGSS and Standards: Observers should share student-centered observations rather than evaluative judgments. Focus on the impact of the observed strategies on student learning and engagement. For example, you can say, "I noticed students each took turns speaking during the group activity and they each contributed to the consensus energy model."

Joy: As Gholdy Muhammad notes in her book *Unearthing Joy*, "Joy can infuse our relationship building with students, as we check in on their hearts and on their wellness. It emerges when we integrate more art, poetry, and music into our instruction and when we create learning experiences that encourage students to have fun and problem solve, with their voices (and perspectives) centered." Explore how the teacher ensured that all students, including case study students, felt a sense of joy and belonging in the learning. Share moments where students celebrated their successes or accomplishments. Discuss how the teacher acknowledged and celebrated both individual and collective achievements, fostering a culture of positivity.

The protocol allows participants to discuss what was observed and what is already known about effective practices. Once you have gone through all of the components of the observation debrief, we can collaboratively develop an action plan for incorporating anti-racist practices and NGSS-aligned strategies into future STEM instruction. But first we should look at how the observed instruction correlates with the assessment that you will be reviewing during you analysis of student work.

How Does Your Observation Connect to the Student Work Artifact?

Now that you have completed the observation, you want to review the student work artifact that you created in the previous chapter. You may have observed some amazing instructional practices; yet the content is not documented in a student work artifact. How can you ensure that the segment of observation is documented in your student work artifact? The most interactive segments of the lesson plan to observe are the *explore* and *elaborate* phases of the 5E. This is because they typically involve the most inquiry when it comes to exploration and messy experiments. However, arguably, each segment has something to offer the observers.

5E	Observation	Assessment
Engage	Observe students asking questions and creating their driving question board	Driving question board questions or Question Formulation Technique brainstorming sheet or Need to Know Questions list
Explore	Observe students exploring beans in a wet paper towel. Pose the discussion question: What factors do you think had the most significant impact on the germination of the beans?	Science notebooks with observations, evidence gathering organizers
Explain	Observe students creating a model and explaining their conceptual models to each other	Discuss the models that they created and revised upon having additional class discussions on the content
Elaborate	Observe design challenges like an engineering design and watch how students approach problems while making connections between concepts.	Analyze their design challenge worksheet with any models, reflection questions, and iterations as they continued to design and model.
Evaluate	Observe students engaging in science talks. Listen for the specific vocabulary terms and answers to the claims as they engage in discussion	Claim-Evidence-Reasoning organizers, index cards with written answers to their discussions, science journal prompts

Generate actionable feedback for the observed teacher based on the discussed observations. Offer suggestions for improvement and enhancement, maintaining a constructive and supportive tone. This shift from evaluative judgments to observations of student engagement, understanding, and participation helps create a more constructive and growth-oriented discussion. By incorporating the do-know-think framework, the debriefing encourages an open and inclusive discussion. Participants share their observations, knowledge, and reflections, creating a collective understanding that is directly aligned to the do-know-think framework and corresponding instructional learning sequence from our lesson planner. The protocol emphasizes student-centered observations, encouraging participants to focus on the impact of instructional practices on student learning. Instead of pointing out shortcomings, participants collaboratively generate suggestions for improvement and enhancement. This approach frames feedback as an opportunity for growth rather than criticism. In the next chapter, we will continue our journey of reflection and unraveling student thinking by analyzing student work.

#4Real Prompts

Building a Culture of Observation

How can we shift the mindset around classroom observations from being primarily evaluative to being opportunities for growth and reflection? Consider your own experiences with observations and how they have impacted your teaching practice.

How might we create a culture where observations are seen as collaborative opportunities to improve student learning rather than assessments of individual performance? Share your thoughts on strategies for fostering a more supportive and growth-oriented approach to observations among educators.

Maximizing Observations for Effective Instruction

Reflect on the observation indicators presented in the do-know-think framework and the #4Real Observation Tool. How might these observation tools support educators in improving instructional practices and promoting student-centered learning? Share your insights on how transparent and collaborative observation processes can enhance professional growth and student outcomes.

Observation and Case-Study Student Analysis

Consider how closely observing case study students during classroom activities can provide valuable insights into their individual needs, learning styles, and responses to instructional methods. Discuss strategies for incorporating ethnographic knowledge gathered from interviews and assessments of the whole child to implement culturally responsive teaching practices during the observation.

CHAPTER 9

Diving into Student Work: How Are Students Demonstrating Their Understanding?

I failed because my binder was messy and I talked a lot in class.

—Seventh Grade Student

Confession time: If you know me by now, you know that I love to talk and am passionate about talking. Wait until you get to the chapter on discourse! As a teacher, my goal was to make sure that everyone else felt passionate about talking, too. For example, in my biology class, I had an assignment where we would discuss news topics. I walked around the room with my clipboard and marked who was participating. I noticed a very quiet student who never participated in class discussions. She completed every other assignment; however, she stayed completely silent for every single class discussion. No matter how many times I walked past her with my clipboard or gave her an awkward look, she stayed quiet. She ended up getting a B+ in my class because of the lack of participation during the science talks.

If there was ever a grade I wanted to change, it would be this grade. I realized that I was not grading her comprehension of the subject matter; I was grading her noncompliance. What I didn't see was the listening skills she was using to actively listen to each of her peers, nor did I see her internal processing of the materials discussed. I was also not being mindful of the different ways that students can express themselves. This student could have written down her responses or shared them using a recorder. Either way, I was focused on grading a behavior, not mastery of the content. In this chapter, we will discuss how we can figuratively dissect a student's brain in order to see how students think and demonstrate their understanding. The goal of this chapter is to witness the students' processing, critical thinking, and sense-making skills to ensure we're teaching (and grading) them accurately and equitably.

Recap of Our Journey: From Connecting to Creating

Let's take a moment to recap our journey. In Part 1, we spent time connecting with our case-study students. We took time getting to know these students on a deeper and more personal level than what we may typically have had the opportunity to do with the hustle and bustle of the classroom. We also spent time getting to know their families and community context. We created a vivid and complete picture of the whole child. We then used this information to inform our culturally responsive teaching practices. We created a culturally responsive phenomenon based on the information from connecting with our students and community, further informed by the ethnographic research of our case-study students. We actively built connections to social justice and anti-racism. After observing and debriefing the lesson, we are now at the stage of lesson study when we see the rubber hitting the road. There are two guiding questions as we enter this process:

1. How will I assess student learning?
2. Was this a joyful experience?

As Gholdy Muhammad states, joy is something more than having fun or celebrating. Joy is a sustained effort to recognize and honor the beauty of and within the Earth. Joy means coming together for advocacy and problem solving to make the world better. Joy is wellness, healing, and justice. Therefore, if joy has the power to ignite our relationships with students, it has to be something that we think about in terms of assessment and analysis of learning. In the following infographic, you can see how the entire 3D5E instructional learning sequence comes together. The instructor launches the learning sequence with the culturally responsive phenomenon using standard-hook-society (SHS). We then explore the concepts through inquiry-based activities that help students gather observations, ask questions, and engage in the doing of learning. This is referred to as ABC, "activity before content." Even though the activity *is* the content, we mean that the activity comes before the formal lecture or explanations. This allows students to attach the concepts to experiences. Educators can then formally introduce the concepts, vocabulary, formulas, and core ideas by creating opportunities for academic talk. Explanations can go from the teacher to the student, student to the teacher, or student to student. In the elaborate phase, we see this as an opportunity to bring in diverse perspectives, ideas, and counternarratives. Perhaps it is the showcasing of BIPOC STEM professionals, or the cultural stories that are connected to the science and STEM topics. Finally, we round out the lesson with communication strategies that help students formulate claims based on evidence and reasoning. Educators can also incorporate service learning, youth action, and project based learning as dynamic assessments to evaluate student progress.

In each of these categories, teachers can collect a student artifact that will capture student sense-making.

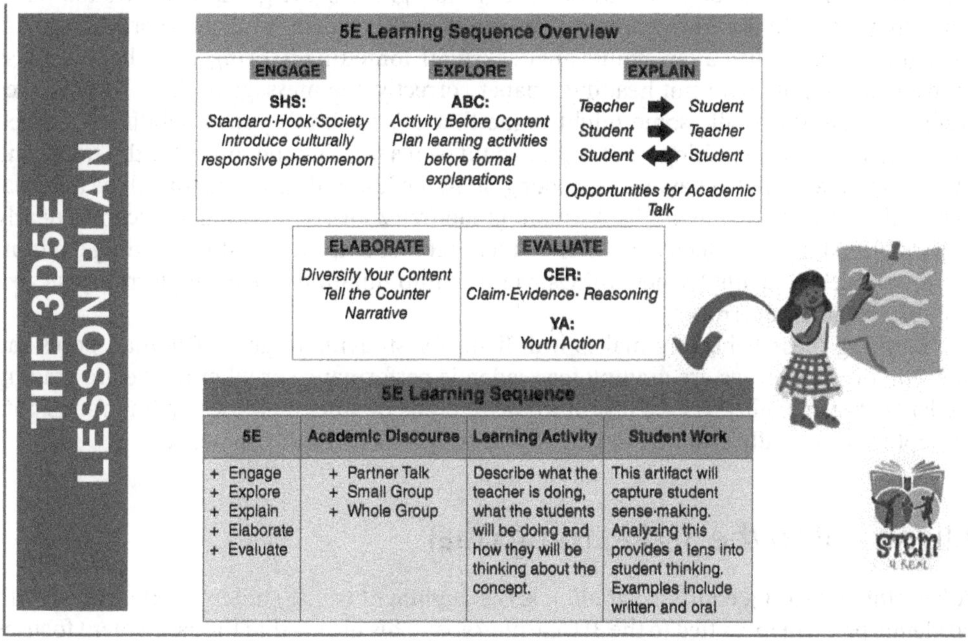

As one can see, a multiple -choice Scantron sheet may tell us whether a student got the right answer; however, it does not reveal the thinking about why they chose a certain answer. Moreover, amongst the wrong answers, we are unable to see the value in the mistakes that were made because we cannot see the thinking behind them. Shana Pyatt-Buckner, a STEM educator of over 30 years and founder of See Different Consulting, states that "One way that I get to know my students is first by modeling vulnerability and humility for them. Making wonderful mistakes out loud, and always being humble enough to acknowledge errors and apologize for mistakes helps them realize that all of those behaviors are part of growth and okay to experience in the classroom learning community." Analyzing mistakes and errors is crucial for cultivating a culture that prioritizes learning over solely pursuing correct answers. We may be celebrating a right answer for the wrong reasons. Mistakes can reveal so much more in student learning and thinking. Embracing mistakes enables educators to uncover deeper insights into student thinking and encourages the development of a growth mindset, promoting resilience, grit, and exploration.

A Note on Equitable Grading

Before we define the analysis of the student work process, let us discuss equitable grading. When I shared about docking my student for not participating in class discussions, that was not equitable grading. According to Joe Feldman, author of *Grading for Equity*:

Teachers often assign grades based on mistakes in students' behaviors as well: downgrading a score if an assignment is late, subtracting points from a daily participation grade if a student is tardy to class, or lowering a group's grade if the group becomes too noisy while they work. In this environment, every mistake is penalized and incorporated into the final grade. Even if just a few points are docked for forgetting to bring a notebook to class or losing a few points for not heading a paper correctly, the message is clear: All mistakes result in penalties. While some might argue that this is simply accountability—"I asked the students to do something, so it has to count"—it's missing the forest for the trees. The more assignments and behaviors a teacher grades, the less willing a student will be to reveal her weaknesses and vulnerability. Without grade-free zones of learning, it becomes nearly impossible to build an effective teacher–student relationship and positive learning environment in which students try new things, venture into unfamiliar learning territory, or feel comfortable making errors.

Limiting these behaviors makes it difficult for students to grow. Feldman poses the question of whether we are grading for academic performance or whether we are grading students' responsibility. As we dive into the analysis of student work, Feldman's insights prompt us to critically examine the factors influencing our grading practices.

Alignment to the 3D Learning Goal

A key clue indicating equitable grading is the alignment of the student work artifact with academic performances tied to the 3D learning goal. This means that the assessment focuses on measuring the students' understanding and mastery of the academic content, ensuring that grades are reflective of their knowledge and skills rather than incorporating behavior or compliance.

In-Class Completion of Work

Equitable grading is also signaled when student work is completed in class rather than assigned as homework. This is because we have to recognize the potential inequities associated with homework, such as varying home environments, access to resources, and stability. Shifting assessments to in-class activities levels the playing field. This approach helps to mitigate external factors beyond the teacher's control, ensuring that students are evaluated based on their understanding and efforts during class time.

Transition to a 0–4 Scale and Growth-Supportive Algorithms

Another indicator of equitable grading is saying goodbye to the traditional 0–100 point scale and instead opting for a mathematically realistic 0–4 scale. This shift acknowledges that learning is a dynamic process and allows for a finer-grained assessment of student performance. Additionally, incorporating algorithms that support student growth rather than punitive measures signifies a commitment to fostering improvement. This approach rejects the notion of consigning students to failure and instead focuses on providing opportunities for development and progress within a supportive grading framework.

While grading and the analysis of student work may serve distinct purposes, it is imperative to pause and deliberate on the principles of equitable grading. Equitable grading revolves around fairness, justice, and a holistic approach to student assessment. It promotes transparency and clarity in communication. Students should understand the criteria used for assessment, the learning goals associated with each task, and how their performance aligns with these expectations. Clear communication helps students take ownership of their learning and actively engage in the improvement process. That way we can acknowledge the potential biases and external factors influencing grading decisions. Many of the student work assessments and artifacts we explore inevitably find their way into gradebooks, shaping the academic journey for students. The foundational step in rectifying inequities within the grading system is a deep understanding of what we are measuring.

Grading versus Analyzing

Put your red pens away because, during this process, we are not grading. The reason we discuss equitable grading is to ensure that the student artifact chosen is a direct reflection of the 3D learning goal. The goal of this artifact is to capture student sense-making. Analyzing this artifact provides a lens into student thinking. Examples can be written and oral. That is why, here, a Scantron bubble test would not work. The answers would not reflect what the student was thinking behind the answer.

Grading and analyzing student work are distinct and have different goals when assessing student learning. They both serve a unique purpose in understanding student performance. Grading is centered on completion, participation, and compliance. It is a quantitative evaluation that categorizes students based on the product or outcome of students' efforts. Analysis of student work is about having an artifact that captures the learning journey of a student's thinking. The process allows for someone to go through the student work and pull out the conceptions and misconceptions that exist. In this process, the evaluator could provide targeted feedback based on what was demonstrated in the learning journey. Analyzing student work delves into the qualitative aspects of the learning process. The focus shifts from the product to the process, emphasizing the intricacies of students' thoughts, reasoning, and decision-making. Analyzing student work explores the *how* and *why* behind their actions, capturing the learning journey rather than just the end destination. Whether formative or summative, the emphasis is on understanding the nuances of student thinking and the developmental path they traverse, ensuring that the product authentically reflects the depth of their learning experiences. At times, after an entire session of analyzing student work, the student may not even have a grade on their paper. *Gasp* This is because the goal of grading is to label an end result or product, whereas analyzing is seeking out information from students' thought processes.

For example, when I was an undergraduate biology major at UC Berkeley, I think I may have been one of the only students who graduated with a biology major but failed introductory "Biology IA." Most people who fail introductory biology switch majors. I was committed to my major and decided to give it another go. When looking at grading, I received an F; I failed. In grading, there was no discussion of what I learned, the journey I was on, or how I thought about the material. However, in analysis of student work, the professor could have looked at one of my laboratory reports and actually gone through the process of my thinking, where I modeled the genetic patterns of the fruit flies, and how I demonstrated understanding of sex-linked traits to see that, despite my failing grade, my comprehension was not completely missing. In a weeder class of over 600 students, analysis of student work is an impossible practice and that is why grading is about completion, participation, compliance, and the "right answers." But it is important to remember that test taking is a skill (in fact, some people happen to be master test takers) and it does not necessarily demonstrate mastery of content knowledge.

Refer Back to Your 3D Learning Goal

Remember that your 3-D learning goal is created directly from the do-know-think framework. Your learning goal should include the practices, the core ideas, and the cross-cutting concepts (CCCs). A possible template adapted from the STEM Teaching Tools website is as follows:

"((practice verb clause)) to ((content element)) highlighting that ((CCC element))."

Example: Students will ((compare models)) to ((electricity and currents (parallel versus series)) highlighting that ((patterns of performance of designed systems))."

Recall that this is the format of your 3D learning goal:

Phenomenon		
DO What are students doing?	KNOW What is the core content?	THINK How are students thinking?
	Standards-Based Goal	

Prairie Dogs and the Snake Alarm (When a snake is present)		
DO Students are constructing explanations of observed relationships	KNOW What is the core content? Group behavior has evolved because membership can increase the chances of survival	THINK How are students thinking? Patterns can be used to identify cause-and-effect relationships.
Standards-Based Goal: Students will explain how patterns of group behavior on individual species' can increase chances of survival and reproduction		

In the following table, the alignment of the *do, know, think* dimensions in student work is crucial for assessing the depth of understanding in science and STEM lessons. To ascertain that students are actively engaging in *do* practices, we can look for evidence of key practices such as hands-on experimentation, data analysis, and constructing explanations. This may include observing students designing experiments, analyzing graphs, or constructing explanations based on their findings. For *know*, specific keywords or phrases indicative of comprehension of core ideas are vital. These could encompass vocabulary terms, summarizations of informational texts, or debates centered around key concepts and disciplinary core ideas. To gauge how students *think* about CCCs, we look for evidence revealing students' ability to diagram patterns, model energy cycles, or discuss cause and effect relationships.

DO: Practice	KNOW: Core Idea	THINK: Cross-cutting Concept
What evidence will demonstrate that the student is DOING this practice in the student work?	*What key words or phrases will you be looking for in order to understand that the student KNOWS the given standard?*	*What evidence will demonstrate that the student is THINKING about this concept to make sense of the content?*

As we analyze the student work, we will be looking for opportunities to collect information on each dimension. For the *do* (practices), we are looking for evidence that will demonstrate that the student is doing the practice as reflected in the student work. This is why there has to be coherence between what is observed in the lesson and what is analyzed. For the *know* (content knowledge), you are looking for key words and phrases in order to understand that the student knows the given standard. Identify key words and phrases within the student work that directly align with the specified content standards. For the *think* (CCCs), we are looking for evidence that will demonstrate that the student is thinking about his concept and highlight how they are making sense of the content. Ensure that there is coherence between observed practices, content knowledge, and thinking skills in both the lesson and the analyzed student work.

Analysis of Student Work: The #4Real Process

1. **Revisit the SHS Learning Goal:** Now that you have reviewed the standards-based learning goal and have solidified the three dimensions you are seeking to analyze, you are ready to have a grounded discussion on the student work. Remember that the analysis of student work process provides a window into the unique approaches and perspectives each student brings to problem-solving. The goal sets the stage for the multiple responses you are about to review.
2. **Recall the 5E Sequence:** Review your 5E sequence and make a quick reference guide for your squad (and yourself) so that as you analyze student work, you have an idea of where the learning took place within the learning sequence. This also helps analyzers in identifying where the student is in their learning journey. Emphasizing that mistakes are part of the learning process and can be valuable for improvement helps create a supportive environment where students feel safe to take risks.

3. **Divide and Number:** Divide the stack of papers among your team. (Pro tip: You always want a partner or group to analyze student work so that you can bounce ideas off of each other and continue the magic of collaboration.) Number each of the papers in your stack before you begin. This ensures that you are solely looking at the work and not necessarily naming students yet. When analyzing a stack of work, you will be recording trends so adding numbers aids in the flow of the process versus adding full names.
4. **Trends and Categories:** On a set of sticky notes, write down each trend or category of information that you see in the responses. Each trend should go on a separate sticky note. *One* trend equals *one* sticky note. Here is an example: When looking at a student's work, we saw the following in their responses:
    a. Sticky note 1: Explains the benefit of group behavior for survival against predators
    b. Sticky note 2: Connects observations of prairie dogs' behavior to reason for why they survived the snake
    c. Sticky note 3: Describes how group behavior works

    These statements would each go on their own respective sticky note. During this phase, you can write down numbers of all of the student responses that say this same sticky note.
5. **Affinity Grouping and Sorting:** Next, as you come back as a large squad, you will sort and gather the multiple responses as you move through each of the student papers. Perhaps there are various versions of the sticky notes that show up in multiple students' papers. For example:
    a. Five responses sound similar to sticky note 1: Explains the benefit of group behavior for survival against predators
    b. Six responses sound similar to sticky note 2: Connects observations of prairie dogs' behavior to reason for why they survived the snake
    c. Four responses sound similar to sticky note 3: Describes how group behavior works

    You will now have three to four trends that are representative of the entire stack of papers that you just analyzed with your team.
6. **Outliers:** As you are going through many of the student responses, you might get a response that is quite the outlier. These responses have nothing to do with the learning goals or the trends that you are seeing. For example, perhaps the response starts discussing the impacts of lice. This has nothing to do with the learning goal and thus can be placed to the side. You can always refer back to these responses at a later time. Typically, the outlier responses are only one or two per stack of student work and do not qualify as a trend in student thinking.
7. **The magic is about to happen:** You will now choose one student from each of the pile of trends that you created. Be sure to include any case-study students so you can pay extra attention to their answers. Take a deep dive into each of the samples. You will be asking yourself the following questions:
    a. How did the student demonstrate the 3D learning goal? Do (SEP)-know (DCI)-think (CCC)?
    b. What questions would you ask this student? What more information would you like to know?
    c. What are your next steps with this student?

By deliberately selecting one student from each trend pile, including case-study students, the teacher ensures that a diverse representation of voices is heard. This process avoids favoring certain perspectives and promotes equity in the analysis. I like to think of Question B as the question where you are sitting down one on one with your student at a coffee shop and had the opportunity to ask this student any follow-up questions. Sometimes I want to ask general questions like, "What did you think?" However, this is your opportunity to ask more specific questions like, "Why did you mention survival against predators? Are there any other factors that contribute to the animal's survival? How does a group help?" The focus on a one-on-one deep dive into each student's work reflects a commitment to understanding individual contexts and experiences.

Regularly analyzing student work helps educators refine teaching strategies. It enables a continuous improvement cycle where educators adapt their methods based on the evolving needs and responses of a diverse student body. Analyzing student work also aligns with anti-racist pedagogy by uncovering potential biases, challenging traditional evaluation methods, and creating a more just and equitable learning experience. The questions posed to students during the deep dive go beyond surface-level assessments. They encourage a deeper understanding of the students' thought process, inviting them to articulate not only what they know but also how they approach problem-solving and critical thinking. Anti-racist pedagogy emphasizes the importance of recognizing and addressing individual needs. The process of determining next steps for each student, based on their unique responses, aligns with this principle. It acknowledges that different students may require tailored support for their growth and understanding.

Reconnect to the Lesson Debrief

You have now observed instruction, debriefed the observation, and comprehensively analyzed student work. This pivotal moment is the moment where you started with the case study student analysis and longitudinally monitored them from designing instruction, to observing instruction, to analyzing instruction. You now have the opportunity to ask yourself the following questions:

1. **How would you modify the assignment?** This prompts reflection on the inclusivity and accessibility of the assignment. Anti-racist pedagogy encourages educators to critically examine whether assignments cater to diverse learning styles and backgrounds. This is an opportunity to identify and rectify any unintentional biases or barriers present in the assignment.
2. **How would you differentiate for your case-study students?** Addressing differentiation is central to anti-racist pedagogy, emphasizing the importance of recognizing and responding to individual student needs, especially based on Individualized Education Program (IEP), 504, and emergent multilingual instruction. This question directs attention to tailoring instructional methods for the case-study students, ensuring that they receive the support necessary for their unique learning journeys. Use this opportunity to reflect on case study students and the quantitative/qualitative information that we have collected throughout this cycle.

3. **How would you change the lesson?** This encourages a critical examination of the lesson's effectiveness and inclusivity. It prompts educators to assess whether the lesson promotes diverse perspectives and experiences, ensuring that it resonates with a broad range of students. By addressing potential biases and refining the lesson, educators actively contribute to dismantling systemic inequalities within STEM education.
4. **How would you modify your learning goals?** This question prompts educators to reevaluate their learning goals, ensuring they are relevant, accessible, and supportive of every student's growth. This goes back to the idea of equitable grading. Equitable grading starts with equitable learning goals. By modifying learning goals to be more inclusive, educators set the foundation for fair assessment practices.

Netty Spotlight

Selected Student: Cynthia Learning Goal: Design an experiment to determine how a plant grows and observe the effects of water and sunlight	
How did the student demonstrate the 3D learning goal? DO (SEP)-KNOW (DCI)-(THINK) (CCC)?	The student is making connections to oxygen and understanding that humans need oxygen. The plant grew slower and made a connection to the lack of sunlight. She's making connections to the causes and effects of plant growth.
What questions would you ask this student? What more information would you like to know?	How do you know that there was oxygen in the bag? How did it end? Did she plant and replant the bean? She replanted this in the soil. Why didn't one of the beans grow? Why do you want to take out all of the dead plants?
What are your next steps with this student?	Have students grow the plant in soil and in the bag at the same time. Eliminate one process (sunlight or water) to have students see what they notice.

The questions posed by the teacher go into understanding the nuances of Cynthia's experiment by inquiring about the presence of oxygen in the bag and the end result of the experiment. Questions about why one bean didn't grow and the motivation behind removing dead plants reveal the teacher's interest in uncovering Cynthia's thought processes. The information sought about replanting the bean in soil provides insight into Cynthia's problem-solving approach. The teacher's proposal to have students grow plants in soil and in a bag simultaneously, while eliminating one variable, builds on Cynthia's current understanding and encourages her to explore more intricate aspects of experimental design.

When asked how the teacher would differentiate for her case-study students, she said this: "Lots of talking and counseling students to reduce the academic pressures of right vs. wrong. Having to change the mindset of students of exploring, failing, and making mistakes. Emphasizing the process. Mitigating academic anxiety—need for one-on-one or two-on-one conversations." By providing counseling to reduce academic pressures and emphasizing the exploration process, the teacher is actively working to mitigate academic anxiety. The one-on-one or two-on-one conversations reflect understanding each student's unique mental health needs and creating an inclusive environment that allows space for these struggles. This teaches persistence.

Tools for Self-Assessment

Two tools that can ensure standardization and a common language for debriefing, reflection, and sharing best practices are the UDL Guidelines (**https://udlguidelines.cast.org/**) and the NGSS Evidence Statements (**https://www.nextgenscience.org/evidence-statements**). These provide educators with powerful tools for reflection, discussion, and strategic planning in their instructional journey. The UDL guidelines, which emphasize multiple means of representation, engagement, and expression, serve as a guiding framework to create learning environments that accommodate diverse learner needs. Simultaneously, the NGSS evidence statements offer a clear roadmap, delineating the expected outcomes and the three dimensions (do-know-think) for science education. Combining these tools allows educators to critically assess the alignment of their teaching practices with both the principles of inclusive design and the specific expectations outlined in the NGSS to create a common language.

Universal Design for Learning and the CAST UDL Guidelines

UDL emphasizes providing multiple means of representation, engagement, and expression to accommodate diverse learning styles and abilities. Modifying assignments, differentiating for case study students, and providing flexible means to learning goals all resonate with UDL's core tenets. The Center for Applied Special Technology (CAST) UDL guidelines are a valuable indicator that complements the questions raised during the observation debrief. It reinforces the idea that a well-designed learning environment accommodates a range of learner variability. This aligns with the CAST UDL Guidelines by placing an emphasis on flexibility, providing options, and embracing variability. Assessments that consider diverse pathways to demonstrate understanding reflect a UDL-aligned approach to evaluation. By adopting the CAST UDL guidelines as a guiding framework, educators ensure that their teaching and assessment practices are intentionally designed to address the variability in their students' learning needs and preferences, creating a truly inclusive STEM learning experience. As Andratesha Fritzgerald discusses in *Antiracism and Universal Design for Learning: Building Expressways to Success*, there are three keys to leveraging UDL as a tool for anti-racism.

- In step 1 of incorporating anti-racist UDL in STEM, we must self-assess. Teachers assess the inclusivity of their STEM curriculum design and representation, ensuring that diverse voices, including those of mathematicians and scientists from underrepresented groups, are acknowledged. This step promotes reflection on STEM teaching practices within the do-know-think framework by looking at the practices, content and CCCs outlined throughout the assessment. This step also considers the diverse ways students engage in scientific inquiry, investigation, and engineering design practices.

- In step 2, we must confront biases and that is why we number the papers during the sticky notes assessment practice and focus on the number versus the student when we start choosing trends in student thinking. Step 2 aligns with UDL's goal of challenging educators' expectations and promoting intentional design for inclusion and belonging.
- In step 3, we ensure that the analysis caters to a diverse student body with varied backgrounds and interests in STEM. When educators can craft activities that leverage students' strengths while reducing potential obstacles, the resulting outcomes are more likely to genuinely showcase their capabilities.

Universal Design is essential for both instruction and assessment. Beth Laktrez is a special education educator and founder of Lakretz Creative Support Services, which specializes in inclusive education and co-teaching in special education. She recalls the following experience of a student with Down syndrome:

The first thing that people need to do when they take on a unit, when they're including somebody who's very different, is to really delve deep into the objectives and the concepts of that unit and pick a couple that you're going to have this student learn. Let's get ahead of it. Let's be proactive, and let's create concrete reasonable objectives for this person. The general education teacher decided to have the TA verbally give the student parts of the unit test. And the first two questions were things like name two things that conduct electricity. The student didn't have to write, she didn't even have to speak. She pointed to her TA's earrings and necklace which were metal. And then when asked if she could tell us two things that don't conduct electricity, she went in her desk and pulled out a crayon and an eraser. She had clearly understood the concept even though she wasn't going to take the test. So instead, the student, with the collaboration of the occupational therapist (OT) was able to put the circuit together at the circuit building station in the room. When the student's mother heard about her daughter's experience, she just started to bawl. The mother said that if she was in that separate class for kids who are all intellectually disabled or who all have Down syndrome, the only thing about electricity that she would have learned is "*Don't* put your fingers in the socket." This is what inclusion can look like and the diversity in assessments allow for the student to demonstrate their learning and understanding through the collaboration and co-teaching of the special education team. I am not saying that this work is easy; however, it is possible.

NGSS Evidence Statements

Use the NGSS evidence Statements as a benchmark to assess how well your teaching practices align with the intended outcomes. You can also analyze student performance in alignment with the NGSS evidence statements. Consider whether the assessments and activities implemented in your classroom allow students to demonstrate the desired proficiency in scientific practices and understanding of core concepts. Think of the NGSS evidence statements as a tool for reflection versus a checklist to complete your lesson plan. Evaluate whether your instructional strategies effectively address the skills and knowledge outlined in the statements.

- **Analyze NGSS Evidence Statements:** Begin by thoroughly analyzing the NGSS evidence statements associated with the specific performance expectations you are addressing in your instruction. Break down each statement to understand the outcomes and the scientific practices and cross-cutting concepts embedded within.
- **Discuss Instruction with Evidence Statements:** Discuss and reflect on your instructional strategies and activities directly with the NGSS evidence statements. Ensure that your lessons provide opportunities for students to engage in the scientific practices outlined in the statements and develop an understanding of the core concepts.
- **Design Assessments Reflecting Evidence Statements:** Construct assessments that directly reflect the expectations outlined in the NGSS evidence statements. Assessments should not only measure students' content knowledge but also evaluate their ability to apply scientific practices and connect concepts across the disciplinary core ideas. Use the evidence statements as a guide for crafting assessment questions and tasks that authentically capture students' proficiency in three-dimensional science learning.

Metacognition

Metacognition is referred to as how students will self-monitor their learning. This contributes to ensuring that the students are taking ownership of their learning and becoming independent learners. For example, when my infant was nine months old, she wanted to live on the perch of my hip. The pediatrician told me to encourage her to play by herself. Doing so helps her to develop independence as she explores by herself, makes connections, and continues to learn and grow without depending on my presence. Most importantly, it gives me a bit of sanity as I juggle motherhood and my other roles. That is exactly what we are doing here as educators. We want to offload the cognitive thinking and reflection to our students. Tools such as self-assessments, assignment completion records, and student reflections are perfect additions for students to self-monitor.

1. Have students set learning goals. These learning goals can be directly aligned to the goals you created from the SHS. By participating in goal-setting, students gain a clearer understanding of what is expected, develop a sense of purpose, and are more motivated to achieve their objectives.
2. Create an assignment completion record. This can be the evidence gathering organizer that lists all of the learning activities within the instructional sequence.
3. Create reflection questions that encourage students to reflect on the difficulty, strengths, and areas of growth. This encourages a growth mindset and serves as a visual tool to track and organize learning activities within an instructional sequence.
4. Create self-assessments so students can quiz themselves within the learning unit. This can include exit tickets and short one- to three-answer quizzes to encourage learning and mastery. Regular self-assessments enable students to monitor their growth, identify areas for further study, and celebrate their achievements.

Example Meta-Strategic Questions

- Where is my learning now in relation to the learning goals for this lesson?
- Am I on track to meet the learning goals?
- What difficulties am I experiencing in my learning?
- What can I do about these difficulties?
- What are the strengths in my work?
- Where do I need to do to improve?
- I need more support here . . .
- Reflect on this: I feel smart in STEM.

Metacognition is about providing space for students to reflect and connect. The concept of smartness in STEM is something that we have to actively define and redefine. Traditionally, the term smart has often been associated with cognitive abilities, academic achievements, and proficiency in standardized testing. However, this narrow definition fails to capture the multifaceted nature of intelligence and competence required in STEM, especially when it comes to people of color feeling like they belong in STEM. In STEM, being smart goes beyond rote memorization or excelling in traditional academic metrics. A truly smart STEM community values diversity of thought, background, and experience. Embracing different perspectives allows for mistakes, exploration, creativity, and innovation, leading to more comprehensive and equitable solutions.

When I was in college, I remember being very confused on the topic of prions, or abnormal proteins. I just couldn't get the concept and I kept asking questions about it. One male student gasped in frustration and said, "Are we done talking about prions, already?" I remember never asking a question in our discussion class again. I felt dejected and deflated. It felt like I did not belong in this space of learning. These moments are happening all the time and as educators, we have to continually check in on the emotional quotient of our students. Having self-assessments provides capacity for students to monitor their progress and reflect on the content. Moreover, it provides a space for students to ask for help and support.

Analysis of Student Work as an Act of Justice

Most of our schools have an ongoing issue of bias and inequitable grading that has historically been weaponized against students. When we think about grades, there is a connection to worthiness and self-worth. Ebony Omotola McGee, author of *Black, Brown, and Bruised: How Racialized STEM Education Stifles Innovation*, describes how competition-induced stress in the sciences can be exacerbated for students of color. She states, "You have what I refer to as racial battle fatigue, where you're just tired of defending or proving your value in STEM over and over again."

When I went through my entire schooling, I was an A student with an occasional B here and there. I remember being so upset with each B because it made me feel further and further away from attending university. When I went to university, I prayed and wished for Bs. There was a moment when I received my first F. I fell to the floor crying, sure that my time at college was over and any career aspirations I had were immediately halted. Of course, looking back, I made it and I survived. However, those grades were not reflective of what I learned as a biology student. Moreover, I felt that I had lost the battle of proving myself as a viable student in STEM. Because grades are directly connected to being "smart," trauma and emotional violence are often attached to grades. The process of analyzing student work redefines what it means to be "smart" in STEM. It is a process that is enlightening and serves as a window into student sensemaking. This is a two-way process where the students are demonstrating what they have learned while we, too, are learning from the students about *how* they have learned.

#4Real Prompts

Understanding Mistakes in Learning

How can educators create a classroom culture that embraces mistakes as integral to the learning process? Discuss how educators can shift their mindset from penalizing mistakes to leveraging them as opportunities for growth and deeper understanding. Consider strategies for creating a classroom environment where students feel empowered to take risks, make mistakes, and learn from them. Share examples of how you've embraced mistakes in your teaching practice and the impact it had on student learning and engagement.

Grading versus Analyzing Student Work

Discuss the potential benefits of shifting from a grading-focused approach to one that prioritizes the analysis of student thinking processes. How might this shift create a deeper understanding of student learning and promote equitable assessment practices? Share your thoughts on how educators can integrate regular analysis of student work into their teaching routines to inform instructional decision-making and support diverse learners effectively.

Justice and Equity through Student Work Analysis

How does the process of analyzing student work contribute to redefining notions of intelligence and competence in STEM education, particularly in addressing systemic biases and encouraging inclusive learning environments? In what ways does the analysis of student work challenge historical biases in grading and instead affirm the worth and potential of every student? How can our feedback practices allow for students to feel smart in STEM?

PART 3

Cultivate

CHAPTER 10

Classroom Culture, Discourse, Identity, and Belonging

I'm not a STEM person because that's for smart people and I've never been smart in STEM.

—Anonymous student

Audit

In the last chapter, we discussed the power of self-assessment as a tool to encourage meta-strategic thinking in students. We will now use that same power of self-assessment for us as educators as well. An audit is an official examination of a system or our personal practices. Therefore, the first step includes an internal audit. These audits are helpful in identifying where common experiences may have formed stereotypes which then turned into implicit biases. These unintentional, unconscious attitudes impact how we relate to our students and their parents. Moreover, it affects how we choose curriculum, assess learning, and plan lessons.

1. **How are you operating as a teacher? (Are you truly supporting students, or do you see your profession as "I'm here to just teach content"?)**

   This question addresses our mindset and approach to teaching. It challenges us to reflect on our role beyond merely delivering content knowledge. Teachers who view their profession as more than just content delivery are likely to be more open to understanding and addressing the unique needs of their students, cultivating a more equitable learning environment.

2. **Are you holding your students, regardless of identity, to high standards?**

   It is crucial to ensure that all students, regardless of their background or identity, are held to high academic standards. Anti-racist instruction emphasizes providing equal opportunities for success to all students, challenging any preconceived biases that might influence expectations based on identity. This is where you may hear, "These kids can't do this activity" or "This student can't complete this assignment. Here is an easier worksheet." Identify those places in your instructional planning where you might have allowed your implicit biases to prevent you from pushing your students to achieve at optimal levels. Sepehr Vakil, Associate Professor of Learning Sciences in the School of Education and Social Policy at Northwestern University and Faculty Director of the Technology, Race, Ethics, and Equity in Education (TREE) Lab, discusses the impact of detrimental narratives on student's identity. He stated:

   "In computing education, the notion that underrepresented students are unmotivated to learn computer science (CS) due to a perceived clash of values has become a powerful narrative with implications both for how diversity is conceptualized as well as for how interventions are designed to create more inclusive learning contexts."

3. **Has your past interaction with a particular race of people impacted your ability to communicate with parents?**

   This question addresses our self-awareness and ability to reflect on potential biases. Anti-racist instruction requires educators to be aware of any biases that might affect their communication with parents, especially parents from different racial backgrounds. By acknowledging and addressing these biases, teachers can ensure that they are building positive and effective communication with all parents.

When I was a teacher, I had a Pakistani American student. He received a D on one of the exams and was quite distraught. He had not been practicing and instead had been exhibiting off-task behaviors that allowed for many distractions. When we went over his grade, I said, "Sharif, what are your parents going to say? You have to make them proud." What I ended up doing was projecting my own South Asian upbringing and connecting guilt and shame to grades and performance. I reflected on how my experience as an Indian American affected the communication I had with this student because of the prior experiences I was holding on to. I spoke to him the next day and apologized for making his performance about his parents. The experience highlighted a need for me to reflect on my past experiences and also audit how I communicate with other South Asian students and parents.

An easy way to highlight your own biases is by taking Harvard University's Implicit Association Test (IAT) which measures attitudes and beliefs that we may be unwilling to self-report. Take a moment to take the test on the website at **https://implicit.harvard.edu/implicit/**. Are the results surprising? What did you learn about yourself?

Belonging

Dr. Victor Rios has captivated audiences with his story as a former student caught up in the juvenile justice system and what he refers to as street life. Whether you are labeled as a "decent kid" or a "street kid," Rios says, "Instead of thinking of people as fixed types, we should view them as actors dynamically responding on a stage with constantly shifting backdrop and scenery, their performances influenced by different settings and different actors they encounter."

One of my eighth-grade students, Elijah, was quite the challenge as I began my teaching career. He was truant in my class, never completed assignments, and had a string of girlfriends. A few years later, when I was teaching 11th grade, in walked Elijah, three years older. Elijah had become a teen parent and actually took it as an opportunity to do everything he could for his daughter. He ended up working hard to be at one of the top grades of my class, attentively listening and ensuring he obtained all of the class materials. I asked him how he changed so significantly. He said, "I think I just grew up. I am a father now, so I have to be responsible for my little girl." When I had this same student as an eighth grader, he had a different backdrop and scenery. A change in that backdrop impacted many aspects of Elijah's life, ultimately leading to a changed student. Considering the impact that these changing backdrops can have on our students, how can we create conditions for belonging that could allow students to feel included with their multiple identities? Below are a few conditions we encourage teachers to adopt to allow students to feel smart in STEM and to reimagine smartness as an attainable attribute for all.

1. **Embrace a culture of mistakes:** I recently taught a class of aspiring science teachers and we were discussing antibiotic resistance. When I read a related article in class, it said "antimicrobial resistance." Now I am a successful undergraduate in biology and for that moment, I did not know the difference between bacteria and microbes. As I was thinking out loud, I said I forgot the difference, I'll have to go back and look it up. As we moved on to another topic, the students started talking about a non-Newtonian fluid. When we concluded the class, one of the students spoke up and thanked me for demonstrating that it is okay as scientists not to know all of the science concepts. She said that she looked up "non-Newtonian fluid" while everyone was discussing it so that she knew what we were talking about. Inadvertently, I was able to create a culture where the students had permission to not know all of the answers. There is so often so much judgment around not knowing the answer that when you land in a moment like that, it can affect your mindset and the way you show up in the classroom.
2. **Be a motivational facilitator:** Being a motivational facilitator, as opposed to a motivational speaker, involves an interactive and student-centered approach to redefining the concept of being smart in STEM. Motivational facilitators highlight the varied ways in which individuals can excel in STEM, reinforcing the idea that smartness is not confined to a specific stereotype. Once, while working with an administrative assistant at a school office, she said, "You know, it's not like my son is going to go to Harvard, let's

be realistic." He was 10 years old when she said that. This is not just a deficit mindset, it takes a complete reengineering of our mindsets because people can only attain what their environment encourages. That is why it is not just facilitation, it is motivation to keep reinforcing that students belong. The following image is one of our STEM4Real teacher's whiteboards. They teach in a community school where students who have faced expulsion from mainstream educational settings now attend. This message serves as a beacon of encouragement and affirmation, creating a positive atmosphere where every student feels valued and supported in their academic journey.

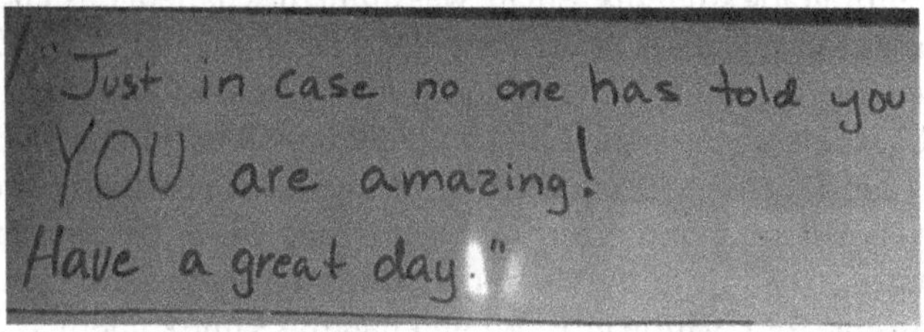

3. **Do more than posters on a wall:** Posters of diverse role models in STEM have been touted as a way to model diversity and inclusion in STEM. While I absolutely agree, what we need to normalize is the experiences, cultures, and pushback that these same role models have received throughout their careers. Merely showcasing diverse role models on the wall may not encourage meaningful interactions or discussions about the contributions of individuals from different backgrounds. Design interactive activities that encourage students to explore the stories and accomplishments of diverse STEM role models. Share personal narratives of diverse role models, emphasizing the challenges they overcame and the impact of their work. This humanizes the individuals on the posters and helps students relate to them on a deeper level. When I was at UC Berkeley retaking introductory biology, I had Professor Rine. In one class, Rine was discussing Mendelian genetics and shared that Gregor Mendel had discovered genetic recombination using pea plants; however, he had major test anxiety and failed his qualifications. In fact, when he went to present his paper, no one showed up to his room because they were all in Charles Darwin's session on natural selection. Although Mendel looked nothing like me, I connected to his story because I had failed biology. I didn't feel like I belonged in STEM or was smart enough to be there. However, when I found out that the father of genetics experienced this same failure, I thought that perhaps I could stick it out. What if we could replicate these moments for our students that have never had an identity of "smartness" in STEM? Some teachers address their students as scientists. Others purchase lab coats for them. It is the job of the teacher to recreate an identity of smartness in their students.
4. **Create a positive STEM identity:** When students are in school, they hear things like "I am not a math person." However, you rarely hear, "Well, I just can't read." There is such an urgency and alarm when it comes to literacy. However mathematics literacy is not valued as much. There is a mindset that normalizes math inabilities. Moreover, students obtain a fear of judgment or ridicule that may haunt them. When I was in

> second grade, I had a similar experience. After running to get to the front of the line, I gasped, held my heart, and said, "Oh wow! I'm running so fast, my heart is beating!" Then a student next to me, Donald, said, "Your heart is always beating." I replied, "Oh, right!" But I actually did not know that. I learned that the heart beats all the time at that moment from Donald. How did I not know that? I thought the heart started beating only when you exerted some exercise. This is because I felt it beating harder when I exercised harder. All of these interstitial experiences contribute to forming a STEM identity. At that moment, I did not feel smart. Over the course of many decades since then, I have had opportunities to learn and grow. Having positive reinforcement to celebrate the small learning achievements helps boost confidence.

When Mr. Gonzalez, also known as the Lab King, began his 14th year of teaching, he came across a young girl who did not feel like she was smart enough for his class. He started a STEM club on campus and invited her to join. In casual conversations with the students, she expressed she loved rocks. On a whim, Mr. Gonzalez found a fossil kit and gifted it to her. He says that the power of giving a child something goes very far. The student replied with a note saying:

> I want to thank you for all that you have done. Every day I always looked forward to going to your class because I knew I would have a fun time in there. I am going to miss your class and especially your science club. Again, thank you so much for the fossil kit. It's one of the coolest gifts, and maybe even the only gift I've gotten from a teacher.

While it's unrealistic to purchase a gift for every student, when the opportunity comes up and you have something cool to give away, it can have a significant impact.

Cultivate the Culture

Remember that teachers set the climate and culture in the classroom. I had one student, Jose, who was polite, studious, and very well-mannered in the classroom. One day, all of the students came in laughing and Jose had a smirk on his face. Then, the other students said, "MISS! Jose climbed out of the window of Mr. Gordon's class." I was very perplexed. My sweet Jose? He looked at me and said, "Nah, Miss, I would never do that in your class." While I took that moment as a pat on the back for the classroom ecology that I had created, it also validates our power in being able to set the tone and cultivate a class culture. Here are three ways to cultivate a culture that is tailored to your own teaching and learning:

1. ***Have a routine that is unique to your own identity:*** My students knew that every Monday we would spend time reviewing relevant news articles and having a discussion on implications for society. We called it Monday News. You can also incorporate Hip Hop Fridays with the use of Hip Hop Education Techniques.
2. ***Incorporate mindfulness techniques such as breathing, journaling, gardening, and other dynamic activities:*** Introducing dynamic activities breaks the monotony

of traditional classroom settings, making learning more engaging. It also provides students with tools to manage stress, anxiety, and other challenges they might face. Stress and pressure can be common in STEM subjects. Mindfulness activities offer students tools to cope with challenges, creating a positive mindset and resilience in the face of difficult problems.

1. ***Allow for multiple languages, abilities, and perspectives:*** Embracing multiple languages in the classroom acknowledges and celebrates the linguistic diversity of students. Students with disabilities also bring unique perspectives and problem-solving approaches to STEM. Sepehr Vakil discusses:

    > Learning environments that approach equity from this lens create new possibilities for the learning and doing of computer science in ways that not only broaden access to underrepresented groups, but redefine the field itself—thus leading to designs, practices and technologies that are socio-politically aware and rooted in concerns and values of populations that have been historically neglected in STEM disciplines. Inclusion of all of these allows for a diversity of thought and experiences, enriching the overall learning environment. For example, during Black History Month, teachers flock to DEI resources to promote Black role models in STEM. This can be done and practiced all year to actively include multiple perspectives.

Once we reflect on the audit, set the conditions for belonging, and cultivate our classroom culture, we must accept the reality of our schools and classrooms: Certain groups of students do not have equal access to STEM courses and rigor. Special education classes are sequestered in a different classroom and building. General education teachers do not have adequate time to collaborate with the special education teachers. Emergent multilingual learners or English learners are tracked together and are removed from core content class time in order to practice their English proficiency. Students in alternative education are furthermore removed from access to STEM. In the next few sections, we will dig deeper into the systemic issues that exacerbate these student inequities.

It's Never Too Early for STEM!

With so much emphasis on reading and mathematics, science and STEM instruction is oftentimes relegated to later grades. Young children are naturally curious and eager to explore the world around them. Science and STEM learning provide opportunities for students to satisfy this curiosity and wonder. Yi Chin Lan, teacher educator and researcher of early childhood science education discusses family and educational strategies that support children's science learning. The themes are as follows:

1. **Embrace curiosity and inquiry:** As you have read in these subsequent chapters, asking questions and embracing the natural curiosity of our students is an easy leverage point for designing science and STEM instruction. Encourage our youngest

learners to ask questions and explore their surroundings. By valuing and nurturing children's natural curiosity, educators can spark a sense of wonder and inquiry that drives scientific learning. You can create a wonder wall, or a designated space in the classroom where students can post questions or observations they have about the world around them. For the young learners, you can document their thoughts and add to the wall throughout the week. During class discussions, select a few questions to explore further, sparking curiosity and inquiry among students.

2. **Promote hands-on exploration:** Provide opportunities for students to engage in hands-on experimentation and discovery. By allowing children to explore materials, make observations, and test hypotheses, educators can create an environment that encourages deeper understanding of scientific concepts and principles. Embracing the messiness of exploration and learning from mistakes helps students develop critical thinking skills and resilience in problem-solving. For example, you can set up STEM stations and rotate the stations around the classroom with different hands-on activities related to STEM concepts. For example, one station could involve experimenting with magnets, while another could focus on making slime. Provide students with exploration guides or worksheets to record their observations and findings at each station. Recording can be as simple as a yes-or-no checklist or a list of observations.
3. **Keep the simple conversations going:** Encouraging academic discourse among your young learners may require a more simplified approach tailored to their developmental level. Instead of relying solely on verbal explanations, incorporate visual aids such as pictures or simple diagrams to support preschoolers' understanding. For example, you can implement emoji reflections after completing a STEM activity or experiment by distribute emoji cards to students, each representing a different emotion (e.g., happy, sad, confused). Ask students to select the emoji that best represents how they feel about the activity or their understanding of the concept. Use these reflections as a springboard for class discussions, allowing students to share their thoughts and perspectives with their peers. This approach not only strengthens students' communication skills but also deepens their understanding of STEM concepts and promotes a culture of collaborative learning.

A researcher studying advanced materials and solar technology hosted a demonstration for preschoolers by showing the solar-powered cells motorizing a fan. When the solar panels were covered, the fan stopped. He said that this mimicked a cloud covering the sun. Each of the students were able to pretend to be a cloud by covering the solar panels. This is how we start the pathways to STEM. Disparities in STEM learning and attainment often mirror broader educational inequities, with marginalized students disproportionately affected by lower academic performance and limited access to advanced coursework and opportunities further down the line in their education journeys. Early exposure to science and STEM learning helps close these opportunity gaps by providing all students with the foundational and memorable experiences necessary for exposure and access to STEM fields.

Special Education: Co-Plan, Co-Teach, Co-Assess, Co-Conspire

Many times when general classroom teachers have students with special needs, they may be partnered with a special education teacher and when this occurs, there is language such as "your kids and my kids." Establishing a co-teaching plan means completely dismantling this mindset. Both teachers need to connect with every single student in the classroom and it is important for both the teachers to build relationships with the students as a united front. I do not know who needs to hear this but the other adult in the classroom is not your aide, they are your partner. Following are strategies to bridge the gap between general education and special education.

Collaboration: Set up a time to meet with your special education teaching partner. Better yet, bring the special education teacher into the lesson study cycle. This allows for preplanning with a common goal and having time for collaboration to co-plan and co-teach. Establish role assignments and have a clear discussion on who will be doing what during the lesson. This can also work for classrooms that have classroom aides. Establish a clear understanding of teaching assignments based on expertise. Incorporate when there will be teaching, modifying of instruction, and checking for understanding. Use the 3D5E Learning Sequence planner to assist with these role assignments. Special educator and consultant Debbie Glazner Sharp writes in her book *I See You, I Hear You: and I Understand*:

Remember, collaboration comes from lots of partnerships & relationships: From Admin to teacher, Teacher to teacher, Teacher to student, Teacher to parent, Parent to student, and Student to student. It's not about curing someone or fixing them. No one is broken. It's about seeing the student for their strengths for who they are. Then we shift the environment, the method of instruction and the expectation of how they show their knowledge. This is special education and requires collaboration.

Assessments: Refer to the chapter on assessments and decide who is designing the assessment. Discuss how you will modify the assessment based on each specific disability and still maintain the rigor. Most importantly, how will you distribute grading? Work collaboratively to provide accommodations and modifications that are sensitive to the needs of students with disabilities from different racial and cultural backgrounds. Recognize that certain accommodations may need to be culturally nuanced for maximum effectiveness. Fair and inclusive assessments contribute to a positive learning experience, promoting the active engagement and participation of SPED students in STEM activities. Researchers Jiwon Hwang and Jonte Taylor wrote a STEM Education Framework for Students with Disabilities (2016) and discuss integrating visual support to facilitate student access to STEM knowledge. They state that when students are allowed to create their own visual representations of science concepts, this allows them to be visually creative and provides teachers an opportunity to determine what students may or may not have learned. Graphic organizers and concept maps have shown to be successful visual tool for students with disabilities.

Administration and Systems: Work with your administration to have a master schedule that provides collaboration time, common preps and the opportunity to combine classes. Administrators should work to provide time, resources, and substitute teachers if necessary. Ensure representation of diverse voices, including those of educators working in STEM and SPED, in decision-making processes at the administrative level. Teachers may lack the professional development to effectively address the diverse needs of SPED students in STEM education and that is why both general ed and special ed teachers should learn together (Florian, L., Black-Hawkins, K., & Rouse, M., 2010). For example, the principal from Valentino High School took proactive steps to encourage collaboration and professional development (PD) between special education teachers and science teachers, aligning their instruction with the Next Generation Science Standards (NGSS).

Family Communication: In Part 1 you established systems for family engagement. This takes it a step further by ensuring the attendance of the general education teachers in the Individualized Education Program (IEP) and 504 meetings. Take the time to understand the family background to obtain a larger context. Science teachers are rarely represented at these meetings, and the IEP documents do not include accommodations and modifications specific to science and STEM. Advocate for anti-bias practices in IEP documentation. Ensure that accommodations and modifications specific to STEM are considered and documented.

Negative attitudes and stereotypes about the capabilities of SPED students in STEM fields persist, affecting their opportunities and experiences (Subban, P., & Sharma, U., 2019). Historically, SPED students have faced exclusion from STEM fields for various reasons, such as limited access to resources, curricular inflexibility, and attitudinal barriers. Addressing historical exclusion requires intentional planning to dismantle barriers and create a supportive environment where SPED students can thrive in STEM (Heron and Williams, 2023). Co-teaching allows for the differentiation of instruction based on individual student needs, providing SPED students with tailored support and accommodations. This is crucial in addressing the diverse learning styles and abilities of SPED students, ensuring they can access STEM content at a level that suits their needs. As STEM teachers, we have a responsibility to read every new student's IEP or 504 plan. Note their present levels of performance, their goals, their accommodations, modifications, methodology and performance criteria.

Emergent Multilingual Learner (EML) Instruction and Newcomers

When I taught middle school mathematics, the English language learners (ELL), as they were labeled, were grouped into one track and took the same courses. I had one student that was a newcomer from Mexico. He did not speak any English; however, he displayed advanced proficiency in the mathematics content. Grouping all English learners together can inadvertently contribute to stigmatization and labeling. Students may feel stereotyped or singled out based on their language proficiency, potentially leading to feelings of inadequacy or exclusion. Though my student displayed advanced proficiency in the content, he was labeled as an ELL and was not moved into the advanced mathematics course.

Okhee Lee emphasizes the importance of integrating language development and science learning; they should not be separated. She advocates for instructional approaches that recognize and leverage the linguistic diversity of students, including emergent multilingual learners. In her guest talk to the STEM4Real "Unspeaker Series" where teachers have the opportunity to collaborate on and design instruction, Lee discusses changing the term from ELL to Emergent multilingual learner (EML). It reframes how we look at language as an asset versus deficit. Lee supports interactive and collaborative learning strategies that allow emergent multilingual learners to engage with scientific ideas through discussion, collaboration, and hands-on activities. This can be seen in the unit she developed on trash, where the anchoring phenomenon was that the school, home, and neighborhood make large amounts of garbage every day. As we discussed, the phenomenon should be grounded in the local context of EMLs' homes and community, which capitalizes on everyday language and experience. In answering the driving question of the unit "What happens to our garbage?" students investigate a series of subquestions (e.g., "What is that smell?" and "What causes changes in the properties of garbage materials?") As students engage in science, they use language in the context of the inquiry. In Project SAIL (Science and Integrated Learning), she refers to the intersection of equity and science. For equity, the primary objectives are to create relevance, utilize funds of knowledge, provide context for language and promote inclusion of all students. When addressing science, the objectives are to integrate science disciplines, link engineering to the local context, and reflect current concerns using science.

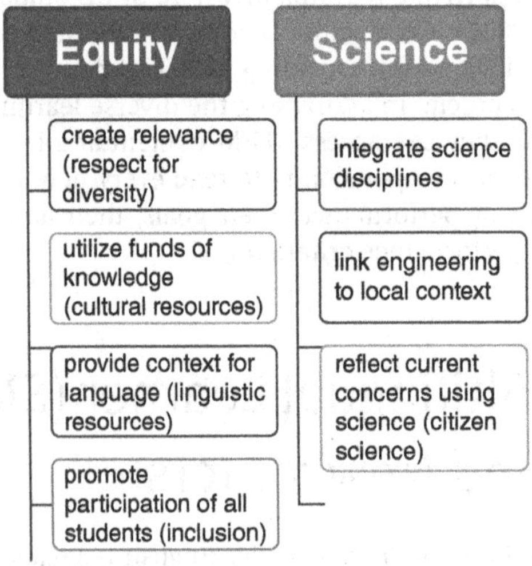

Okhee Lee, Science and Integrated Language (SAIL, 2017)

In Project SAIL, the intersection of equity and science is not only recognized but actively nurtured, with a focus on ensuring that scientific inquiry reflects the lived experiences and diverse perspectives of all students, thereby promoting a more inclusive and accessible learning environment. The culturally responsive phenomenon that is in a local context integrates equity through place-based learning and project-based learning. The use of these practices allow for EMLs to do analytical science tasks, receptive language functions, and productive language functions.

Analytical Science Task	Receptive Language Function	Productive Language Function
Construct an argument	Comprehend arguments made by others orally or in writing	Communicate (orally or in writing) ideas, concepts, and information related to the arguments

(Adapted from Lee,O, Quinn, H, & Valdes, G., 2013)

These EML-specific strategies will help create a welcoming atmosphere for your students:

Welcoming Classroom Culture: Create a welcoming and inclusive classroom culture that celebrates diversity. From diverse posters to multiple languages represented, establish for a place where the students feel comfortable, excited, and safe. Joyful Disruption is an education consulting company that creates inclusive classroom ecologies. The trash unit, when designed with cultural relevance in mind, ensures that language learners see their own experiences in the curriculum. Invite questions and have a place where students can feel comfortable knowing that they can participate in iterative cycles to learn, relearn, and revisit and reflect.

Get Messy! Hands-on inquiry activities provide EMLs with concrete experiences that can help them understand scientific concepts even when faced with language barriers. Engaging in activities allows students to use language in context, enhancing their vocabulary and communication skills. Integrating language learning with science instruction helps language learners see the interconnectedness of language and content. It supports the development of academic language skills, allowing students to articulate scientific ideas and explanations.

Provide Visual Aids and Sentence Starters for Academic Language Support: Offer sentence starters and academic language support to help newcomers express their thoughts and ideas in a scientific context. This assists in developing their language skills while engaging with scientific content. Visuals provide additional support for comprehension, especially when linguistic input may be challenging. Leverage science notebooking and modeling from the assessment chapter to incorporate additional visual assessments. When one teacher opened her lesson, she posted the following questions: "Which food is more nutritious? What is your evidence?" Underneath, she added this: "*¿Qué alimento es más nutritivo? ¿Cuál es tu evidencia?*" One simple question in her students' home language can create an inviting pathway to ignite learning.

Supporting the home language: Encouraging EMLs to speak and develop proficiency in their home language has been recognized as a positive approach in language acquisition. The historical oppression of indigenous languages, such as Navajo and Hawaiian, by English-only policies has had detrimental effects on language preservation. Recent efforts to revitalize these languages, as seen in language immersion programs, contribute to a renewed interest and pride in students' cultural and linguistic heritage. Krashen (1996) argues against English-only instruction, suggesting that bilingual education is more effective in promoting language acquisition and academic success for ELLs. He emphasizes the importance of meaningful content instruction in both the home language and English. The teacher can provide multilingual resources. With the onset of AI, machine learning, and ChatGPT, there are many resources that can be translated into multiple languages. Offer multilingual resources, such as glossaries or translated materials, to help newcomers grasp scientific vocabulary and concepts in their home language.

A Case for Detracking Emergent Multilingual Learners: Tracking all EMLs together, also known as homogeneous grouping, can have several disadvantages. While the intention may be to provide targeted language support, it's crucial to consider the potential drawbacks that can affect the academic and social experiences of EMLs. EMLs often come from diverse cultural backgrounds. Homogeneous grouping may result in reduced cultural diversity within the learning environment, limiting students' exposure to a variety of perspectives and experiences. Homogeneous grouping may inadvertently perpetuate tracking and inequities, as students could be kept in the same group based on their initial English proficiency levels, potentially hindering their access to more challenging coursework. According to the 2017 report from the Education Trust-West titled "Unlocking Learning: Science as a Lever for English Learner Equity," a middle school principal from Calipatria Unified School District "refocused the academic content delivery across all grade levels and eliminated tracking students based on their status as English learners, special education students, or GATE students. The principal instituted a schoolwide daily science period and daily classroom visits to support teachers." In this decision alone, the principal lifted the gates for all learners to obtain access to daily science instruction, regardless of language proficiency levels.

Alternative Populations, Community Schools, and Court Schools

Students in alternative populations may have diverse educational backgrounds, and needs, requiring tailored approaches to engage them in science learning effectively. Alternative schools often face resource constraints, including budget limitations, which may impact the availability of science laboratories, equipment, and materials. Teaching STEM to alternative education students has to go beyond traditional approaches like laborious packets and online courses. It involves creating engaging and relevant experiences that cater to the unique needs and backgrounds of students in alternative settings.

We posed this question at the last state science conference, "Is Science a Right or Privilege for 'Those' Kids?" The resounding answer is that it should be a right. However, we are seeing that access to science is systematically worsened in lower socioeconomic and high needs areas. Dr. Victor Rios does not call these students at-risk students; they are at-promise students, and it is the promise that we should keep paramount.

Netty Spotlight, Principal Douglas Corbin

1. ***Adopted STEM curriculum:*** *Mr. Corbin adopted a science curriculum and incorporated professional development using Lesson Study with his teachers. He did not just rely solely on the curriculum and asked his teachers to prioritize student relationships to transform their lessons to be culturally responsive.*
2. ***Provided culturally responsive professional learning:*** *He ensured that every single staff meeting had professional learning that equipped teachers to teach science in their classrooms and instructional strategies to cultivate an equitable learning environment for every student. For example, this school year, teachers focused on increasing academic discourse and began the school year with a baseline discussion on what this practice meant and how it actually looked. Additionally, he facilitated teacher observations where teachers not only taught the curriculum but also observed each other and analyzed student work from each session.*
3. ***Access for special education teachers and instructional aides:*** *He ensured that the instructional assistants were also receiving professional development so that they could best support the teachers and students in the classroom. Each IA participated in the lesson study cycle.*
4. ***Set the vision:*** *Mr. Corbin set a vision for a focus on STEM at his school. He ensured that his investments and priorities were aligned with a vision for equity and justice in STEM at his school. He also realized that he couldn't passively spend money and hope that the program runs on autopilot. He regularly met with PD providers and community members to ensure that the program was truly servicing his students.*

One of the biggest challenges in the alternative education world is chronic absenteeism. I am no expert on attendance, however I am very sure that students are not going to rush to school to complete a packet. These are the strategies we have seen in place to address students from alternative schools:

1. **Ditch the packets:** Experiential and inquiry-based learning: In one of the units, students created their own fossils using bread, paper clips, pencils, and other solid artifacts. The students sandwiched the solid materials and created imprints in the bread. This simulated creating fossil skeletons. The objective is to move away from rote memorization and passive learning and toward sensemaking to encourage critical argumentation and thinking.
2. **Projects over computer clicks:** Project-Based Learning (PBL): Project-based learning opportunities allow students to connect with career experts in STEM fields and create

real-world projects. There is a factor of mentoring and career advising built into the learning. Students apply scientific concepts to solve authentic problems, making learning more meaningful.

3. **Community over completion:** While credits are vital in completing your high school diploma, having a *why* is imperative. Various online programs keep students in front of the computer with rote memorization. We are instead advocating for community-embedded STEM. As we have discussed, implications for the community and society make the learning relevant. This is why we took the time to conduct an ethnographic study of the surrounding school community. Infuse cultural relevance into science lessons by incorporating examples, contexts, and practices that resonate with the diverse backgrounds of alternative education students.

Putting It All Together: Discourse: Giving Them Something to Talk About

Now that we have systematically removed the barriers that are keeping our most vulnerable populations out of the classroom, we can now create our culture of discourse that not only includes every student but also embraces their entire identity. The first step in building a culture of discourse and academic talk is ensuring that students feel like they are capable and that they belong in STEM. There are various reasons why students, particularly those who do not feel smart in STEM, may be reluctant to participate in class. Some students may lack confidence in their abilities, feeling they are not smart in STEM subjects. This lack of confidence can be reinforced by past academic experiences that have formed their identity. It is our role to encourage a growth mindset by emphasizing that intelligence and success in STEM can be developed over time through effort and learning. Students can overcome misconceptions with every opportunity to talk and make sense of the information. Students may fear judgment or ridicule from peers if they make a mistake or express uncertainty. I still have this fear of judgment. Here are a few ways to mitigate that:

Fostering a growth mindset: This is something that has to be done consistently and daily. When working with my preservice teacher, Ernesto, he expressed his fears rooted in traumatic flashbacks from his chemistry class. He said that his worst memory was his high school chemistry class. "I felt like my teacher never gave me a fair chance. She wouldn't grade my tests the same as others. I would give the same answer as others. I just gave up and didn't pass the class. Visibly saw that I wasn't welcomed, other classmates told me this too. Went for help after school and felt she didn't want to help me. When I retook the class, she told another teacher that she wasn't excited to have me in her class again." This experience stuck with Ernesto throughout high school, college, and now his professional life. Students who have experienced failure or difficulty in STEM subjects in the past may carry negative associations.

Address stereotypes and biases: Students who belong to groups traditionally underrepresented in STEM may experience stereotype threat, fearing they will confirm negative stereotypes about their group's abilities. Teachers can be aware of and challenge stereotypes, promoting diversity and inclusivity in STEM by sharing positive role models and showcasing diverse achievements in STEM. Language or cultural differences may also pose barriers for some students in understanding STEM concepts. Provide additional language support and multilingual resources to ensure all students can communicate, access and understand STEM content. Linking STEM topics to social justice issues can engage students by showcasing the societal impact of STEM knowledge, especially when discussing the impacts on community and cultures.

Build authentic relationships: The foundation of creating a culture of discourse lies in the educator's ability in building relationships with each of their students. Artificial intelligence and online programs are just waiting to take over and replace the teacher. A job posting on LinkedIn from a company called Alpha touted the following: "Teaching is done through technology, not teachers. Why? Because learning apps take advantage of decades worth of learning science, including spaced repetition, forced recall, mastery-based progress, and adaptive algorithms, which speed up and slow down to match the speed of each individual student." This startup can potentially and completely dehumanize education with their special technology. As I have experienced firsthand, teachers can have significant and life-changing relationships with students. My teachers' names are etched in my brain. Mr. Peterson. Mrs. Aguilera. Dr. Hayes. These teachers and so many more have positively impacted my life and shaped the person that I am today. They taught me things that no technology, software, or adaptive algorithm could ever replace. Once the foundations of relationships are established, we can create a culture of discourse that promotes a space where students feel safe enough to embrace mistakes, speak with their entire identities (including their hair and skin color), and have their statements honored and valued.

If your students are anything like my students, I could not get them to talk about the content and I could not get them to stop talking about frivolous topics. I knew I needed to implement a protocol that gave the students something to talk about: Either pose a question to your students or have students generate a question to explore. Then, use the following protocol:

Individual Reflection on Question: Each student takes a few minutes to independently jot down their thoughts on how they would design an experiment to explore the impact of light on plant growth. They consider variables, controls, and potential outcomes in their reflections.

Partner Talk: After individual reflection, students pair up to share their thoughts with a partner. They take turns discussing their experimental design ideas, providing reasoning for their choices, and seeking feedback from each other. The focus is on constructive dialogue and refining their initial ideas. Ensure protected time for each student to share.

Small Group Talk: Students are then organized into small groups of three to four individuals. In these groups, they share their reflections on the experiment's design, listen to their peers' perspectives, and collectively discuss the strengths and weaknesses of each proposed approach. The goal is to collaborate on refining their experimental plans.

Whole Group Discussion (Teacher as Referee): The teacher initiates a whole-group discussion where students, without teacher involvement, present their refined experimental designs to the class. The teacher serves as a referee, ensuring that the discussion remains respectful and focused. Students ask questions, provide feedback, and engage in a collective conversation where they refine their ideas further as a group.

Revise Individual Reflections on Question: Following the whole-group discussion, students return to their initial individual reflections. Now armed with insights gained from partner talk, small group discussions, and the whole-group dialogue, they revise their individual reflections, incorporating new ideas and considerations into their experimental design plans. Each step contributes to refining students' understanding and experimental designs through interaction, sharing of perspectives, iteration, and constructive feedback.

This allows students to have something to talk about when they engage in group discussions. Jumping directly into discussions without any research or preparation time doesn't equip them with the adequate time they need to process the information.

Academic Discourse around Social Justice Issues

There is a misconception that social justice issues may be too complex and political for students. Having a protocol ensures that your conversations stick to the standard and topic.

1. Build a Social Justice Culture: This is an ongoing process that must be built from the beginning. Craft norms for your classroom and use sentence stems to help students make claims based on evidence and facts. Collaboratively create the norms so that the class is building the culture together and you are creating buy-in.
2. Phenomenon: Choose a phenomenon that ignites curiosity and has societal implications using the standard-hook-society (SHS) method. Ensure that all topics will be connected back to your state standards using the SHS method.
3. Questions/Observations: Pose the (unjust) situation to the students and have students come up with questions and observations. Relate discussions to current events or issues relevant to students' lives. This connection helps students see the real-world implications of social justice topics.
4. Do the Science (Explore, Elaborate): Brainstorm activities that allow for students to generate evidence that can ultimately support their arguments. Sources of evidence include observations, experimental results, simulation data, graphs, diagrams, and charts. Incorporate activities that encourage students to see issues from different

perspectives. Empathy-building exercises can help create a more compassionate and understanding atmosphere.

The following table outlines various discourse strategies connected to the Science and Engineering Practices (SEPs) and offers structured protocols and sentence starters for engaging students in academic discourse. These practices, including asking questions, engaging in argument from evidence, constructing explanations, analyzing and interpreting data, and planning and carrying out investigations, serve as essential pillars of STEM inquiry. These practices can also serve as powerful tools for encouraging academic discourse around social justice issues. This table explores how each practice can be leveraged to facilitate discussions on social justice topics within the classroom context.

Discourse Connected to the Science and Engineering Practices (*Do*)

Practice	Discussion Protocol	Sentence Starters
Asking Questions (SEP 1)	Recall that QFT is a structured process where students generate, improve, and prioritize their questions. It encourages curiosity and active engagement in scientific inquiry.	Why did . . .? How does . . . . .? What would happen if . . . .? Who is . . . .? What does ________ mean? First I noticed ____________, then I saw ____________. I observed that ____________ when ____________.
Engaging in Argument from Evidence (SEP 7)	Socratic Seminars involve students in a structured discussion where they collaboratively explore and critically analyze arguments related to a specific scientific question or issue.	One piece of evidence for _____ is . . . . As you can see in our lab . . . . The data shows _____ which I believe means ______. When we carried out the ______ experiment, we saw________. My idea is similar/related to yours, in that ___________. To build upon your idea, ____________. I agree with you that ____________. However, I feel that ____________. I had a different answer: ____________.

Practice	Discussion Protocol	Sentence Starters
Constructing Explanations (SEP 6)	CER is a structured framework where students make a claim, support it with evidence from their investigations, and provide reasoning to explain the connection between the claim and evidence.	My claim is that ____________. My observations support this because ____________. My reasoning is supported by the text because ____________. Will you explain that again/Will you explain that in a different way? So are you saying that ____________? Now I understand . . . . This makes sense now . . . . No, I think it means . . . . I agree with you. This means . . . At first I thought this (________), but now I think (________).
Analyzing and Interpreting Data (SEP 4)	Students analyze and interpret scientific data displayed in a gallery walk format. They engage in discussions about patterns, trends, and potential relationships within the data sets.	This reminds me of . . . I've never experienced . . . I wonder what it feels like . . . I could really picture . . . The description of ____ helped me visualize . . . In my mind I could really see . . . When it said ____, I could imagine . . . If this were a movie . . .
Planning and Carrying Out Investigations (SEP 3)	Students engage in a Think-Pair-Share activity to collaboratively plan and discuss experimental designs. This includes identifying variables, controls, and procedures.	I hypothesize . . . I imagine . . . Based on . . . I infer . . . I observe . . . In my opinion . . . I think . . . I predict that . . . Since this happened (________), then I bet the next thing that is going to happen is . . . Reading this part makes me think that this (________) is about to happen . . . I wonder if . . .

When having discussions on cultural and societal issues, it is vital to start with lessons or activities that build foundational knowledge on the social justice issue. Provide background information, historical context, and perspectives to ensure a shared understanding among students. Discuss how to disagree respectfully. Encourage students to challenge ideas rather than attacking individuals. Teach strategies for expressing disagreement constructively. When I was observing Mr. Davis's class in the Lower East Side of New York City, there were two second-grade students engaging in discourse.

Prompt: What happens when you use rubbing alcohol wipes?

STUDENT 1 The alcohol disappeared because I don't see it anymore.
STUDENT 2 I don't think it disappeared. It's still there even though you can't see it.
STUDENT 1 If it were there then you would be able to see it and you can't see anything.
STUDENT 2 Yes, it evaporated into the air. Just because you can't see the air doesn't mean it doesn't exist.
STUDENT 1 I DON'T LIKE YOU.

This conversation took a wrong turn. Although it was hilarious to witness two second graders having such an authentic and sense-making discussion on evaporation, it was clear that as we continue to teach students how to argue, we must teach how to disagree effectively. Model how to engage in respectful and thoughtful discussions. Demonstrate active listening, empathy, and the use of evidence to support opinions. Emphasize the importance of creating a safe and inclusive space for everyone to express their thoughts. Make it clear that differing opinions are welcome, but disrespectful behavior is not. Collaboratively develop discussion norms with students. These crucial steps allow for collaborative community building when having discussions.

Social justice discussions also encourage students to think critically about systemic issues, fostering an awareness of the root causes of inequities. Based on Ibram Kendi's children's book *Antiracist Baby*, we crafted these sentence frames to support classroom discussions:

Anti-Racist Discussion Frames

- "When I opened my eyes to all skin colors, I noticed that ______ people were more/less affected by______________ compared with _______ people because ______."
- "When I hear people talk about race I feel_______________."
- "When the government blames______________ on the people, I say_______________."
- "Blaming ______________ exposes evidence like__________________."
- "_________ should be celebrated because _____________."
- "This person or event helped others grow by__________."
- "I thought that this person would ___________ but they____________."
- "I talk about race because__________."
- "Today I did ______________ to help other people that are different than me.

By exploring different perspectives and understanding the impact of social injustices, students develop empathy, a key component of anti-racist teaching. The journey toward a thriving STEM classroom culture prioritizes values rooted in antiracism. Moving beyond rote memorization and impersonal packets, the emphasis is on cultivating a sense-making environment, nurturing curiosity, and embracing empathy. This recognizes the intelligence and potential for growth in every student, irrespective of abilities, ethnicities, or languages. It hinges on creating an inclusive atmosphere that not only accommodates mistakes but actively encourages them as opportunities for learning and growth. Imagine being a newcomer to the United States and saying the wrong word with a foreign accent. In the anti-racist classroom, this student would shrug off the word, collaborate with his partner, and try again without any ridicule or shame. The foundation is the establishment of meaningful relationships that instill a profound sense of belonging, where students feel smart in STEM and are empowered to express their identities authentically. Tina Cheuk, Assistant Professor from California Polytechnic University at San Luis Obispo, discusses the "messy middle" of partnerships in science education and poses the following questions: "How do we empower learners and shake up the status quo power structure? In what ways can I amplify student voices and their ideas, especially communities who have been historically excluded from the science knowledge-building enterprise? How can I take these diverse perspectives and connect the dots?" Such a classroom ethos celebrates diversity, embraces joy, and actively contributes to dismantling systemic barriers, paving the way for a future where all learners, regardless of background, can engage with STEM disciplines in a way that is both personally fulfilling and socially impactful.

#4Real Discussion Prompts

Reflecting on Teaching Practices

How are you operating as a teacher? Do you see your role solely as delivering content, or do you consider yourself a supporter of students' overall growth and development? Share instances where you have gone beyond content delivery to support your students' unique needs and identities.

Special Education

Share your experiences or insights on the shift from a "your kids and my kids" mindset to a collaborative co-teaching approach in inclusive classrooms. How can establishing a united front between general education teachers and special education teachers benefit both educators and students? Discuss specific strategies for building strong relationships and collaboration within co-teaching environments.

Detracking Emergent Multilingual Learners

Consider the advantages and disadvantages of tracking or grouping Emergent Multilingual Learners together. What potential drawbacks might homogeneous grouping have on the academic and social experiences of EMLs? Discuss alternative approaches that ensure language support while maintaining cultural diversity within the learning environment. How can educators address potential inequities associated with tracking?

Principal Corbin's Story

Reflect on the provided case study of Principal Douglas Corbin's initiatives in an alternative education setting to promote STEM learning. Discuss the importance of adopting a STEM curriculum, providing culturally responsive professional learning, and ensuring access for special education teachers and instructional aides. Share your insights on how such initiatives align with the goal of making science education a right for all students, especially those in alternative populations. Consider how community-embedded STEM and experiential learning can address challenges like chronic absenteeism and create a sense of community.

CHAPTER 11

The Culture of STEM: Indigenous and Ancestral Knowledge

You don't really believe in that, do you?

—A teacher in New Zealand

One of our teachers shared a vulnerable story. While she was teaching in New Zealand, part of the teaching requirements was to teach Indigenous knowledge as well. The teacher took the time to weave in the stories of Māori people as they pertained to her science course. While teaching on the geology of the islands, there was an indigenous story about the creation of the islands. One of the god's canoes had sunk and each end of the canoe was sticking above the water, which ended up being the North and South islands of New Zealand. After presenting the story of how the islands were created, she then proceeded to tell the scientific story. When one of her Māori students was discussing the story, the teacher asked, "You don't believe that, do you?" And the student's face fell. The teacher felt awful and still reflects on this moment even though it happened 20 years ago. The question this brings up is how we as educators honor the history, stories, and legends of Indigenous cultures, especially when they can be very opposed to Western explanations.

It is crucial for educators to approach the integration of Indigenous knowledge with sensitivity, respect, and cultural understanding, but how do we grapple with the conflicting theories posed by multiple different worldviews? Future technology produced from the cycle of questioning and investigating may show that continental drift was wrong and a canoe-shaped asteroid impact actually formed Aotearoa, the Māori name for New Zealand. The reality is, who knows? Right now it might feel like an unrealistic and silly thought, but to think like a scientist you have to be open to the fact that sometimes "silly" thoughts are actually the best explanation and may have the most supporting evidence.

Honoring Indigenous Cultures

Aboriginal Elders are the wisdom-keepers of Indigenous science, also known as traditional knowledge, while PhD-trained scientists are the gatekeepers of Western science, or STEM, in North America. However, both may be key to the attraction and retention of the next generation of scientists in STEM (Alkholy, Gendron, McKenna, Dahms, Ferreira, 2017). This study suggests "there is value in exposing post-secondary STEM students to Indigenous science through culturally competent course design and content delivered by Indigenous science educators alongside STEM-trained PhDs."

Netty Spotlight: Hālau Kū Māna Public Charter School

Hālau Kū Māna provides a culturally enriched learning environment through grounding in the ancestral knowledge and practices of Hawai'i.

One of our netties, Kumu (Teacher) Lehua, had one-on-one coaching sessions with our lead instructional facilitator, Dr. Sheri Fitzgerald. They worked on a 10th grade biology conceptual flow map that included topics on genetics and heredity, with layering of Hawaiian cultural values, mo'olelo, and connected to the three dimensions of NGSS using the do-know-think frame. *Mo'olelo* is a Hawaiian term that traditionally refers to stories, myths, legends, history, and narratives. The word itself can be broken down into *mo'o*, which means succession, and *olelo*, which means word or language. Therefore, *mo'olelo* can be understood as a succession of words, representing the transmission of knowledge, culture, and tradition through storytelling. The final topic of human impacts and innovations related to genetics will include GMO impacts on the local food system, sustainable and organic agriculture, and human health. In addition, the class would discuss the topic of banning genetic modification of sacred crops like kalo (taro), which would undermine the genetic integrity of the Hawaiian varieties. These topics would be discussed with haumāna or the students. With the need to support haumāna with bridging Indigenous knowledge and culture with Western knowledge, Sheri connected Lehua with Eric Tong, a teacher and coordinator at 'Iolani School in the 'Āina-Informatics program. Eric conducted a lab activity about GMOs using papaya and led discussions about bioethics, food security, and food sustainability. This aligns with the NGSS PE: MS-LS3-1: "Develop and use a model to describe why structural changes to genes (mutations) located on chromosomes may affect proteins and may result in harmful, beneficial, or neutral effects to the structure and function of the organism." *Do*: Analyzing and Interpreting Data: Students will analyze data from the papaya GMO lab activity conducted by Eric Tong to understand the impact of genetic modification on the local food system, food security, and food sustainability. *Know*: LS3: Heredity: Inheritance and Variation of Traits (DCI): Students will explore how genetic traits are passed down through generations and how variations in genes contribute to biodiversity, connecting this understanding to mo'olelo (stories) and cultural values of Hawai'i. *Think*: Systems and System Models (CCC): Students will examine the interconnectedness of the local food system, sustainable agriculture practices, and human health, considering how genetic modifications can influence these systems.

We can honor Indigenous cultures by promoting Indigenous science even in a primarily Western science class using the following ways:

Acknowledge the violent and traumatic history: "You are teaching on stolen land." Director of Educational Studies at Claremont Graduate University, Dr. Samara Suafoa opened her keynote address with this statement to the teachers of the STEM4Real Summer Institute in Hawai'i. She did not lie, and it was a hard reality for our teachers to accept. As a researcher from University of Washington, Anastasia Sanchez, states:

> Before setting a pathway ahead of us for engaging in dreaming and designing for liberatory pathways toward science education transformation, we must first face the nightmares that colonial schooling has brought to life. This requires remembering forward to be critically cognizant of the white supremacy of colonial schooling that has been designed to continuously erase and silence Black, Brown, and Indigenous livingness, rightful knowledges, and ways of knowing—to speculate, dream, and design forward, toward a just otherwise.

In the next chapter, we will discuss the politicization of education, book bans, and the limiting of knowledge. However, the first step in reconciling the gaps in Indigenous STEM is to address the elephant in the room—the violent and traumatic history of Indigenous peoples. This is a world issue that impacts so much of the world from Australia and New Zealand to the United States and Canada. Establish safe spaces for students to share their feelings and reflections on the historical trauma experienced by their communities. This could be facilitated through group discussions, writing exercises, or art projects. In looking at the state of Hawai'i, for example:

Throughout the turbulent nineteenth century, Hawaiian language schools and newspapers supported the transmission of cultural knowledge. But Hawaiian voices were nearly silenced after economic and political change culminated in the 1893 overthrow of the Hawaiian kingdom and Hawaiian as a language of instruction was prohibited from 1896 to 1978, a span of four generations (Chinn, 2007). For histories like this, it is important to develop empathy and understanding, creating an environment where students support one another in processing historical trauma and building resilience. Mary Ann Ng, a veteran high school biology, anatomy, environmental science, and computer science teacher, leverages the following resources for her lesson planning:

- *The Great Thirst: California and Water: A History* by Norris Hundley, Jr.
- *The Owens Valley Paiute: A Cultural History* by Gary R. Varner
- *An American Genocide: The United States and the California Indian Catastrophe* by Benjamin Madley
- *We Are the Land: A History of Native California* by Damon B. Akins and William H. Bauer, Jr.

You can also invite Indigenous guest speakers or elders to share their perspectives directly with students. Hearing directly from those who hold these cultural beliefs can deepen understanding and foster respect. Encourage students to research and present on Indigenous knowledge within the context of their subjects. This promotes inclusivity and allows students to take ownership of their learning. As Isabel Wilkerson, author of *Caste: The Origins of Our Discontents* states:

> Many people may rightly say, "I had nothing to do with how this all started. I have nothing to do with the sins of the past. My ancestors never attacked Indigenous people, never owned slaves." And, yes. Not one of us was here when this house was built. Our immediate ancestors may have had nothing to do with it, but here we are, the current occupants of a property with stress cracks and bowed walls and fissures built into the foundation. We are the heirs to whatever is right or wrong with it. We did not erect the uneven pillars or joists, but they are ours to deal with now.

We may have not been present; but we owe it to ourselves and our students to rectify the broken pavement in the pathway to STEM.

Immerse in the Culture

Collaborate with local Native communities to identify STEM initiatives that address community challenges or opportunities. This fosters a sense of relevance and applicability. Learn about historical STEM practices such as traditional agricultural methods, engineering techniques, or medicinal knowledge. Incorporate these practices into STEM lessons to showcase the historical contributions of Native communities. Learn about historical STEM practices such as traditional agricultural methods, engineering techniques, or medicinal knowledge. Incorporate these practices into STEM lessons to showcase the historical contributions of Native communities. Respectfully approach community leaders to seek advice on incorporating Indigenous perspectives into STEM education. Elders can provide valuable insights and ensure cultural authenticity. Pauline Chinn, a researcher in the department of curriculum studies at the University of Hawai'i, Manoa, discussed decolonizing methodologies and Indigenous knowledge. She states, "If mainstream school science is viewed as immersion in the culture of Western science, perhaps immersing mainstream teachers in Indigenous or sustainability-oriented cultures and communities holds the potential to help them teach a more complex, systems-oriented science that supports environmental literacy and recognizes the role of culture in learning" (Chinn, 2006).

Middle school science teacher Pia Cummins-VanHerreweghe, who is from the Big Island of Hawai'i, teaches her lessons as follows: I do incorporate phenomena that kids can observe here on the Big Island: acid rain from volcanic emissions that make the water in the catchments acidic and can damage lead plumbing here in South Kona. This is why we add baking soda to our catchment tanks to prevent damage from happening. When I use these types of activities or inquiries for chemistry, students are more interested and more vested in their learning because they are familiar with the phenomenon. The most exciting part is when we start Earth Science. Although we might not be part of a plate boundary, we do have a lot of volcanic activity and earthquakes, and students are so much more engaged when I use local events and local phenomena as the tool for them to access learning. I also add Hawaiian Mythology to my lessons, as it helps students understand why we have certain cultural protocols when Kilauea erupts or when we enter different districts or sites.

Redefine the Native Narrative

Emphasize the historical achievements of Indigenous communities in STEM fields. Integrate examples of Native advancements in science, technology, engineering, and mathematics into the curriculum. Showcase the brilliance of Indigenous ancestors as researchers, scientists, architects, and more. Illustrate how traditional practices, such as ethnobotany, agriculture, and astronomy, align with modern STEM disciplines. Showcase the relevance and sophistication of Indigenous knowledge systems. This is in the passage of the AISES (Advancing Indigenous People in STEM) College and Career Guide:

> *Your Indigenous ancestors were brilliant researchers, scientists, chemists, farmers, architects, and doctors long before our current professionals in these fields. You may not have been taught that they practiced ethnobotany through using plants for medicinal or artistic use or that Biology was present in the agronomy and agricultural techniques of Native people, most notably in the practice of planting corn, beans and squash next to each other. Technology can be found in how Native people used natural waterways to design and utilize irrigation canals for their farms many years ago. Engineering can be found (then and now) in the architecture of homes and ceremonial structures – the portable teepee or traditional Navajo hogan. Math can be found in the traditional counting systems of Indigenous people through pictures or knots on a counting rope. Anatomy and physiology were (and still are) taught in the butchering of a deer, sheep, or buffalo. Astronomy and cosmology are also crucial to how Native people tell the changing of the seasons and forecast weather and are also used by Native Hawaiians to navigate across the oceans."*
>
> *(Bitsoi and Lowe, 2018)*

Highlight the achievements of Indigenous scientists, engineers, and STEM professionals. Showcase role models to inspire the next generation of Indigenous students to pursue careers in STEM fields. When we brought this up as a teaching tool, one teacher, a white woman, stated, "Isn't that prejudice?" Highlighting the achievements of Indigenous scientists, engineers, and STEM professionals and showcasing them as role models is not prejudice; rather, it is a proactive and positive step toward fostering inclusivity and representation in STEM. It is important to distinguish between efforts to highlight the accomplishments of underrepresented groups, such as Indigenous communities, and prejudiced attitudes or actions. The goal is not to elevate one group over another but to create a level playing field where everyone has the opportunity to pursue and succeed in STEM. I have to warn that while we are having this discussion, pushback and protest may occur as many deep-seeded attitudes are rooted in fear and bias.

Explore the Similarities and Differences

Explore the similarities and differences between Indigenous stories and scientific explanations. Highlight the ways in which different cultures approach and understand natural phenomena. Indigenous stories are not just explanations of natural phenomena but are also important cultural heritage. They contribute to the identity and worldview of Indigenous communities. Encourage critical thinking by discussing the cultural and historical contexts of both Indigenous stories and scientific theories. Help students understand that different knowledge systems emerge from unique cultural contexts. Share Indigenous stories that explain natural events or phenomena. Use multimedia, guest speakers, or traditional storytellers to enhance engagement. Highlight the narrative elements, symbolism, and cultural values embedded in the stories.

Dr. Manulani Aluli Meyer serves as the director of Indigenous Education at the University of Hawai'i – West Oahu and describes herself as "the fifth daughter of Emma Aluli and Harry Meyer who grew up on the sands of Mokapu and Kailua beach on the island of O'ahu and along the rainy shoreline of Hilo Palikū." In my efforts to properly cite her full title, I saw that her biography begins with her ancestral lineage. She states:

> Existing in relationship triggers everything: with people, with ideas, with the natural world. It was a cornerstone inspiration to the people I listened to. It marked a consciousness of the dialectic, a reckoning with what one brought to other. Relationship gave mentors opportunities to practice generosity with others, harmony with land, and ways to develop their own pathway to an idea.

This perspective underscores the interconnectedness of all things and serves as a foundation for Indigenous ways of knowing. In line with this ethos, educators can implement the following "Storytelling and Wayfinding Protocol" to integrate Indigenous knowledge systems with STEM education. This protocol encourages students to analyze Indigenous stories alongside scientific explanations, encouraging an appreciation for diverse perspectives and knowledge systems.

Storytelling and Wayfinding Protocol

Compare: Encourage students to analyze and compare Indigenous stories with scientific explanations. Guide students in identifying similarities and differences in how different cultures approach and understand natural phenomena. Discuss the cultural context, symbolism, and scientific principles embedded in both narratives. Reinforce the idea that both knowledge systems contribute unique insights.

Question: Encourage students to ask questions and engage in discussions about the similarities and differences. Emphasize the importance of respecting diverse perspectives and recognizing the validity of different ways of knowing.

Discuss: Discuss how Indigenous stories contribute to cultural heritage, passing down knowledge, values, and identity. Explore the role of storytelling in preserving cultural wisdom and fostering a sense of belonging.

Invite Community: Create connections with the local Indigenous community. Invite community members, elders, or cultural experts to share their perspectives and insights. Facilitate a respectful exchange of knowledge and experiences.

There is a movement to bridge the gap between Indigenous cultures and STEM; however, this terminology insinuates that indigenous culture and STEM knowledge is disjointed. Rather than viewing Indigenous cultures and STEM knowledge as separate entities needing reconciliation, it's crucial to recognize that STEM is inherently embedded within Indigenous cultures. Communities attempt to shore up insecurities and validate what their ancestors accomplished by adding math and science to it. Had the culture not abruptly collapsed from disease, war, and politics, it would have adapted math and science to make more efficient fishponds, wetlands or lo'i, transportation, and electricity. As written by associate professor of music at the University of Hawai'i Maui College Joseph Keola Donaghy describes that, the Hawaiian monarchy is described as prioritizing making Hawai'i one of the most advanced countries on earth per capita and succeeded at that as shown by the nearly 100 percent literacy rate in the late 1800s (in Hawaiian). They were particularly fond of the sciences, which is why the Iolani Palace had electric lighting before the White House.

Storytelling and wayfinding serve as powerful tools for educators seeking to create engaging and culturally inclusive learning experiences. Storytelling transcends mere narration; it is a vehicle through which cultures pass down knowledge, values, and traditions. Wayfinding, often rooted in Indigenous navigation techniques, offers a unique approach to spatial understanding and problem-solving. Educators can use wayfinding concepts to teach skills such as critical thinking, resilience, and adaptability. By inviting community members to share their insights and experiences, educators can create culturally inclusive learning environments that honor Indigenous wisdom and heritage. Additionally, storytelling and wayfinding serve as powerful tools for teaching critical thinking, resilience, and adaptability, empowering students to navigate complex challenges with confidence and creativity.

Netty Spotlight: Meet Pua Pali

"During the STEM4Real Institute, the facilitators shared the importance of social justice and incorporating culture into lessons and I agree 100%. I have always incorporated the Hawaiian culture into my lessons. As a native Hawaiian educator who teaches in Hawai'i, it has always been important for me to share mo'olelo and both modern and ancient cultural practices with my students. For example, when covering, NGSS standard for understanding the Big Bang Theory, I share with them the Kumulipo, an ancient Hawaiian genealogical chant that begins in darkness and then eventually describes the evolutionary process from the first coral polyp to the birth of the first human."

This teacher created a unit dedicated to this. In her unit summary, she planned for students to explore what happens during a bad hair day: Why does hair get "big" during rainy or humid weather? The learning outcome of the lesson is that students will be able to describe patterns in the periodic table to explain the phenomenon. In addition, students will engage in Hawaiian culture and review why weather is an important part of stories in Hawai'i. Students will also look at alternative ways of electricity as a means to see that not all people on Hawai'i have access to

(continued)

(*continued*)

electricity. They will experiment to see what else can power an object, like a light bulb or charging their cell phones. She included a representative from the University of Hawai'i and Bishop Museum to help explain how Hawaiians have used some form of electricity and retell the significance of Pauahi in Hawaiian culture.

By incorporating culture into lessons, many students find personal connections and develop a sense of pride in what they are learning. They are also highly encouraged to go home and talk with family members to learn more about their own family history and cultural background and some come back to class excited to share their families' stories with their peers. She connected her lessons to the Indigenous practice of storytelling, bringing in the story of Pauhi's name chant to show the role of electricity. For NGSS HS-PS-1 and HS-ETS-1.2, she incorporated youth action as an assessment by asking her students to advocate for alternative energy sources to get electricity in remote areas of Hawai'i with low socioeconomic communities. Pua strives to combine her love of Science and Hawai'i in her classes. She has made her students aware of the importance of environmental and cultural stewardship and incorporates core values such as: mālama 'āina, mālama kai, mālama wai, and mālama 'ohana to drive passion and love for Mother Earth.

The Nā Hopena A'o (HA) Framework

The Nā Hopena A'o (HA) framework was developed by the Hawai'i State Department of Education and provides a valuable guide for educators to integrate culturally responsive and place-based instruction in their teaching practices. This framework is designed to emphasize the interconnectedness of academic success and the well-being of students. The five general learner outcomes outlined in the HA framework are:

1. Sense of Belonging: Students develop a strong foundation of relationships, understanding their lineage, place, and connection to past, present, and future. Engage students in exploring their local community, emphasizing its historical and cultural significance. Connect academic content to the stories and traditions of the community.
2. Sense of Responsibility: Students actively carry responsibility for themselves, family, community, and the larger society, demonstrating commitment and concern for others. Connect this to service-learning projects that address community needs. This allows students to actively contribute to the well-being of their community, fostering a sense of responsibility for others.
3. Sense of Excellence: Students believe in their ability to succeed in school and life, pursuing skills, knowledge, and behaviors to reach their potential. Design project-based learning experiences that allow students to pursue their interests and showcase their skills.
4. Sense of Aloha: Students exhibit care and respect for themselves, families, and communities, fostering empathy, appreciation, and a symbiotic relationship with others. Integrate activities that promote cultural appreciation and understanding. This can include art projects, language lessons, or events that celebrate the diversity within the community.

5. Sense of Total Well-Being: Students learn about and practice a healthy lifestyle, making choices that improve the mind, body, heart, and spirit while contributing to the well-being of family, ʻāina (land), community, and the world. Leverage the local environment for outdoor learning experiences. Connect lessons on ecology, sustainability, and environmental science to the well-being of the land and community.

Even though this framework was created at the state level, systems at the regional and local levels must encourage the implementation of this framework. Therefore, we must explore other avenues of legislation and initiatives that can encompass these same principles. As the international movement for climate education literacy and environmental justice continues to grow, we can see this as an opportunity to incorporate place-based instruction through the lens of Indigenous STEM.

Is the Environment Racist? Environmental Justice

The lack of diversity in the field of environmental science is a critical issue that hampers inclusivity and representation. Students, especially those from underrepresented backgrounds, benefit from seeing scientists who look like them. Diverse representation helps in forming a sense of identity and belonging in STEM. Highlighting the work of scientists of color like Dr. Tyrone Hayes and Dr. Ayana Johnson challenges stereotypes and demonstrates that environmental scientists come from a variety of racial and ethnic backgrounds. Sharing the stories of scientists who have made significant contributions, like Dr. Hayes' groundbreaking atrazine research, provides students with role models who are redefining what it means to look like a scientist. I wrote my children's book, *There's Something in the Water*, to begin a revolution to diversify the curriculum and engage the community in environmental issues. This creates awareness for the community issues that take place, especially when environmental issues adversely affect populations of color.

The impact of human activities on the environment goes beyond individual behaviors or blatant sources of pollution. In fact, pause for a moment, step outside, and draw in a deep breath. Are you inhaling a refreshing breeze, or is it in reality a lungful of fresh pollution? Our human impact extends to government regulations, urban planning, and legislative decisions that intricately shape our daily lives. Regrettably, the tendrils of systemic racism persist in these very measures. Take, for instance, the diesel truck routes in West Oakland, California, where around 21,000 residents, predominantly Black and from lower-income households, reside. This scenario prompts critical questions for our students such as who determined these routes and whether air quality was a consideration in their city and housing planning. Did decision-makers take into account the well-being of Oakland residents when routing these trucks through their neighborhood? Was there diversity represented in the decision-making process? Encouraging students to explore the complexities of such environmental issues is crucial for them to grasp the underlying causes of environmental racism. It is our responsibility to teach environmental principles and spark dialogues among students that explicitly address environmental racism and justice.

As described in *Braiding Sweetgrass*, author Robin Kimmerer proclaims that "We need acts of restoration, not only for polluted waters and degraded lands, but also for our relationship to the world. We need to restore honor to the way we live, so that when we walk through the world we don't have to avert our eyes with shame, so that we can hold our heads up high and receive the respectful acknowledgment of the rest of the earth's beings." We can look at the California Environmental Principles and Concepts as a guide for teaching environmental injustice and leveraging Indigenous knowledge in STEM:

- Principle 1—People Depend on Natural Systems: Displacement of Indigenous Communities:
  - Large-scale development projects, such as dam construction or mining operations, often lead to the displacement of Indigenous communities from their ancestral lands. This disrupts their connection to natural systems, impacting their traditional ways of life. Educators can explore traditional ecological knowledge within these displaced communities, showcasing how Indigenous STEM practices are intimately connected to the local ecosystem. Students can learn about sustainable practices that were disrupted by such environmental injustices.
- Principle 2—People Influence Natural Systems: Pollution in Marginalized Communities:
  - Industries with hazardous waste or pollutants are often situated in or near marginalized communities, disproportionately affecting the health and well-being of residents due to exposure to environmental toxins such as in Oakland, CA. Indigenous STEM perspectives can be highlighted by discussing traditional methods of resource extraction and land management that were sustainable and respectful of the environment. Students can explore how modern industrial practices deviate from these traditional approaches, leading to environmental injustice.
- Principle 3—Natural Systems Change in Ways That People Benefit from and Can Influence: Disruption of Natural Cycles in Agriculture:
  - Intensive monoculture practices and excessive use of agrochemicals disrupt natural cycles in agriculture, affecting both the environment and the health of communities, often impacting marginalized groups more significantly. Indigenous agricultural practices, like agroforestry or polyculture, can be introduced to students, showcasing how Indigenous communities historically worked in harmony with natural cycles. This comparison provides insights into sustainable land use and the impacts of deviating from these practices.
- Principle 4—There Are No Permanent or Impermeable Boundaries That Prevent Matter from Flowing Between Systems: Contamination of Water Sources:
  - Industrial activities often lead to the contamination of water sources, affecting both aquatic ecosystems and communities that depend on these water bodies. Indigenous communities may be disproportionately impacted due to their reliance on traditional water sources. Educators can delve into Indigenous water management techniques and their deep understanding of the interconnectedness of water systems. Students can explore the implications of modern pollution on Indigenous communities and their traditional STEM practices related to water.

- Principle 5—Decisions Affecting Resources and Natural Systems Are Complex and Involve Many Factors: Unequal Resource Distribution:
  - Decision-making processes that favor certain communities over others in resource allocation, such as land rights or access to clean air and water, can lead to systemic environmental injustice. Educators can guide students in understanding how Indigenous communities historically made decisions about resource use, considering a holistic approach that integrates ecological, cultural, and social factors. This comparison highlights the complexity and importance of inclusive decision-making processes.

Netty Spotlight: Embracing Indigenous STEM as a Tool for Healing

The focus on Maui schools in Lahaina through the BWET project exemplifies the intersectionality of environmental principles and the unique context of Lahaina's community. The devastating fires have not only left a visible impact on the flora, fauna, and human structures but have also deeply affected the teachers and students emotionally and mentally. As part of a grant, the emphasis on place-based learning becomes a powerful tool for trauma-informed practices and healing. By centering the professional development on rebuilding the ahupua'a, the grant recognizes the profound connection between the community's trauma and the need for healing through engagement with the environment. This approach aligns with Principle 1, highlighting that the health of individual lives and communities is intricately tied to the health of natural systems. Through a holistic strategy that integrates environmental science, diversity, equity, and inclusion, the project acknowledges the complexity of Lahaina's situation, providing a unique opportunity for teachers and students to collectively heal and engage in the regeneration process of both the land and the community. This approach to professional development using the MWEE framework is designed to be "student" directed. In this case, the teachers are the haumāna. We realize through personal experience that returning to the location of former homes and the fire scar may be distressing to people. We have included a licensed clinical social worker, embedded in each day, who will work alongside STEM4Real staff as we engage teachers (and their students) in the healing process).

Community, Culture, and Normalizing STEM

National nonprofit organizations have manifested to address the lack of Indigenous access to STEM. Alaskan Native Science and Engineering Program, the Society of Advancement of Chicanos/Hispanics and Native Americans in Science, and The American Indian Science and Engineering Society all have a collective mission to increase the school-to-STEM-career pathway for Indigenous students. ANSEP, SACNAS, and AISES exemplify impactful initiatives that build a sense of community, culture and normalize STEM in Indigenous settings. These programs share common themes centered around identity, representation, outreach, and honoring ancestors. The success of ANSEP, for instance, lies in its sequential education model that spans from kindergarten to PhD, ensuring continuous support and inspiration. Dr. Herb Ilisaurri Schroeder founded the organization in 1995 while working on a sanitation research project. He realized that there were no Alaskan Native engineers and decided to create a pipeline of Alaskan Native engineers using his role as a professor. If there are more Alaskan Native engineers working in areas like sanitation, there wouldn't be people from outside making big decisions about their communities. The engagement of over 100 Alaskan communities underscores the significance of community involvement in STEM education. SACNAS and AISES, with their commitment to fostering the success of Chicanos/Hispanics and Native Americans, similarly highlight identity and representation in STEM.

Educators can draw valuable takeaways from these programs to replicate microcosms in their classrooms. First and foremost is the recognition of the importance of identity; understanding and incorporating students' cultural backgrounds into STEM education creates a welcoming atmosphere. Representation is key—showcasing successful role models from similar backgrounds inspires students to pursue STEM careers. Outreach initiatives, whether through internships, conferences, or scholarship programs, make STEM accessible and attractive. Lastly, emphasizing the connection to ancestors and heritage instills pride and a sense of purpose in students, making STEM an integral part of cultural narratives. By incorporating these strategies, educators can create inclusive STEM environments that empower Indigenous students to thrive academically and professionally.

Tokenization of Indigenous Cultures

Avoiding the tokenization of Indigenous cultures in STEM education requires a thoughtful and sustained effort to move beyond performative gestures toward genuine normalization and a sense of belonging. One teacher was invited to be on a panel and felt like she was invited so that they could report back that they considered Native perspectives. We must embed Indigenous perspectives within the curriculum in a meaningful way.

Introduce traditional ecological knowledge and Indigenous scientific practices alongside conventional scientific concepts. In Hawai'i, the installation of the TMT (Thirty Meter Telescope) was a scientific advancement that would compromise the sacred land of the people. The ongoing controversy led to the Mauna Kea Stewardship Oversight Authority, an 11-member panel that would include representatives from the university and observatories along with two seats for native Hawaiians. While this opened the door for native Hawaiians to obtain a seat at the table, it serves as another example of politics that seeks out voices for the sake of meeting quotas or grant requirements. This tokenization is also seen in institutions of higher education. Author Ebony McGee warns that "institutions often expect these faculty of color to lead the charge when it comes to anti-racist efforts. They are approached to mentor students of color, to serve on diversity committees, and to speak on panels about diversity—activities that are tangential to their research. Although many people of color in STEM have a fervent desire to make their field and workplace more equitable, pressure to perform duties unrelated to their research creates a service burden that many of their white colleagues do not bear."

Nurturing and Creating an Authentic Sense of Belonging

Nurturing and creating an authentic sense of belonging for underrepresented groups in STEM, such as Indigenous students, is crucial for their success and long-term engagement. Several programs, including the Biology Scholars Program at UC Berkeley, the Native Hawaiians in Engineering Program, and initiatives like Black Girls Code, have demonstrated success in encouraging a supportive environment for students from diverse backgrounds. They focus on increasing the representation and success of Black and Indigenous students in the science and engineering fields through mentorship, community-building, and cultural integration. Creating a sense of belonging in STEM involves implementing strategies to support underrepresented groups and mitigate feelings of otherness. Affinity groups, cultural integration, mentorship programs, and community events are effective approaches used to promote diversity and equity in STEM. These initiatives aim to address the unique challenges faced by underrepresented students, providing opportunities for growth, mentorship, and community engagement. Embracing these strategies empowers educators to nurture a supportive environment where students from diverse backgrounds can thrive academically and professionally in STEM. The following is a summarized list of strategies and tools to nurture this sense of belonging.

- **Affinity groups:** Establish affinity groups or clubs focused on STEM for underrepresented students. These groups offer a sense of belonging and provide a platform for shared experiences and support. Share resources and success stories highlighting individuals from underrepresented backgrounds who have excelled in STEM.
- **Cultural integration:** Infuse cultural elements into STEM lessons. Explore the intersection of Indigenous knowledge with scientific principles, making the content more relatable and culturally enriching.
- **Mentorship programs:** Develop mentorship programs connecting students with professionals in STEM who share similar backgrounds. Mentorship provides guidance, inspiration, and a sense of community.
- **Throw a party:** So much of building community is about connecting through joy and justice. Organize events, workshops, and guest speaker sessions that engage the local community. Many of these organizations host conferences in order to come together to create a place for belonging, inspiration, and community.

The culture of STEM and embedding Indigenous wisdom into our STEM lessons has to go further than a few special lessons during Black History Month, Women's History Month, and Native American History month. If you are seeking out resources for these months, consider teaching like that all year. Alberto J. Rodriguez, distinguished professor of education at the University of Houston, along with Marianela Navarro-Camacho discusses the importance of claiming your own identity and positionality as the first steps toward establishing equity and social justice in science [and STEM] education. He encourages teachers to "experience different ways of doing and understanding science from culturally diverse perspectives, such as ways of knowing from Indigenous, Afro-descendants, and other traditionally marginalized peoples. For example, student teaching placements in culturally diverse schools, and/or visits to sites where students can gain new insights (e.g., visiting an Indigenous Peoples' school; visiting museum exhibits on Indigenous Peoples' rich place-based knowledge of metallurgy, agriculture, conservation, engineering, and so on)." In the spirit of cultivating an inclusive and culturally enriched STEM education, embracing the achievements and traditions of diverse communities should not be confined to designated months or observances. Reimagining a STEM culture involves recognizing and celebrating the valuable contributions that different cultures, including those of Native American and Indigenous communities, have made to the fields of STEM all year long. By capturing the joy in traditions and showcasing the brilliance of various cultures, educators can inspire a sense of belonging and curiosity that extends throughout the entire academic year, enriching the STEM experience for all students.

#4Real Prompts

Navigating Conflicting Perspectives in the Classroom

Consider the complexities and challenges of honoring Indigenous cultures while teaching scientific concepts. How can educators navigate conflicting perspectives between Indigenous stories and Western scientific explanations in the classroom? Share your thoughts on strategies for fostering cultural understanding, respect, and inclusivity while promoting critical thinking and scientific inquiry among students.

Honoring Ancestral Wisdom in Science Education

Explore the "Storytelling and Wayfinding Protocol" outlined in the passage as a framework for promoting cultural inclusivity and appreciation for diverse perspectives in your classroom. Discuss the importance of creating a learning environment that honors Indigenous wisdom and heritage while empowering students to engage critically with both Indigenous stories and scientific explanations. Share your thoughts on how you can implement these strategies to create engaging and culturally inclusive STEM learning experiences for your students.

Inclusive STEM Communities: Strategies and Challenges

Discuss the importance of identity, representation, outreach, and honoring ancestors in establishing a welcoming and supportive environment for Indigenous cultures in STEM education. Additionally, explore the concept of tokenization of Indigenous cultures in STEM education and strategies to move beyond performative gestures toward genuine normalization and a sense of belonging. Discuss the significance of nurturing an authentic sense of belonging through strategies such as affinity groups, cultural integration, mentorship programs, and community events, and share your ideas for implementing these strategies effectively in your teaching practice.

CHAPTER 12

STEM Teachers Are Not Exempt: Anti-Racism, Anti-Bias, and Cultural Responsiveness

Can you just teach STEM and leave out all of the anti-racism stuff?

—District Administrator

I was on a call with a district partner, and our lead advocate had just received a promotion to site principal and was changing roles. Our team at STEM4Real always gets nervous when there is a change of guard because decision-makers have to be 100 percent committed to anti-racism, anti-bias, and social justice when they hire us. However, when the new person came onto the role and took over the contract, she said, "Can you just teach STEM and leave out all of the anti-racism stuff?" When we hear that, it reminds us of when political pundits would tell basketball player and activist LeBron James to "shut up and dribble." Just teach STEM and omit all of the work on equity, justice, and anti-racism. On an episode of the widely popular show *Ted Lasso*, one of the soccer players was speaking up for Nigeria and immigration rights. Then someone destroyed his restaurant and spray painted "Shut up and dribble" across the wall. There is a reason why STEM lacks diversity, and we as educators have to take responsibility for our place in the school-to-STEM-career pathways.

Use of Street Data versus Standardized Data to Inform and Revolutionize

While education systems faun over quantitative data measures, they blatantly ignore the qualitative measures that make students whole. Authors Shane Safir and Jamila Dugan refer to this as street data. Leveraging street data, also known as community-based or grassroots data, to inform policies can bring a more nuanced and inclusive perspective to decision-making compared to relying solely on standardized data. As they say:

> Street data is the qualitative and experiential data that emerges at eye level and on lower frequencies when we train our brains to discern it. Street data is asset based, building on the tenets of culturally responsive education by helping educators look for what's right in our students, schools, and communities instead of seeking out what's wrong. Street data embodies both an ethos and a change methodology that will transform how we analyze, diagnose, and assess everything from student learning to district improvement to policy.

Standardized data can sometimes perpetuate existing biases, as it may reflect historical disparities or under-represent marginalized communities. Street data considers the lived experiences of students, providing insights into their socio-emotional challenges. This understanding helps educators implement targeted support systems that address the specific needs of racially diverse student populations. It also opens our eyes to the deep-rooted anti-Blackness that persists in education systems.

Black Students Matter

The underrepresentation of Black individuals in STEM fields underscores the importance of integrating anti-racist principles into STEM education and workplaces. Addressing racial disparities in STEM is not only a matter of equity but also crucial for fostering innovation, diversity of thought, and social progress. According to *The Journal of Blacks in Higher Education*:

In 2021, Blacks were about 12 percent of the adult population in the United States but made up only nine percent of the STEM workforce. In 2011, Blacks were seven percent of all STEM workers. About 18 percent of all Black workers were employed in STEM fields compared to 25 percent of all white workers and 39 percent of Asian workers. Black workers, on average, had lower wages than white or Asian workers in STEM fields. Educators must be aware of and actively address implicit biases that may affect teaching, mentorship, and evaluation. Antiracist training helps educators recognize and counteract biases, ensuring fair treatment and opportunities for Black students.

Black-Escalation Effect

A disturbing phenomenon called the Black-escalation effect, revealed by a study from Stanford University, indicates that teachers tend to view Black students more harshly than white students, potentially contributing to racial disparities in school discipline. This bias can lead to a destructive cycle where teachers' responses may influence students' behavior and perpetuate stereotypes. Ultimately our discipline measures keep students out of the classroom and out of learning. Dr. Julia Aguirre, a mathematics professor from the University of Washington, facilitates an activity that elicits stereotypes from the following student groups: Black boys, Muslim girls, students with disabilities, foster youth, LGBTQ youth, and Chicano students. It is a triggering and jarring activity that we have conducted with various leaders across the United States, gathering responses from the following prompt: "What have you heard about working with these groups of students and/or their families?" Each participant takes a few moments to reflect on all of the stereotypes and then lists them on the wall. We then ask for volunteers to read each statement written about each student group out loud. Hearing the statements is the heavy part of the activity. One district coordinator said, "I can't believe how easy these statements came out of people." The truth is that these statements, whether they are said out loud or not, are ever present on the shoulders of our students. This is why we cannot "just talk about STEM." Knowing that these deficit-framed messages are hanging over the heads of these students and families, our role as educators is to take an active stand to ensure that we are changing and reframing these messages.

Arash Daneshzadeh is the lead organizational coach and project specialist with **Traumatransformed.org**, a social services organization in Oakland, California, that cultivates systems change and provides capacity-building strategies and tools for agencies that serve historically marginalized children and families across the United States. In his research on restorative justice (RJ), he states:

> Stakeholders must be willing and ready to examine the principles of RJ through a lens of community activism. In the participatory ethos of RJ, counter-narratives and equitable stakeholdership between youth and adults create spaces unsanctioned by common Western systems of financial incentives or carceral punishment. Neoliberal appropriations of RJ in schools have flattened the community-centered texture and critical lens in which conflict is framed. If Black and First Nation youth are seen solely as restoration projects, then RJ will ascribe to a deficit-lens that hyper-individualizes activism as an issue of Black 'respectability', while simultaneously absolving subtle and pervasive violence wrought within historically-blighted communities by the legacy of settler colonialism.

Changing the Narrative through Reframing

According to Dr. Julia Aguirre, we have the power to change the messages from a deficit-frame to a strength-frame. Here are the messages about Black boys and mathematics:

Deficit-Framed	Strength-Framed
Don't feel they need math	High expectations
Want to be successful at sports	Successful graduates
Lots of energy	High energy to learn
Low attention	Knowledgeable and mature
Families don't support	College bound
Not math people	Love math
Not interested in math	Scholar athletes
Candidates for high dropout rates	Interested in math
Not motivated/ambitious	Families support
Low attention span	Families care
Haven't heard positive or negative things	Mathematical thinkers
Pipeline to prison	Care about learning
Adult-ified	Highly capable
Live in the "ghetto"	Leaders
Low expectations	Motivated
Held back	
Low learners	
Poor math students	

The "Racial Stereotypes Activity" was initially developed by Julia Aguirre in her teaching methods course and was modified for STEM4Real. It is designed to create awareness and stimulate discussion about racial stereotypes that may exist within educational settings, particularly in STEM. By engaging participants in reflecting on what they have heard about working with different student groups and their families, the activity prompts them to recognize and acknowledge common stereotypes that may impact their perceptions and interactions with students. Not only do these perceptions persist, they are amplified in STEM spaces. Through group discussion and reframing the narrative with a counternarrative approach, participants are encouraged to challenge and reframe stereotypes to promote a more inclusive and equitable learning environment. This activity highlights the importance of addressing implicit biases and stereotypes in STEM education. By facilitating conversations around racial stereotypes and encouraging participants to rethink their perceptions, educators can work toward creating a more supportive and inclusive environment for all students, ultimately promoting equity and diversity in our STEM spaces.

Conduct the Racial Stereotypes Activity (Modified for STEM4Real)

Materials:

- 10 pieces of chart paper
- 10 signs with each of the student groups of your choice
- Sticky notes
- Sharpies (for the end)

Directions:

1. Set the Stage: "What have you heard about working with these groups of students and/or their families?"
2. Recording: Allow participants 5–7 minutes to go around and write down everything about each student group
3. Read Aloud: Have 10 volunteers read each statement word for word out loud.
4. Discussion: Discuss how these are the lived realities of our students in each of these student groups.
5. Reframe with the Counternarrative: Have participants take their Sharpies and reframe the narrative that they hear. Example: Student doesn't speak English --> Student speaks multiple languages.

In her book *Cultivating Mathematical Hearts*, Aguirre states, "We see children as whole people; they are not extensions of content or data, or solely adults in the making: They are living, breathing, thinking, emotional, and social—they are full human beings." We as STEM educators have the power to reframe the narrative and tell the counternarrative by recognizing the importance of teaching full humans and the whole child, embracing their emotional, social, and cognitive development alongside STEM content knowledge, and promoting a holistic approach to education.

LGBTQ in STEM

When I was at the Institute of Astronomy at the University of Hawaii, I came across the following poster that highlighted prominent figures in space from the LGBTQ community. Not only does this image showcase LGBTQ space scientists, it highlights the plight of their journey because of their identities. Sally Ride, for example, kept her relationship a secret in the fear of losing corporate funding and facing societal backlash.

SPACE IS GAY
Ready to Go Stargazing?
Sally Ride
James Pollack
Frank Kameny
Astrophysicist & Astronaut
- First and only KNOWN queer astronaut AND first American woman and youngest person to go to space
- Ride received her PhD in Physics from Stanford University in 1978, for her thesis on the interaction of X-rays with the interstellar medium.
- Selected for NASA Astronaut Group 8 where in 1984 she flew to space as a crew member on the shuttle Challenger for NASA's seventh space shuttle mission.
- Started the company Sally Ride Science and authored many children's science books with her partner, professor of psychology Tam O'Shaughnessy (kept their relationship private in fear of losing corporate sponsorships).
Planetary Astrophysicist and Space Scientist
- Pollack is a gay 20th century NASA researcher who established himself as a prominent figure in atmospheric science.
- Pollack obtained his PhD in Astronomy from Harvard in 1965, where he was the first graduate student of astronomer and science popularizer Carl Sagan.
Astronomer and Gay Rights Activist
- Dr. Frank Kameny was an American astronomer-turned-gay rights activist, after being forced to leave the profession due to his sexuality.
- Kameny earned his PhD in astronomy from Harvard in 1956, where he studied under the eminent stellar astronomer Cecilia Payne-Gaposchkin.
- Conducted photometric studies of variable stars, taking over 500 observations of yellow semiregular variables and RV Tauri stars.
- Success in fighting to remove the designation of homosexuality as a mental illness, and for coining the famous "Gay is Good" slogan.
George Takei
George Takei played Sulu in the original 'Star Trek' TV Series.
Star Trek Actor and Gay Rights Activist
- Acted as astrosciences physicist Sulu in the second pilot for the original Star Trek series
- Takei and Altman were the first same-sex couple to apply for a marriage license in West Hollywood
- In May 2011, in response to a Tennessee State Legislature bill that prohibited school teachers or students from using any language that alludes to the existence of homosexuality, he offered up his name, suggesting that people could just substitute that for 'gay'.
- For ex: They could support Takei Marriage or watch Takei Pride Parades; or even use slurs such as That's so Takei.
"THAT'S SO TAKEI!"

Jennifer Janzen, an openly trans science education leader, stated this as a guest writer for the STEM4Real Blog: "As educators we should be working not only on mastery of the

NGSS performance expectations, Math practices and Common Core literacy standards for science, & technical subjects in our STEM/STEAM education, but also connecting with our youth, especially the LGBTQI+ youth who face harmful amounts of discrimination and fewer support structures. How do we do this, you might ask. What I appreciated in my transition was the showing of empathy by others. There were people in my life that were willing to express appreciation and respect towards me, which validated my core identity." Professors Gary William Wright and Cesar Delgado found that students who identify as LGBTQ continue to report feelings of being unsafe at school because of their sexual orientation, gender identity, and gender expression." "According to Gay, Lesbian, and Straight Education Network, "Over eight in 10 (85 percent) of LGBTQ students experienced verbal harassment based on a personal characteristic, and nearly two thirds (66 percent) experienced LGBTQ-related discrimination at school." Access to a gender and sexual diversity (GSD)-inclusive curriculum and supportive teachers may positively improve the school climate for LGBTQ students, but these supports are often not included in STEM classrooms. One response is to ensure that STEM teachers are prepared to integrate GSD-inclusive STEM teaching into their classrooms. Additionally, creating a safe and welcoming classroom environment where all students feel respected and valued is essential. This can involve implementing anti-bullying policies, establishing LGBTQ-affirming classroom norms, and providing resources and support for LGBTQ students, such as access to LGBTQ student groups or counseling services. When I was a high school teacher, I served as the Gay-Straight Alliance Advisor. The simple act of having a space on campus and having a place for their full identities was powerful enough to embrace the need for their sense of belonging.

Bev Berekian, a veteran secondary science teacher who identifies as part of the LGBTQ community, said that one of the professors in her credential program also identified as LGBTQ and that immediately made her feel comfortable. She learned early on that in order to make folks feel like they belong, you must show them that there is space for them and you must show up in authentic and genuine ways. Allyship can be modeled for our students. It can be as simple as having a rainbow flag in our room or wearing a button. There are opportunities to be inclusive with Trans Awareness Day, LGBTQ+ History Month, Pride Month, and so on. In our lessons, we should include models from the LGBTQ+ community such as George Washington Carver, Dr. Sara Josephine Baker, Alan Turing, and most notably Sally Ride. It needs to become as commonplace to talk about LGBTQ+ figures in STEM as it is to mention folks of any other underserved or represented groups. The "Queer STEM History Podcast" created a series that highlights the lives and science of queer scientists throughout history.

Revolutionary STEM Teaching

Now that we have discussed the anti-Blackness that persists in education systems, we can explore revolutionary and out-of-the-box teaching that will pull our students into STEM and increase the number of open doors and entry points. Dr. Jeremiah Sims, author of

Revolutionary STEM Education, states, "Critical pedagogy in STEM seeks to re-empower traditionally oppressed students by presenting them with the necessary tools to come to consciousness so that they can begin to exercise their power to deconstruct the ideological and juridical bulwarks of inequity that wreak havoc on and in their lives." Revolutionary STEM teaching ideas allow for increased entry points and belonging in STEM. By providing students with varied ways to make sense of STEM, these approaches can break down traditional barriers and empower learners from diverse backgrounds to see themselves as capable contributors to the world of STEM that goes beyond textbook learning.

Service Learning as an Act of Anti-Bias in STEM

Service learning, particularly when integrated with a focus on anti-racism and anti-bias, serves as a powerful tool for promoting equity in STEM education. In our most recent partnership with a school district located in the Inland Empire of California, we leveraged their implementation of the State Seal of Civic Engagement. The State of California had earmarked a set of funds for service learning aligned to the History and Social Science Framework. I saw this as an opportunity for interdisciplinary instruction and leveraging service learning as a tool to address chronic absenteeism and access to STEM through community and civic engagement. Service learning, particularly when integrated with a focus on anti-racism and anti-bias, can be a powerful tool for promoting equity in STEM education and place-based learning. Juanita Chan Roden, a district administrator and leader in environmental education, said this:

> I have witnessed firsthand the benefits of place-based learning on developing relationships with students and each other. Vibrant and engaging learning requires strong relationships, and these relationships often need to traverse generation gaps, socioeconomic differences, racial and political incongruence. So how do we find common ground? We have to believe that diversity is strength when our common values define our noble purpose. In spite of all of the differences that you find in a classroom or school there is one thing that binds us together; we are all here, in this place, and at this time.

Because we are in these shared spaces, service learning naturally brings in place-based learning. Integrate service learning into the lesson study process to encourage collaborative planning and reflective teaching. Teachers could incorporate community service elements into their lessons, ensuring that they align with academic goals and provide students with opportunities for real-world application. Connect the evaluation to a youth-action plan. After the lessons are taught, conduct collaborative reflections to discuss what worked well, challenges faced, and potential improvements for future service-learning integration. Invite community leaders, service organizations, or professionals who have successfully incorporated service learning into their teaching practices to share their experiences. Conduct discussions on the importance of community connections in education and how service learning can enhance both teaching and student outcomes.

STEM or STEAM?

If I have to choose between STEM or STEAM, I am most definitely in the STEM lane. Does this mean I have something against the arts? Absolutely not! I have seen the evolution from STEM to STEAM to STREAM, and next thing you know, we may have an entire alphabet on our hands! Let's regroup and go back to what STEM education is. STEM is inclusive of the following subjects: science, technology, engineering, and mathematics. According to the National Science Teaching Association (NSTA), STEM education is an interdisciplinary approach to learning where rigorous academic concepts are coupled with real-world lessons as students apply science, technology, engineering, and mathematics in contexts that make connections between school, community, work, and the global enterprise enabling the development of STEM literacy and with it the ability to compete in the new economy. For example, students explore the relationship between music and mathematics, creating compositions based on mathematical patterns. Therefore, art, history, civics, ethics, reading, and writing are all vehicles that STEM relies on to make connections to the real world *and* create opportunities for application. We need civics to ensure policies are transferred into our society and economy. Plus, art is *everywhere* in STEM education as it is our vehicle for modeling, designing, and iterating our sense-making. STEM is our *how* in order to do the *why*: art, reading, writing, history, civics, and any of the 26 letters in our alphabet. The ultimate goal is to make the content relevant without teaching these concepts in isolation.

Make It Happen with Maker Education

Maker education empowers students to become creators and innovators, breaking away from traditional passive learning. It revolutionizes teaching by promoting hands-on exploration, problem-solving, and collaborative learning. Students can design and build prototypes of solutions to community challenges using 3D printing, robotics, or other maker tools. This approach not only develops technical skills but also instills an entrepreneurial mindset and a sense of agency in addressing real-world problems. To create a makerspace, start by designating a dedicated area within the classroom, whether it's a corner, a table, or an entire section. Next, gather a diverse range of materials and tools that encourage exploration and experimentation, such as art supplies, craft materials, robotics kits, and coding resources. Incorporating a variety of STEM-related elements ensures that students can engage in a broad spectrum of projects. Additionally, consider involving students in the setup process to cultivate a sense of ownership and inclusion. Implementing flexible seating and storage solutions allows for easy reconfiguration and accessibility. Finally, encourage a culture of collaboration and problem-solving by incorporating group projects and challenges.

Netty Spotlight: Bringing Literacy to Life with Maker Education

STEM4Real created the following protocol to connect Maker Education with Literacy:

Find Curiosity within the Story

1. Create Curiosity
   a. List 10 things you are curious about with the story.
2. Storyboard: A storyboard artist is someone who takes a script (or just a concept) and turns the words into a visual story. Storyboard artists are in control of how others perceive the project. It can be a tool others look at for reference.
   a. **https://www.getmecoding.com/storyboards_and_pseudocode/**
   b. Storyboard Artist 101: The Complete Guide to Beginners, **GameDesigning.org**

The Design-Thinking Process

1. **Empathy:** Sharing Your Story and Connecting to the Reading
   a. Journal about your own story that relates to the story you just read.
   b. Bring your own identity into the story.
   c. Share your story with a partner.
2. **Define the Problem:** Redefine and focus your question based on your insights from the empathy stage. The problem is the problem or challenge in the story or literary work that you are reading.

Title	Main Character	Setting	Major Event
Another Character	Problem/ Challenge	The End	Lesson or Message

3. **Ideate:** Returning to your original user group and testing your ideas for feedback
   a. What are the elements of a good model? How can you implement this practice?
   b. **Developing and using models progression:** Create a student-generated list of what to include in your model or prototype.
   c. **Classroom Management Tips**
      i. Have students show you a 2D model first before you show them all of the materials.
      ii. Organize your materials by material "type." Have students assist with the setup if possible.
      iii. Assign a materials manager for each group.
      iv. Have a cleanup process ready. Organization will be your best friend!
      v. Be ready with your attention-getting tricks such as the "Waterfall, Waterfall, shhhhhh" technique.

4. **Prototype:** Brainstorm and come up with creative solutions
   a. Honor time to ideate, brainstorm, and tinker.
   b. Connect your solution to the story.
5. **Test:** Build a representation of one or more of your ideas to show to others
   a. Read the story again: How does the story change with your device?
   b. Did you solve the problem? Retell the story with your story partner.

Computer Science, Coding, and AI in STEM

As we explore the use of artificial intelligence, some districts have stepped in and started creating policies to outlaw AI and ChatGPT. This sets the stage for some districts to have access to AI tools while others don't. No matter how much we resist, these tools are here to stay with more to come. We have to embrace these technologies and incorporate them into our curriculum. Incorporating CS, coding, and AI is vital to ensure that we are equipping students with essential digital literacy skills and promoting diversity in tech-related fields. Students can collaborate on coding projects that address societal issues, such as creating an app for local community services or using AI to analyze data related to social justice.

Ruha Benjamin, author of *Race After Technology and Viral Justice*, states, "Like segregated water fountains of a previous era, the discriminatory soap dispenser offers a window onto a wider social terrain." The proverbial soap dispenser she is referring to are the modern-day soap dispensers that cannot recognize darker skin tones. The soap dispenser example underscores the urgency for diversity and inclusion in the development of technology, especially in fields like computer science, AI, and tech. Benjamin powerfully highlights how seemingly mundane technological artifacts can reflect and perpetuate existing inequalities in society. When diverse voices are not adequately represented in the creation of these systems, the resulting technologies may inadvertently reinforce existing social hierarchies and discriminate against certain groups.

Rudy Escobar, a STEM and computer science coordinator from California, shared a recent aha moment when discussing computer science. He was part of a series of workshops called "Conchas and Computadoras." In these workshops, they provided underserved Latinx parents in an area that does not receive much attention with education about computer science and what they should be seeing in their children's schools in respect to computer science in their own community. He recalled:

> One of the parents told me that she was thankful that someone like me had come to their community to provide them with the information they needed. In one of the workshops, we had them come with their family. The aha moment came when I saw the enjoyment of the parents with their children working on a computer science concept. Note that there were no computers involved during this workshop and they still interacted with computer science concepts and computational thinking. Commonly we do not see fathers showing up for these events, and we even had fathers participating

> and having fun with their children. This confirmed for me the importance of investing in our underserved communities and not having them come to us, but for us to go to their community so they feel safe.

This is why increased exposure to computer science and technology education allows students to reimagine and reshape technology to be more just, unbiased, and reflective of the diverse world we live in.

Hip-Hop Hooray!

Hip-hop education brings cultural relevance to STEM by incorporating elements of hip-hop culture into the teaching approach. One science teacher found this out and created a whole movement. Meet the rapping science teacher and world sensation, Mr. Matt Green. Green, a teacher out of London, found a way to use his creativity in rap music and combine it with scientific topics such as electrolysis. He began making videos to help students pass the General Certificate of Secondary Education (GCSE). He says:

> I'm keen to use music to show what science teaching is all about and reach as many young people as possible. When I went back to school after the viral video was posted my pupils had all seen and commented on the video. One thing that was said quite a few times is that they had learned more in 30 seconds watching the videos than they had in the previous four weeks. And that was what I wanted, for them to remember the information really easily.

You can find his video titled "Science Raps: GCSE Physics – Electricity" on his YouTube Channel (**https://www.youtube.com/@MattGreenJGM**).

One student commented, "Bro teaches me what I'm confused about after a full term, in 40 seconds that I understand completely. Only Matt can do that!" Through the use of culturally relevant avenues like hip-hop, we are expanding the doors and entry points to STEM education. Inspired by Mr. Green, students can create STEM-themed rap songs or rhymes that creatively explain scientific principles or mathematical concepts. This approach not only reinforces STEM knowledge but also celebrates cultural diversity and encourages students to express themselves through a familiar medium. Hip-hop education leverages the cultural relevance and vibrancy of hip-hop music, art, and language to make STEM concepts more accessible and relatable to diverse student populations.

Christopher Emdin, a prominent advocate for hip-hop education, emphasizes the power of incorporating hip-hop culture into the STEM classroom to engage and inspire students. His work, including his book *For White Folks Who Teach in the Hood . . . and the Rest of Y'all Too*, underscores the potential impact of hip-hop pedagogy on STEM education. He argues that by tapping into the rhythm, language, and storytelling elements of hip-hop, educators can create a dynamic and inclusive learning environment. This approach not only addresses the cultural disconnect that some students may feel in traditional STEM settings but also fosters a sense of belonging and empowerment. Aligning with Emdin's vision, this Hip-Hop Ed Argumentation Protocol offers a structured framework to seamlessly integrate hip-hop culture into the STEM content, facilitating engaging and collaborative learning experiences. Teachers can integrate the Hip-Hop Ed Argumentation Protocol into their STEM lessons by introducing the hip-hop track selected for the session. Choose a song that relates to the STEM concept being taught and captures students' attention. Allow students to listen to the song and encourage them to identify any scientific content or relevant themes in the lyrics. This sets the stage for the lesson and piques students' interest. Provide students with the lyrics of the hip-hop song and guide them through a close examination of the text. Encourage students to identify scientific concepts or evidence embedded within the lyrics. Facilitate a discussion where students share their findings and collaborate to extract relevant evidence related to the STEM concept. Students can then work collaboratively to create rhymes integrating the scientific evidence identified earlier. Divide students into small groups and provide them with the opportunity to craft rhymes that effectively communicate scientific arguments.

Hip-Hop Ed Argumentation Protocol

Hip-Hop Ed Argumentation Protocol

1. Intro Rhyme Session (10 mins):
   - Start with an engaging hip-hop track related to STEM.
   - Identify evidence in the lyrics and discuss. I love "Insane in the Membrane" by Cypress Hill
2. Lyric Analysis & Evidence (15 mins):
   - Analyze lyrics for scientific content.
   - Extract evidence related to the STEM concept.
3. Group Rhyme Construction (20 mins):
   - Small groups create rhymes integrating evidence.
   - Emphasize collaboration and clear scientific argumentation.
4. Performance Preparation (15 mins):
   - Rehearse rhymes, focusing on rhythm and clarity.
5. Hip-Hop Showcase (20 mins):
   - Groups present, combining evidence and creativity.
   - Facilitate constructive feedback.
   - Set up the battle stage.
6. Reflection & Discussion (10 mins):
   - Reflect on using hip-hop for scientific argumentation.
   - Discuss engagement and understanding.

Revolutionary STEM teaching methods are poised to redefine education, challenging traditional paradigms and promoting inclusivity. As Jeremiah Sims notes, "Where STEM had initially been neutral and axiomatic, the students began to ask more critical questions by applying the tools of rhetorical analysis to their STEM learning. They wanted to know: STEM for what, and STEM for whom?" (Sims, 2018). These revolutionary methods embody a commitment to equity, diversity, and a vision of STEM education that empowers all learners to imagine, create, and thrive in a rapidly changing world.

Anti-Racist Collaborative Work via Student Grouping

Creating strategies for group work for STEM teachers through an anti-racist lens involves intentionally designing activities and interactions that promote equity, inclusion, and respect for diverse perspectives. Anti-racist and anti-bias group work promotes an environment where all students feel valued, heard, and empowered to contribute meaningfully to the learning process. The following are strategies that STEM educators can take to implement flexible, anti-racist, and anti-bias student group work:

1. **Intentional Task Design:** One key aspect of anti-racist group work is ensuring that tasks and assignments are designed to captivate and maintain students' attention. Stanford professors Elizabeth Cohen and Rachel Lotan refer to these as "groupworthy tasks" where tasks should be rooted in complex issues or problems that can be approached in varied ways that have various solutions. This means providing multiple entry points for participation and allowing students to demonstrate understanding in various ways. A groupworthy STEM task could involve designing and conducting an experiment to investigate the effects of different environmental factors on plant growth. In this task, students would work collaboratively in small groups to plan and execute their experiment, ensuring that each member has a role in the process. One student could be responsible for researching the various environmental factors to test, another could oversee the setup and maintenance of the experimental conditions, while others could collect and analyze data. This open-ended task allows students to engage in complex problem-solving as they design their experiment and analyze their results, providing multiple entry points for participation and opportunities to demonstrate intellectual competence. According to Carol Ann Tomlinson, Professor Emeritus at the University of Virginia, tasks worthy of group work strive to mirror real-life dilemmas and authentic challenges, prompting students to draw from their personal experiences and articulate their viewpoints with conviction.
2. **Promote Collaborative Leadership:** Assigning job roles and rotations in group work can also be done in an antiracist manner by promoting collaboration and shared leadership. Rather than assigning roles based on assumptions or stereotypes, teachers can encourage students to self-select or rotate roles to ensure that everyone

has an opportunity to develop essential skills and contribute their unique strengths to the group. In a science class, particularly in a unit on environmental conservation, students could work on a project to research and propose solutions to a local environmental issue, such as water pollution in a nearby river. Each group member could rotate through different leadership roles throughout the project duration. For example, one week, a student might lead the group discussion on the causes and effects of water pollution, while another student takes charge of conducting research on potential solutions, and another organizes the data collected. The following week, the roles could rotate, allowing each student to contribute their unique skills and perspectives to the project. This collaborative leadership approach ensures that all students have the opportunity to develop leadership skills, engage with the content in meaningful ways, and contribute to the group's collective understanding and success in addressing the environmental issue.

3. **Model Inclusive Communication:** Flexible grouping is crucial for accommodating the diverse needs of students, including those with special education needs and emergent multilingual learners. Teachers can create mixed-ability groups that provide peer support and collaboration opportunities. You can offer graphic organizers, sentence starters, and peer feedback to help students articulate their thoughts effectively. By forming groups based on complementary strengths and needs rather than fixed assignments, educators facilitate peer support and collaboration. For instance, pairing students with varying abilities and language proficiencies allows for mutual learning, with more proficient students providing language and content scaffolding while benefiting from their partners' analytical skills. Encourage respectful debate and critical inquiry by setting clear expectations for communication norms in the classroom.
4. **Building Authentic Community and Conflict Resolution:** This is the most vital one and oftentimes most forgotten. Establishing a culture of trust, respect, and collaboration is essential for building authentic community within groups. Teachers can facilitate team-building activities and establish clear expectations for behavior and communication. Additionally, educators can teach conflict resolution strategies and provide guidance on how to address disagreements respectfully. For instance, students could participate in role-playing exercises where they practice active listening, empathy, and compromise. By equipping students with these skills, educators empower them to navigate conflicts constructively and maintain positive relationships within the group.

When I was coaching cross country, one of my runners came up to me and said how he had one of the best first days of school. He was in his history class and the activity was to use a pipe cleaner to introduce yourself to the class. He said his name was Brian and he made an "R" for *Runner*. I was also a science teacher and I had just finished going over the syllabus and norms for the year. I do not think I was wrong; however, I recall Brian's excitement and how he could not wait to go back to his history class the next day. In my class, I had skipped the community building thinking it would naturally happen throughout the year. When I saw that my history colleague was intentional about creating this classroom ecology and remembered Brian's excitement, I realized that building community is not a fluffy optional task; it is a requirement for functional student collaborative relationships.

Creating a supportive classroom ecology begins with establishing a culture of trust, respect, and collaboration. Teachers can create this environment by setting clear expectations for behavior and communication, promoting empathy and active listening, and encouraging students to value each other's contributions. Building a sense of community within the classroom helps students feel connected and supported, making them more likely to engage positively in group work. Additionally, providing opportunities for students to reflect on their experiences and express their thoughts and feelings increases a sense of belonging and ownership over the learning process.

Expanded Learning Needs to Expand

In order to address STEM for ALL, we have to analyze the impact of expanded learning programs. These programs have actually saved many students, especially programs such as Math and Science Engineering Achievement that particularly target Black and Brown youth. While after-school programs such as MESA, Black Girls Code, the Hidden Genius Project, and Science Olympiad play a crucial role in cultivating STEM interest and skills among students, relying solely on expanded learning opportunities is insufficient for achieving educational equity in STEM. These programs, though impactful, have limitations in reaching all students and may not address core learning needs. The Hidden Genius project saw gaps in schooling and actually refers to their programming as "un-schooling." This is because the school has historically not served all students in STEM. After-school programs, by design, often have limited capacity to reach all students due to factors such as time constraints, resources, and enrollment limitations. Students who may benefit the most from these programs might face barriers to participation. This list outlines strategies for ensuring that expanded learning programs are expanded to scale and include more students. Schools can integrate after-school and expanded learning elements by providing anti-bias training for educators, designing inclusive curricula, and building community partnerships. Anti-bias training helps bridge the gap between core teachers and expanded learning providers, ensuring that STEM content is delivered in a manner that resonates with all students. These strategies aim to build a sense of belonging and interest in STEM among all students while expanding access to multiple pathways to academic success and future career readiness in STEM.

- **Integrate Aspects into Core Learning:** Embed elements of after-school and expanded learning programs into the regular school day. This could involve incorporating hands-on STEM activities, project-based learning, and mentorship opportunities within the curriculum.
- **Anti-Bias Training for Core Teachers and Expanded Learning Providers:** Provide professional development opportunities for teachers to enhance their ability to deliver STEM education in a culturally responsive and engaging manner. This can bridge the gap between after-school programs and core learning.

- **Curriculum Design and Resources:** Develop inclusive and culturally relevant STEM curricula that cater to diverse student populations. Ensure that resources and materials reflect the experiences of all students, fostering a sense of belonging and interest in STEM.
- **Community Partnerships:** Forge partnerships with community organizations, universities, and industry partners to bring STEM professionals into the classroom. This can expose students to diverse STEM career paths and provide real-world context to their learning.

Despite the commendable work of expanded learning opportunities in STEM, ensuring equitable access to these programs for all students remains a challenge. Factors such as geographic location, socioeconomic status, and school infrastructure can impact participation. We had the opportunity to partner with MESA at the University of Washington and the executive director of the project sought out the STEM4Real Leadership 4 Justice trainings that centered implicit bias and anti-racism in STEM. One of the participants was a middle school teacher who grappled with the power structure and his position as a teacher. He said while reflecting on MESA, "I work as a middle school teacher, not necessarily a MESA program leader, but I am appreciative of the opportunity to reflect on my own instructional and classroom practices as an educator." Another participant reflected on her own faculty: "While most of our faculty are verbally supportive of this work, they are reluctant to alter how they teach. How can I inspire them to make tiny changes in the way they teach to better support DEI efforts?" Because of the divide between expanded learning and core learning, there is a tendency to play hot potato and pass the issue to someone else. This is an issue where all educators, regardless of their place and position in the system, must think about anti-bias and anti-racism. As one director reflected, "As a career-technical education director it has given me the confidence and purpose to stand up for a more culturally responsive curriculum. And as a graduation specialist, it will empower me to fight for more family and community engagement." It is about having the conversations to speak up and stand up when we see these biases manifest.

Critical Race Theory as the Boogeyman

Now that we have discussed tools that can change and revolutionize STEM education systems, we have to address the politicization of equity in these education systems. Critical race theory (CRT) turned into the boogeyman, representing a fear-mongering creature that does not exist as a real issue. There are some schools and districts that actually outlaw equity work based on a misunderstanding of CRT. It has been a subject of intense political debate in recent years, often being weaponized as a tool to deflect from genuine discussions about equity in schools. The misrepresentation and politicization of CRT has led to a distorted narrative that serves specific political agendas rather than addressing real issues of educational inequality. The following framework helps facilitate conversations around CRT when discussing race, bias, and equity in STEM:

Define: I came across a message on social media that said, "My wife who works at our local Catholic school was asked by a parent if the school intended to teach critical race theory. She replied, 'Explain to me what it is, and I'll tell you if we teach it.' The parent had no reply." When we look back at crafting a definition of CRT, there is no unified definition. Defining critical race theory (CRT) is the foundational step in understanding its implications, and the need for a unified definition before engaging in discussions or arguments. I encourage a collective effort to establish a clear definition of CRT and to spend time discussing its actual implications, especially in STEM. Confusion arises when people use different interpretations of CRT, leading to broad and sometimes inaccurate perceptions.

Diffuse: The diffusion stage involves asking questions and engaging in discourse to clarify misunderstandings about CRT. Asking questions is the best way to stay in curiosity mode when faced with accusations or concerns. When confronted with statements such as "CRT is running amok" or "CRT is not developmentally appropriate," use this phase as an opportunity to actively seek understanding, asking questions such as "What is CRT?" and "What exactly is being taught?" This approach aims to bridge the gap between different perceptions and promotes a clearer understanding of the content and its implications. By asking for specific examples and explanations, educators can diffuse misconceptions and provide accurate information.

Deliver: The delivery stage involves providing instruction that is standards-based and culturally responsive. I must emphasize the importance of continuing to deliver education aligned with established standards while incorporating cultural responsiveness. This is framed as a way to navigate challenges, even if there are legislative restrictions or public debate about CRT. As discussed in the previous chapters, many people confuse critical race theory with culturally responsive teaching. The significance behind culturally responsive teaching involves being responsive to students' cultures, backgrounds, and experiences. The idea is to personalize and differentiate instruction, getting to know students and their families and creating a positive and inclusive learning environment. Always come back to the standards to ensure the content is aligned.

The political weaponization of CRT has been used strategically to divert attention from policy discussions and actions that could address educational disparities. By focusing on the supposed dangers of CRT, policymakers may avoid engaging in substantive conversations about resource allocation, school funding, teacher quality, and other critical factors influencing educational equity. When I presented this at a conference, I had a participant come in with a body camera to film my talk and troll the discussion. When I used the define, diffuse, deliver method, he was quiet and did not have much to protest.

The Systems Game

The educational system, while designed to be a platform for equal opportunities, often exhibits systemic inequities that hinder students' access to rigorous STEM instruction. For example, the practice of tracking and gatekeeping in education, particularly in math prerequisites for science courses, has far-reaching adverse impacts, often resulting in systemic inequities. As Dr. Julia Aguirre states, "We acknowledge the dual role that mathematics has played as gatekeeper and gateway to various opportunities in society, and we recognize that mathematics has often been used to make judgments about intelligence. We call on teachers to reflect on these uses of mathematics." The following table presents a series of systemic policies that contribute to unequal access to STEM and learning overall:

Policy	Situation	Impact
Tracking Based on Behavior	Black boys have been suspended for three days and will miss the Friday science lab.	Missing science labs disrupts their learning continuity, setting them on a trajectory of potential disengagement from STEM subjects.
Gatekeeping of Math Prerequisites	All low-performing students in either English Language Arts or Mathematics are removed from elective or prep classes to take additional ELA and math preparation.	Students facing challenges in math are further isolated from enriching elective courses, limiting their exposure to diverse learning experiences and potential STEM pathways.
Economic Barrier to Field Trips	A student whose parents are unable to afford a school field trip due to the cost and were unable to fundraise.	The economic barrier hinders the student's participation in hands-on STEM experiences, contributing to a lack of practical exposure and opportunities for exploration.
Disciplinary Actions for Dress Code Violation	A student is sent to the office for a school dress code violation.	Focusing on disciplinary measures for nonacademic issues detracts from valuable classroom time, widening the educational gap for the student.
Consequences for Incomplete Homework	A student serves lunch detention for incomplete or "lost" homework assignments.	Punitive measures for incomplete homework may disproportionately affect students facing external challenges, further hindering their academic progress in STEM subjects.

These examples highlight how tracking, gatekeeping, and punitive measures can lead to cumulative disadvantages for students, particularly those from marginalized communities. Addressing these issues requires systemic changes, including reevaluating disciplinary policies, creating inclusive learning environments, and providing additional support to students facing academic challenges. Let's take a look at what happens when anti-racism initiatives are only in the hands of a select few versus organization-wide:

In a district located with a high agriculture and migrant farming population, Yasmine Banuelos was the assistant superintendent of education services at her district. She wrote a grant on anti-bias education initiatives and contracted with STEM4Real to carry out the work. Ms. Banuelos then received a promotion to work at the regional level. When the new administration came, the new assistant superintendent, a white woman, canceled the contract stating that this was not a district priority at this time. This new assistant superintendent did not mean to commit an intentional act of racism. However, the impact of this decision affected an entire set of teachers and students. The teachers that were slated to receive stipends were dropped from any future programming and the coaches and instructional coordinators were directed to halt services.

Education decisions like this are happening every minute. Now if they had stated that they were continuing the project but not working with our team, the decision would have been fine because it is about the work getting done and the teachers getting served first rather than who completes the work. However, that was not the case. As Robin DiAngelo, author of *White Fragility*, states, "The simplistic idea that racism is limited to individual intentional acts committed by unkind people is at the root of virtually all white defensiveness on this topic." The decision to cancel the contract did not stem from overt racism but had a significant impact on teachers and students, particularly those from Black and Brown communities. As Andratesha Fritzgerald states, "Every act that serves Black and Brown children better is an act of antiracism. When we design with every student in front of us in mind, that is Universal Design for Learning." Removing any act, initiative, or funds that would prevent our Black and Brown students from getting served is an act of racism.

Anti-racism efforts should be deeply embedded in the fabric of educational systems. It calls for a shift from individual actions to collective responsibility, emphasizing that every decision, intentional or not, shapes the educational experience for students, especially those from marginalized communities. For meaningful change, anti-bias and anti-racism must be systemic, continuous, and a shared commitment across all levels of leadership and within the broader educational community.

#4Real Discussion Questions

Revolutionary STEM Teaching Ideas

How do the revolutionary STEM teaching ideas discussed, such as service learning, hip-hop education, maker education, computer science, coding, AI integration, and STEAM and art integration, challenge traditional teaching paradigms and contribute to creating a more inclusive and equitable STEM education system?

Collective Responsibility and Leadership

In considering the impact of leadership decisions on equity measures, what role does collective responsibility play in fostering a culture of anti-racism within educational leadership, and how can educators and administrators work together to ensure sustained commitment to these initiatives?

Street Data versus Standardized Data

In considering the use of street data as a form of antiracism in education, how might leveraging local and community-specific information reshape education policies, practices, and priorities to better address the unique needs and experiences of diverse student populations?

PART 4

Commit to STEM for All

CHAPTER 13

Leading and Coaching 4 JUSTICE: Transforming STEM Education

Are your students and community better off because of you and your work?
—Leena Bakshi McLean (adapted from Principal Baruti Kafele)

When I was seeking administration positions, I interviewed over 30 times. When I finally achieved a leadership position in education, I was given my new title: Science Coordinator. I was very proud of this title. Eventually, I was promoted to Program Director I, and I was even more elated. After working hard to achieve these titles, I could not imagine jeopardizing them. Therefore, I found myself working very hard to maintain the status quo, keep the supervisors content, and complete my tasks. In fact, I was directed, "Lay low, and you will eventually get another promotion." However, at the core of my heart as an educator is the pressing need to make an impact.

Think about your title, whether it is teacher, principal, director, or assistant superintendent. Every single one of these titles required hard work, credentialing, certification exams, evaluations, and commitment to make them possible. With that in mind, would you be willing to give up your title? This is a question I had to face. When I think about having finally achieved a title that I aspired to, this becomes a very difficult question, especially when we may be faced with situations in a system where inequity is present and persists. As we arrive at the final chapter of this book, we have seen that this work takes work. We have to ask ourselves: Are we going to sit down in compliance or are we going to stand up for justice? And sometimes, standing up for justice means perhaps giving up or at least endangering your title.

Recognizing Systemic Racism

Equity is more than using sentence frames in the classroom. It is not a trendy term, it is a movement. The question is whether we can recognize systemic racism within our own context. What does it look like, and how does it manifest? Going back to my previous title of director, our organization was planning a computer science fair and members from our team trained the students from the court schools to code and present at the fair. The supervisor of our team had contacts at the university and set the stage for the whole fair. However, in the planning processes, there were concerns that there would not be enough security present to "handle the students from the court schools." These students were then uninvited from the fair. (See figure.)

What do you do?

- (A) Agree with the leadership. Security is important and we can reflect on how to incorporate increased security for the next event.
- (B) Disagree silently. It's important to recognize this issue but know that these things happen all the time.
- (C) Actively disagree.There may be consequences but it is important that you communicate the importance of the invitation for all students.
- (D) Neither agree or disagree. I would need more information and this doesn't really apply to the scope of my work.

Remember when we said that you might have to give up your title?

I can tell you what we did. Our team came together and spoke up. We advocated for those students' presence, and they eventually were reinvited. However, our advocacy went against the leadership. After the event, we were placed on watch and eventually saw all the cards fall. One team member was passed up for promotion, another team member was constantly interrogated in HR. All of our cubicles were separated from each other so that we would not have the opportunity to collaborate anymore. Upper management instituted cubicle walkthroughs to monitor when we were all at our desks. The focus on compliance and obedience was straight out of a white supremacy playbook. Eventually, the entire team (including me) resigned, and the organization has not seen a computer science fair since. I always look back at this moment and wonder whether I should have stayed quiet. Had I stayed quiet, though, STEM4Real would not have been born. There were people on our team who did stay quiet because of the very concrete reality that they had a family to support. When we stand up, it's not just our title on the line. It is our career and our livelihoods. As Baruti Kafele asks, "Is my school a better school because I lead it?" We followed up with the question, "Are your students and community better off because of you and your work?" The first step is to recognize the following situations and think about whether various situations have a systematically racist connotation.

Recognizing Situations

Situation 1: A fifth-grade teacher is submitting recommendations for an honors science class in sixth grade. The fifth-grade teacher teaches science once a week. She recommended the five top students with the highest grades: three Asian students and two white students. The Black boys in her classroom are very talkative and rowdy during science. She feels that they would not have the maturity for an honors-level science course.

Situation 2: An English-speaking student had just come to the United States and entered kindergarten. She asked for a lid and used the word in her native tongue instead of the English word. The teacher immediately moved her into the English-language learner (ELL) program.

Situation 3: A student with Brown skin was involved in a physical altercation with a white student. Both students were suspended, per the school policy. The same student with Brown skin was involved in another altercation where a white student slapped her. The Brown student did not want to get suspended again, so she immediately went to the dean. The dean held a conference with the two students and decided to talk it out. The white student was not suspended and was given a warning.

Situation 4: Out of 25 members of a state science curriculum committee in California, we saw the following racial breakdown of members: 22 White, 2 Asian, 1 Latinx, 0 African American.

In addressing each of these situations, we are oftentimes compelled to prove that it is not overt racism. Overt racism involves explicit, intentional discriminatory actions based on race. In contrast, systemically racist connotations refer to subtle and often unintentional actions that contribute to a system not set up for equity for all. These situations represent a mixture of both, contributing to inequities in education. As you reflect on the programs and initiatives that you have, ask yourself this question: Are all students getting served? These initiatives can include computer science programs, elementary science implementation, outdoor education camps, emergent multilingual services, special education, mathematics tracking, and gifted and talented programming. There may be programs that are not meant for all students. There also may be programs that are intended for all students, but access is limited. We are calling on leaders to take a closer look at policies and procedures in place. Take the time to analyze how many students of color are suspended based on skin color. Look at the race and ethnicity demographics of advanced course enrollment and discuss how to expand pathways for underrepresented groups. I would also encourage teachers and coaches to reevaluate grading systems and explore ways of equitable, standards-based grading. Educators can also take a closer look at family and community involvement and how it is aligned with different ethnic groups to ensure that we are inviting our families into the school system.

You can also use our STEM4Real Equity Odometer (www.stem4real.org/odometer) to reflect on equity in your classrooms, schools, and districts. Our odometer helps indicate your mileage of equity, knowing that the road to anti-racism is a journey, and we are all going at different speeds. The odometer looks at components of equity in terms of availability of advanced courses, social-emotional learning, discipline, leadership, strength of family/home partnerships, and the joy of teachers in supporting students. Some questions to expect from the odometer include:

Questions	None	Some	Yes
1. Are students giving up, dropping out, or feeling demoralized when they are not succeeding in STEM?			
2. Do you have the opportunity to observe STEM instruction, analyze student work, and reflect on seeing and celebrating student successes?			
3. Is your STEM instruction and curriculum aligned with the Next Generation Science Standards (NGSS) or state adopted science standards?			
4. Do students have the materials to fully engage in STEM learning (labs, resources, technology, hands-on experiences) with full funding for STEM?			
5. Do you have a passion to research the community, resources, families, and neighborhoods of your school and district populations?			
6. Do students with disabilities (SpEd) and emergent multilingual learners get full access to STEM?			
7. Do the STEM lessons incorporate real-world phenomena (like discovering new species in the ocean) and examples that reflect the diversity of students' experiences and their local communities (Flint Michigan Water Crisis)?			
8. Do you encourage students to draw connections between STEM concepts and their own cultural experiences, backgrounds, and learning styles to increase excitement about STEM?			
9. Does the professional development training available to you teach antiracism, diversity, equity and inclusion as it fits into STEM teaching and curriculum?			
10. Do you actively think about stereotypes and biases related to race, gender, disability and other identities when you plan your STEM instruction?			

Deliberate resolve is needed to lead schools through a lens of social justice and equity. The challenge behind this crucial leadership is that when we bring cultural identities (ethnicity, nationality, gender, sexual orientation, religion, ability, and socioeconomic, to name a few) together there is an increased potential for conflict within the organization. The Equity Odometer was designed to give education leaders a starting point. Research points out that equity in education means that personal or social circumstances such as gender, ethnic origin, or family background are not obstacles to achieving educational potential (fairness) and that all individuals reach at least a basic minimum level of skills (inclusion) (Organization for Economic Co-operation and Development, 2012). An equity audit allows you to recognize the school's organizational and personal values and how they are enacted to support *all* students.

Dismantle Inequitable and Racist Systems

Ask yourself: What are some systems in place that need to be dismantled in order to achieve equitable outcomes?

Diversifying your educating force: You obviously can't just change your teaching force, and you cannot choose people simply based on color. So what can you do? Assess your recruiting practices. Tap the shoulders of teachers of color and ask them to take on leadership roles. Create a group of educators that intensively study equity and social justice. A lack of diversity has many implications, which can lead to an unhealthy work environment where people may feel unwelcome or excluded, leading to poor mental health and higher turnover rates. This lack of diversity also leads to a lack of role models for individuals from underrepresented groups, discouraging them from pursuing careers in STEM fields. It is, however, important to ensure that we are not tokenizing people of color to serve as part of a "quota" or "diversity hires." In our Leadership for Justice Program, we play a game called the Counting Game, where we count the people of color in the room. A next step is to count how many people of color speak up and contribute to meetings and ideas. In the state of California, there is a law that requires boards of directors to have at least one female director. Our next step is imagining a diverse world that did this as a way of life versus as a need for compliance. The Center for Black Educator Development reported that "research shows when Black students have Black teachers who reflect their experiences and worldviews, they perform better in school. But most go through 13 years of public education without one." Ensuring a diverse workforce in both teaching and leadership means revisiting recruitment practices, networking with diverse associations of color, expanding the pool of applicants, and most importantly, creating an inclusive culture that values anti-bias and anti-racist practices.

Revisit and revise school and district policies and procedures: Where in your policy do you specify when to have students removed from the classroom? What alternatives to suspension can you look into? Seek out a plan for restorative justice. Reach out to school counselors and leaders of color who specialize in behavior outreach. Reevaluate the counseling department and assess the diversity. As Michael Creekmore of Creekmore Conversations asks, "How many Black male counselors have you met?" Jane Margolis, author of *Stuck in the Shallow End*, notes, "The ineffectiveness of college counseling at the high school level is especially problematic for students of color. The counselors may rely too heavily on assumptions and biased beliefs, and too little on real information about their students' abilities and interests." Many times, students are losing instructional minutes due to behavioral issues. Black and Brown boys are more likely to face adverse discipline. This keeps them out of the classroom more and more. At the elementary levels, there are policies where emergent multilingual learners are removed from the science preparation time and given additional language instruction, hence further limiting access. Advocate for and implement policies that provide equitable access to resources, opportunities, and mentorship programs. Break down financial and logistical barriers that may hinder underrepresented groups from pursuing STEM education.

Ensure Well-Rounded Instruction: When schools teach and focus on mathematics and English language arts (ELA) instruction, they neglect the other parts of education that make a student feel whole. Science, art, music, and social studies are oftentimes pushed aside to meet the demands of math and ELA. These subjects are relegated to the margins because they are not heavily calculated as part of the accountability quotient. Teachers are encouraged to fit in the other subjects when they get a chance. Though this is good for testing, this is detrimental to the students and takes away from their well-rounded education. There also lies a diversity factor here because many of the curriculum companies also lack diversity on their teams, leading to curricular resources that do not include diverse backgrounds or experiences. The ones who miss out the most are students in elementary school or continuation school, students with disabilities, and emergent multilingual learners.

This table presents various scenarios within educational settings, highlighting aspects of the situations that may need recognition, educational implications, and opportunities for dismantling inequities. Use these situations to examine similar situations in their own contexts and consider how they might address issues of equity and inclusion. By recognizing the underlying biases or systemic factors at play, educators can then explore strategies for promoting fairness and sustaining a more equitable learning environment.

Examples of Dismantling

Recognize Situation	Educational Aspect	Dismantle
A 5th-grade teacher is submitting recommendations for an honors science class in 6th grade. The 5th grade teacher teaches science once a week. She recommended the 5 top students with the highest grades: three Asian students and two white students. The black boys in her classroom are very talkative and rowdy during science. She feels that they would not have the maturity for an honors-level science course.	Honors Recommendation	How are students recommended into Honors? Is it only based on teacher recommendation and test scores? How can we encourage all students to choose into honors? How are students tested into GATE? How are they chosen? Do all students have the opportunity to participate?
A student with brown skin was involved in a physical altercation with another white student. Both students were suspended per the school policy. The same student with brown skin was involved in another altercation where a white student slapped her. The brown student did not want to get suspended again so she immediately went to the dean. The dean held a conference with the two students and decided to talk it out. The white student was not suspended and was given a warning.	School Suspensions	What can we do as a school to reduce school suspensions? Identify your root causes. Reach out to organizations that specialize in black mentorship, increase family engagement, create a space for more adults to supervise, and create a task force that represents parents, teachers, and community members to address discipline.
An English-speaking student had just come to the United States and entered Kindergarten. She asked for a lid and used the word in her native tongue instead of the English word. The teacher immediately moved her into the English Language Learner program.	English Language Learner Instruction	How are English Language Learners tracked and taught? Is there the same level of rigor in ELL classes and standardized classes? What are teachers' assumptions about English Language Learners?
Out of 25 members of a state science curriculum committee in California, we saw the following racial breakdown of members: 22 WHITE, 2 ASIAN, 1 LATINX, 0 AFRICAN AMERICAN.	Curriculum Leadership	Have we reached out to any people of color who can better represent our state's demographic populations? When you are on a curriculum committee or leadership team, notice how many people of color are represented. "Can we recruit more people of color on our team?"

Rebuild

At this time, we have recognized inequities within the system and we have dismantled the very processes and policies in place that perpetuate these inequities. It is now time to rebuild. Rebuilding involves a conscientious and deliberate effort to construct new systems, structures, and approaches that actively address the recognized inequities and discrepancies within the educational landscape. This phase calls for a commitment to systematic evaluation and introspection. Leaders must rigorously assess and analyze data on enrollment, academic achievement, and representation, particularly within specialized programs such as STEM. Education leaders gain valuable insights into existing disparities, allowing for the formulation of targeted interventions.

Create a vision grounded in social justice: Your vision should reflect a commitment to addressing disparities in enrollment, achievement, and representation in STEM programs. It involves actively working toward creating an educational ecosystem that embraces diversity, dismantles barriers, and ensures equitable access to resources and opportunities for all students. Here is an example vision:

> *We believe in our ability and responsibility to address the pervasive issues obstructing the well-being of all students without regard to what their social condition may indicate about their chances for success. We set* ***uncommonly high educational goals*** *for all students and commit to equipping the most vulnerable students and those who serve them with the tools to thrive. Our work serves as a* ***model of social justice in action*** *to erase the predetermination of failure for children from communities of violence and poverty.*

Ironically, this was actually the vision of the organization that uninvited the students from the court schools to the computer science fair. That is why having a vision is not enough. Continually revisit the vision and ensure that your work is always aligned.

Build a team of visionaries: Educators of color often bring unique perspectives and experiences to the educational setting. Supporting them involves recognizing their contributions, providing professional development opportunities, and ensuring that their voices are not only heard but actively valued. When teachers feel supported, they can better advocate for the diverse needs of their students. According to Lisette Partelow from the Center for American Progress, "Teachers of color tend to provide more culturally relevant teaching and better understand the situations that students of color may face. These factors help develop trusting teacher-student relationships." Empower the team of visionaries to engage in ongoing professional development focused on cultural competence, inclusive teaching practices, and anti-bias strategies. This team of visionaries serves as advocates for systemic change within the educational institution.

Foster community engagement: Because of the historically racist past of public schools, family and community engagement has to be rebuilt on terms that encourage inviting and welcoming spaces. When we say, "These parents don't care about education" or "These parents can't even speak English," we are continuing a precedent of othering the families within our school community. Collaborate with local communities to understand their unique needs and challenges. Establish partnerships that facilitate mentorship, outreach programs, and exposure to STEM fields from an early age and onto high school. For example, the Hidden Genius Project, based out of Oakland, California, trains and mentors Black male youth in technology creation, entrepreneurship, and leadership skills to transform their lives and communities. Founder Brandon Nicholson sought to address the high unemployment of Black male youth and the enormous amount of career opportunities within the technology sector.

Engage with families: Build partnerships with families; parents and families are your allies. See how you can bring them in and create an inviting environment for them. Build partnerships with community organizations. Look for health and mental wellness organizations and especially focus on students of color, students with special needs, migrant students, and LGBTQ students. Create leadership teams and task forces that involve parents and families to speak up and be involved, even virtually. There are so many stories that surround our families. Invite more parents and families and have them share these positive stories.

Focus on student-centered instruction that is working: When I graduated from my high school, our district was plagued with a reputation of low test scores, crime, and underachievement. However, our teachers amplified the stories of success. Students were receiving college acceptance letters from Yale, Berkeley, and Stanford. Highlight and amplify student voices that are breaking barriers with success. Regularly assess and analyze data on enrollment, achievement, and representation in STEM programs. Use this information to identify disparities and implement targeted interventions to address inequities. Check-ins with specific student populations, such as ELLs, students with special needs (SPED), LGBTQ students, and those from diverse ethnic backgrounds (Black, Indigenous, Latinx), inform targeted interventions and ensure that resources and support are allocated equitably.

Advocate for policy change: Advocate for policies at institutional and governmental levels that promote diversity, equity, and inclusion in STEM education. Engage in dialogue with policymakers to influence systemic change. As Nate Scholten from Baylor University states, "When policies and bills are being passed that forbid the use of instructional strategies, curricular content, or social analyses that invite or prompt students to think about or discuss race, this purposeful instruction of and with CRT requires courage." Equity, book bans, and critical race theory have turned into tools to weaponize political discourse and debate.

Anti-racist professional development: Prioritize ongoing training for educators and administrators on cultural competence, bias awareness, and inclusive teaching practices. This ensures that educational institutions are equipped to foster an environment where every student can thrive. STEM4Real had to take a stand for being an organization rooted in justice and anti-racism. We have been placed on lists of banned organizations for some schools and districts because of this stance. This stance requires bravery in ensuring we are aligned with our vision and taking a stand. According to Dr. Ibram X. Kendi, author of *How to Be an Antiracist* "I would say the most efficient way we can do this is by making sure we ourselves are striving to be antiracist. Because if we as individuals are really ensuring that we are being antiracist as individuals, then that's going to come across in how we act as an educator."

Case-Study Student Analysis: If there is only one takeaway for you from this book, I hope it is our case study student analysis protocol. Choose case study students and conduct a case-study student analysis. If you are out of the classroom, partner with a teacher that has access to a classroom. The further removed we get from the classroom, the harder it is to lead with empathy. If you're in a leadership role, encourage teachers to get to know their students. You can even choose case-study students yourself. Learn as much as you can about those one or two students and truly take a deep dive so that when you make decisions, you have them in mind. This process supports a comprehensive multi-tiered system of support that addresses academic, behavioral, and social-emotional instruction. It answers the following questions:

- How does this student access the STEM academic content?
- How does this student behave in class and school?
- What social-emotional supports are available?

It is impossible for the counselors alone to seek out this information on a large scale. This is why we have to leverage the teaching community to obtain this qualitative information that contributes to teaching the whole child beyond isolated STEM concepts.

Let's see how Susan R. Mosby, an elementary principal from Oklahoma puts this all together to promote and amplify STEM instruction:

> *Science education has always been at the top of my list of important goals for both teachers and students. My teachers know I expect students to get a well-rounded education at our school. This is part of their evaluation. However, I am constantly finding ways to move teachers toward teaching more and better science. I spent a lot of time in the classrooms. When teachers facilitate science learning, I make a huge deal about it. I talk about it to everyone as a good example. Also, I send teachers to professional development to learn how to teach science. I also search for pilot programs to involve my teachers. Finally, for 3rd through 5th grade, I departmentalize them so they have one hour to teach science each day. We are still working on making science important at my school but have made a lot of progress. I also hired a STEM teacher for a weekly rotation.*

It is clear that she not only amplifies the instruction but has also created a vision for science, regardless of the testing pressures at the elementary level. She has allocated resources for a STEM teacher and ensures that the science instruction is part of her policies and procedures with respect to her evaluation.

Multi-Tiered System of Support: Focus on STEM

Schools in the United States have widely adopted multi-tiered systems of support (MTSS) as a form for targeted instruction and intervention. However, many of these conversations systematically leave science and STEM out of the conversations. Just as we had to advocate for science and STEM to be included in special education Individualized Education Program

(IEPs) and discussions, we must do the same for MTSS. School improvement plans and local control accountability plans (LCAPs) often exclude science and STEM from the conversation as well. These critical exclusions make it difficult to fund STEM programming especially when dollars are associated with the accountability goals. This following list outlines key strategies that are essential to a comprehensive MTSS plan for ensuring that all students have equitable access to high-quality STEM instruction and support structures. Many of the discussions surrounding MTSS are centered around mathematics, literacy and social-emotional learning. These tools such as science benchmarks and family engagement interviews allow educators to address individual needs and provide targeted support to ensure student success. Progress monitoring aligned with 3D5E assessments and clear data points for proficiency and mastery further enhance the effectiveness of STEM instruction by allowing educators to track student progress systematically and adjust interventions as needed.

1. Universal Support
   a. First Good Instruction: Ensuring that the foundation of STEM education is robust and inclusive involves providing high-quality, culturally responsive instruction for all students. This includes the integration of diverse perspectives, hands-on learning experiences, and real-world applications to engage students from various backgrounds.
   b. Site-Wide Initiatives: Implementing science instruction at all elementary school sites daily demonstrates a commitment to universal access. This initiative creates an equitable learning environment, ensuring that STEM education is not limited to specific schools but is accessible to every student.
   c. **Anti-racist** Professional Learning: Embedding anti-racist professional development ensures that educators are equipped with the knowledge and skills to recognize and dismantle biases in STEM instruction. This empowers them to create an inclusive classroom environment that values the contributions of all students.
   d. Lesson Study PLC Cycles: Engaging in professional learning communities focused on lesson study cycles enhances collaboration among educators. Sharing insights, refining instructional strategies, and addressing challenges collectively contribute to the continuous improvement of STEM instruction.
2. Interventions and Targeted Supports
   a. Science Benchmarks: Establishing clear science benchmarks guides instructional planning and ensures that students are progressing toward mastery of key concepts.
   b. Intensified Support with Student Interviews: Conducting student interviews provides valuable insights into individual needs, preferences, and challenges. This personalized approach informs the design of interventions and support structures.
   c. Family Engagement Interviews: Engaging families in the learning process through interviews ensures that the home environment aligns with STEM education goals. It also provides an opportunity to address any barriers to engagement.

3. Progress Monitoring
   a. **Connection** with 3D5E Assessment: Aligning progress monitoring with 3D5E assessments ensures that students are mastering the three dimensions of science learning: disciplinary core ideas, science and engineering practices, and crosscutting concepts.
   b. Data Points for Proficiency and Mastery: Establishing clear data points for proficiency and mastery allows educators to track student progress systematically. This data-driven approach ensures that interventions are targeted and effective in promoting STEM proficiency for all students.

The idea is to decolonize the processes of MTSS through storytelling, ethnography, and humanization. As Dr. Sheldon Eakins from the Leading Equity Center states, "Spend time with students outside of school settings. Recognize the importance of spending time with families outside school settings." This is what contributes to teaching the whole child with respect to academic, behavioral, and social-emotional learning. Your advocacy lies in understanding the systems and policies such as MTSS, UDL, and LCAPs that control how the schools and districts operate. Once you know how they operate, you can advocate for the inclusion of STEM.

The "Can't Fail" Experiment: A Tool for Innovation

The "Can't Fail Experiment" by the National Equity Project is an empowering tool for innovation that invites educators to become proactive agents of change in addressing educational inequities at any level. This approach encourages individuals to identify a specific problem related to inequity in education, pose a research question, make predictions about potential solutions, carry out a tangible experiment, and meticulously collect data to assess outcomes. Rooted in a spirit of curiosity and a commitment to inclusivity, the experiment challenges traditional norms and encourages educators to take intentional actions to create equitable learning environments. Through this process, educators become researchers, actively engaging with the complexities of their educational settings to unearth insights that can transform their practice. The following list outlines the steps of the "Can't Fail" experiment following by an example for each action:

1. **Identify a Problem of STEM Educational Inequity:**

   Problem: Limited representation of diverse voices in STEM education materials.
2. **Ask Yourself a Question to Research:**

   Question: What impact would incorporating diverse perspectives in STEM curriculum have on student engagement and achievement?

3. **Make a Prediction:**

   Prediction: If I integrate materials featuring diverse scientists and perspectives into the curriculum, students will demonstrate increased interest and understanding of STEM concepts.

4. **Carry Out Your Experiment and Monitor/Collect Any Data:**

   Experiment: Introduce curriculum materials showcasing prominent scientists from diverse backgrounds. Monitor student engagement, participation, and achievement over a set period. Data collection: Document student responses, participation levels, and academic performance during the implementation of the new curriculum. Consider surveying students for qualitative insights on their experiences.

5. **What Did You Find Out?**

   Findings: Students showed increased engagement, curiosity, and enthusiasm for STEM subjects. They actively participated in discussions, asked questions, and demonstrated a deeper understanding of the material. You can now use this data as leverage for your advocacy.

6. **What Did You Notice?**

   Observations: Not only did students benefit academically, but there was also a noticeable improvement in the classroom environment. Students from underrepresented backgrounds expressed a stronger sense of belonging and identification with STEM fields.

The "Can't Fail Experiment" serves as your starting point for educators at any stage of their STEM implementation. By identifying a specific problem related to equity in STEM education, educators gain a precise focus on an area that requires attention. The subsequent steps, from formulating research questions to making predictions and carrying out experiments, guide educators through intentional actions that address inequities. This experiment's strength lies in its scalability and applicability, making it equally relevant for those taking the initial steps in integrating equity into STEM practices and for those seeking to refine and expand their existing initiatives. Advocates can use the data to inform decision-making processes at various levels, from individual classrooms to district-wide initiatives. By weaving together the stories told by the data, we can create a powerful narrative that resonates with a broad audience and underscores the urgency and importance of addressing equity issues in STEM. As we strive to advance STEM education and create inclusive learning environments, it is imperative to reflect on our organizational practices and approaches. This following list of questions serves as a guide for assessing the current state of STEM instruction, family engagement initiatives, professional development opportunities, and ongoing learning experiences within your organization. By asking these critical questions, educators and administrators can identify areas of strength and opportunities for improvement, ultimately working toward ensuring equitable and impactful STEM education for all students.

Questions to Ask Your Organization

- Is STEM being taught? If so, how regularly? Ensure that science is not forgotten and stands as an equal subject next to Math and ELA.
- How are we connecting with families to facilitate STEM learning at home? Discuss the digital divide and how we can embrace our families as allies.
- How are teachers getting professional learning in culturally responsive and anti-racist teaching? What does standards-based, culturally responsive teaching look like?
- How can we create opportunities for ongoing professional learning that is meaningful and relevant? Let's face it, professional development (PD) can be boring and a waste of time. What if we had a network that could disrupt what PD has been and provide real-time collaboration?

Next Steps: Standards, Initiatives + Anti-Racism & Justice: You Don't Have to Choose

The educator in me has to leave you with your next steps. No matter where you are in your education journey, you are a leader. Whether you are a teacher, instructional coach, principal, or district/complex/state/world-level administrator, we all have a responsibility and call to action to ensure that STEM for All is a reality for ALL. At STEM4Real, we created the STEM for All Leadership Symposium. This is a unique and dynamic event where we call upon teachers, instructional coaches and education administrators to come to the table to make leadership and instructional decisions together in unison. Below is a list of implications we have curated to help you on your journey of making STEM for all:

- Implications for teachers: **Create your anti-racism in STEM content.**
  - Reflect on your teaching practices and any unintentional biases that may exist. How might your instructional decisions and recommendations contribute to or challenge systemic inequities in STEM?
  - Regularly engage in self-reflection on your teaching practices. Consider how your instructional decisions may impact students differently based on their backgrounds. Continuously strive to create a joyful classroom environment that values belonging.
- Implications for **instructional coaches**: **Build your anti-racism STEM toolbox.**
  - Use data analysis to identify any disparities in student outcomes and work closely with teachers to develop targeted interventions that address these inequities. Guide teachers in implementing data-driven instructional changes.
  - Provide teachers with curated resources, literature, and tools that promote diversity and inclusion in the curriculum. Encourage the integration of diverse perspectives and authors into instructional materials.

- Implications for **administrators: Conduct your equity audit of access to STEM.**
  - Conduct equity audits at the district level, analyzing data on enrollment, achievement, and representation across various programs. Use this information to identify systemic issues and implement district-wide interventions for a more equitable educational system.
  - Collaborate with policymakers to advocate for district-wide policies that promote diversity, equity, and inclusion in STEM education. Participate in discussions about curriculum changes, teacher training, and community engagement initiatives.

In addition to groundbreaking shared decision-making, collaboration, and action planning, we use this opportunity to celebrate diversity in STEM by treating real life scientists and engineers from marginalized groups to be treated like the celebrities they are and amplify their voices, research, and impact on the world. That is actually how our name came to be: celebrating and amplifying real-life diversity in STEM and making STEM, #4Real.

STEM and Early Learning

STEM education plays a critical role in early learning, laying the foundation for cognitive development, problem-solving skills, and a lifelong interest in scientific inquiry. Contrary to the misnomer that young children are not developmentally ready for STEM, research and educational frameworks, such as the California Preschool Learning Foundations, demonstrate that early childhood is an optimal time for introducing STEM concepts. For instance, the "Scientific Inquiry" foundation emphasizes Observation and Investigation (3.1): "Children observe objects and events in their environment and describe them." The "Mathematics" foundation highlights the importance of early mathematical experiences, noting that young children can understand and apply basic math concepts through play and exploration (California Department of Education, 2019). Activities like counting, measuring, and pattern recognition are not only engaging but also fundamental to later success in STEM fields. Equating science and STEM education to reading and mathematics at younger levels is crucial; just as literacy and numeracy are foundational skills, early STEM experiences can significantly enhance cognitive and academic development. Vanessa Bermudez, researcher from the UC Irvine School of Education, conducted a study on culturally situated playful environments for early STEM learning, provides a practical example of this integration. She notes that "when discussing their family grocery shopping experiences, parents shared examples of engaging children in mathematical thinking by having them weigh food items, compare prices, add costs, and determine if the total was within their budget. Furthermore, children engaged in scientific thinking by observing the qualities of fruits to decide whether they were ready to be eaten or needed more time." She continues, "*Cuando voy con mis niños les gusta ayudarme. Por ejemplo, les digo cómo agarrar los jitomates, que no estén verdes pero que estén poquito durítos para que nos alcancen para la semana.*" This approach not only supports children's mathematical and scientific learning but also creates joyful family interactions. For example, in a preschool or transitional kindergarten (TK) classroom, teachers can set up a "nature table" with various natural objects like leaves, rocks, flowers, and pinecones. Children are encouraged to observe these objects closely using magnifying glasses and describe their characteristics, such as color, texture, and shape. Teachers can ask open-ended questions to prompt further exploration, such as "What do you notice about the leaves?" or "How are the rocks different from each other?" This activity aligns with the foundation by practicing observation skills and encouraging children to articulate their findings. By actively incorporating STEM learning experiences in early learning spaces, educators can ensure that all students have access to opportunities in STEM, thereby building the school, family, and community foundations of the school-to-STEM pathway.

School-to-STEM Career Pathways

Let us reflect back on Bridget, my former student who started off at the top of my mathematics class in middle school and was later told that she was not a math person. As I remember her story, I think about a lost opportunity to embrace someone's mathematical skills and talent. Though she is successful and thriving in her own right, a moment occurred where she was dissuaded from STEM. She is not the only one. Who else have we shielded from these pathways? The school-to-STEM pathways are losing a critical mass of diversity in its potential scientists and engineers. The Kapor Center, based in Oakland, California, focuses on addressing issues of access, opportunity, and representation, particularly for underrepresented communities in the tech sector. According to the research on the Leaky Tech Pipeline:

- Low-income students and students of color are 12 times less likely to have access to computer science courses in their high schools.
- Men earn 82 percent of bachelor's degrees in CS while women earn only 18 percent, and only 20 percent are Black/Latinx.
- Just 1 in 10 employees across some of the largest and top-grossing tech companies are Black and Latinx.

Taking strategic responsibility for the school-to-STEM pathway is not merely an ethical imperative but a strategic investment in the future of diverse STEM talent. When I posed this question: "What is one thing an educator or mentor did to motivate, encourage, and cultivate your belonging in STEM?" these were the responses:

> "Making STEAM projects, programs accessible and digestible. Exposure was the biggest factor. Not just seeing others that looked like us, being there for us."
>
> – Zephanii Smith Eisenstat

> "Told me that I could do the physics when my entire family said that girls can't do math and science."
>
> – Heather Wygant

"Called me a future mathematician during an assembly. I felt encouraged."

– Kassandra Avelar

"One thing my educator did to boost my interest and confidence in STEM was to treat our class as equals. She made sure we felt valued and encouraged us to enjoy learning, feel at ease with asking questions, and simply being in the class."

– Farrah Marini

"Having a group of educators making me feel like I belonged in STEM was the most impeccable feeling."

– Brandon Davis

The overarching theme was that they each had an educator who believed that they truly belonged in STEM. In an interconnected world, countries with a strong STEM workforce are more competitive. A STEM-for-*All* mentality ensures that a nation's talent pool is diverse and capable, enhancing its global competitiveness in technological advancements and scientific research. It not only prepares students for successful careers but also contributes to a more equitable, innovative, and just society. A STEM-for-*all* mentality in K-12 education is not just a pedagogical approach; it is a strategic imperative in preparing the next generation of students to be problem solvers, critical thinkers, and advocates for justice.

Sitting in Compliance or Standing Up for Justice

When we began this chapter, I posed the question of whether you would be willing to give up your title, to ask yourself the question of whether you were going to sit in compliance or stand up for justice. I personally came to that crossroads and I chose the radical position of resigning and starting STEM4Real, with a vision to diversify the school to STEM career pathway. Our charge grew even greater by creating a professional learning community that truly believed in combating the systemic racism that plagues our classrooms. Anti-racism is not just one strategy. It's not the flavor of the month. Anti-racism is a movement and a revolution for change that seeks to pave the way for access and opportunity to STEM for ALL. When we embody a vision for justice, we are creating systems, structures, and tools that come together for this shared vision. This book is not for those who sit in compliance. It is for those who choose to take a stand. Just know that you are now part of the #4Real community where you will not be standing alone. This work is not individual. This is a collective movement and I honor the moment you picked up this book to take a stand to allow every student to thrive in STEM, for all, #4Real.

#4Real Discussion Prompts

Reflecting on Leadership

How has your perception of leadership evolved after reading about the challenges and decisions faced by the author in maintaining justice in education leadership roles?

In your current or aspiring leadership position, how do you balance the responsibilities of maintaining the status quo and advocating for justice and equity in education?

Recognizing Systemic Racism

In the section discussing systemic racism, how would you navigate situations like the computer science fair incident and the subsequent repercussions faced by the team members? What role does advocacy play in dismantling systemic biases?

Rebuilding for Equity

As the author outlined the rebuilding phase, particularly in terms of community engagement, anti-racist professional development, and advocating for policy change, how can these strategies be applied in your educational context to create a more equitable environment?

A Word by Raven the Science Maven by Dr. Raven Baxter

In the pages of this book, Dr. Bakshi McLean's powerful message resonates clearly: Knowledge is not just power—it's a treasure that, when shared, multiplies and enriches our world. I'm Dr. Raven Baxter, also known as Dr. Raven the Science Maven. As a Black molecular biologist and science educator, I knew that the exploration of culturally responsive science education within these chapters does more than advocate for inclusivity. It illuminates a path forward, where every student can see themselves as integral parts of the scientific and STEM narrative, especially for students like me.

When I was a university researcher in my master's program in molecular biology, I was tasked with creating a poster of our research. I fondly remember decorating the poster with hot pink tones and glitter. When I brought the poster to the poster session, I saw that my poster stood out from the sea of Times New Roman and Arial fonts. However, to my surprise, my poster garnered the most attention as attendees lined up waiting to hear about the immunological strategies to study GRP170 in *Caenorhabditis elegans*. It was at this moment that I realized the power of science communication from education, to research, to the broader public. This book argues compellingly that when education mirrors diverse student experiences, engagement deepens and learning transforms. It's an invitation to view science not as a static collection of facts but as a dynamic story that everyone should have the chance to help write. In doing so, it challenges us to rethink how and why we teach science, emphasizing the importance of connecting with each learner's unique background.

At The Science Haven our mission is focused on sparking curiosity and reinterpreting science into engaging experience, regardless of their scientific knowledge or background. That is why we set out to ensure that 100 students and their families would be given 100 telescopes in order to increase opportunities in the field of astronomy. 100 telescopes. 100 families. 100 dreams. You can learn more at thesciencehaven.org. The notions shared in this book provide a beacon for all involved in education. They remind us that to truly unlock the potential within each student, we must ensure our teaching reflects the myriad of cultures and experiences they bring to the classroom. This approach doesn't just benefit learners; it enriches the entire academic community by ensuring a deeper, more comprehensive understanding of the world.

The conversation doesn't end here. Each one of us—educators, students, policymakers, and community members—has a role in nurturing an environment where the sciences are accessible, engaging, and representative of all voices. This is why I created "The Science of Life Podcast." It is my invitation to the world to explore the intricacies of life that are rooted in STEM and how they socially and scientifically intersect. These invitations are exactly what our young people need to know that science and STEM makes up our entire livelihood and society. By committing to this vision, we can ensure that the pursuit of knowledge remains a vibrant, inclusive, and empowering journey for everyone. Cheers, to a future where the power of knowledge brings us closer together, lighting the way to discovery and belonging in STEM for all.

With hope and determination for what lies ahead,

Dr. Raven

THE

SCIENCE MAVEN

STEM for All, #4Real

Did you know that you can book Dr. Leena Bakshi McLean and the STEM4Real Team to facilitate your next event or training?

Dr. Bakshi McLean has been behind both the teacher and the administrator desk. She knows the unique challenges and opportunities of both, and what it's like to want to make a difference but not know where to start. She is not just inspirational; she's relatable. Using her years of experience combined with her passion for change-making, Dr. Bakshi McLean invites us to reimagine the impact that we all can have on every single one of their students.

Her vibrant energy, humor, and authenticity actively engage and captivate audiences and are guaranteed to inspire, entertain, and encourage positive change. If you are looking for a speaker and facilitator to ignite transformation and action, contact our team for more information.

This is not just about checking the equity box; this is about moving from learning to action. Let's make STEM for all, #4Real!

www.stem4real.org

References

Adah Miller, E., Berland, L., & Campbell, T. (2023). Equity for Students Requires Equity for Teachers: The Inextricable Link between Teacher Professionalization and Equity-Centered Science Classrooms. Journal of Science Teacher Education, 35(1), 24–43. **https://doi.org/10.1080/1046560X.2023.2170793**

Bell, P. (2019). Infrastructuring Teacher Learning about Equitable Science Instruction. Journal of Science Teacher Education, 30(7), 681-690. DOI: 10.1080/1046560X.2019.1668218

Williams, H. L. (2016). Street cred: A hood minister's guide to urban ministry. Soul Shaker Publishing.

Rodriguez, A.J.; Navarro-Camacho, M. Claiming Your Own Identity and Positionality: The First Steps toward Establishing Equity and Social Justice in Science Education. Educ. Sci. 2023, 13, 652. **https://doi.org/10.3390/educsci13070652**

Index